Group-Based Modeling of Development

Group-Based Modeling
of Development

DANIEL S. NAGIN

Harvard University Press

Cambridge, Massachusetts

London, England

2005

Library of Congress Cataloging-in-Publication Data

Nagin, Daniel.
Group-based modeling of development / Daniel S. Nagin.
p.   cm.
Includes bibliographical references and index.
ISBN 0-674-01686-6 (alk. paper)
1. Longitudinal method.   I. Title.

BF76.6.L65N34 2005
300'.72—dc22   2004053925

For Risë and Emily

Contents

---------------------------------- ❖ ----------------------------------

Acknowledgments

Without the support of many individuals, this book would not have been possible. The initial inspiration for using groups to approximate population heterogeneity came from a suggestion by John Engberg. John has always been generous in giving statistical counsel. Without this recommendation, I would never have begun the line of research reported in this book. My initial collaboration with Ken Land and Kathryn Roeder in developing group-based trajectory modeling was instrumental in moving the methodology forward. For this I thank them both. My ongoing collaboration with Richard Tremblay in applying still more recent advances has also been crucial to the evolution of the methodology. Just as important have been Richard's encouragement and support for the method's development and his generosity in making available some of the data that is used in the book.

I have received much valuable advice from colleagues for improving the manuscript itself. I thank Ronet Bachman, Avshalom Caspi, Elizabeth Cauffman, Steven Durlauf, Wayne Osgood, Ray Paternoster, Alan Taylor, and William Vogt for valuable suggestions and encouragement. Gretchen Hunter provided superb secretarial support from afar while I was drafting the manuscript at the Institute of Criminology, University of Cambridge. Special thanks go to Leslie Johns and Henry Reese. I engaged Leslie to copyedit the prepublication drafts of the book. However, she provided far more than copyediting services. She made countless suggestions for improving both the exposition and the reasoning. To her great credit she was also relentless in prodding me to develop and clarify key arguments. Henry Reese took over where Leslie left off. Not only did he make innumerable suggestions for improving the exposition, he himself skillfully developed key conceptual arguments. Both Leslie and Henry moved this book to a higher level than I would have achieved on my own.

I am grateful for permission from *Criminology* and the Society for Research in Child Development to draw on two earlier articles in revised form: "Age, Criminal Careers, and Population Heterogeneity: Specification and Estimation of a Nonparametric Mixed Poisson Model," *Criminology* 31 (1993): 327–362, coauthored with Kenneth Land; and "Trajectories of Boys' Physical Aggression, Opposition, and Hyperactivity on the Path to Physically Violent and Nonviolent Juvenile Delinquency," *Child Development* 70 (1999): 1181–1196, coauthored with Richard Tremblay.

The research reported in this book has received generous support from the National Science Foundation (NSF) (SES-9210437, SBR-95-11412, SES-9911370), the NSF-supported National Consortium on Violence Research, and the National Institute of Mental Health (RO1 MH65611-01A2). It has also made heavy use of data collected with support from Quebec's CQRS and FCAR funding agencies, Canada's NHRDP and SSHRC funding agencies, and the Molson Foundation.

Group-Based Modeling of Development

1

❖

Introduction and Rationale

1.1 Overview

All social, behavioral, and biological processes evolve over time. Psychologists call the evolution of an outcome over age or time its "developmental trajectory." I borrow this term to describe the progression of any phenomenon, whether behavioral, biological, or physical. Charting and understanding developmental trajectories are among the most fundamental and empirically important research topics in the social and behavioral sciences and medicine. A few prominent examples include: psychological studies of the course and antecedents of psychopathologies, criminological analyses of the progression and causes of criminality over life stages, economic models of the accumulation and use of human capital, sociological investigations into the interaction between human behavior and social context over time, and medical research on the impact of treatments on the progress of diseases.

Longitudinal data—data with a time-based dimension—provide the empirical foundation for the analysis of developmental trajectories. Most standard statistical approaches for analyzing developmental trajectories are designed to account for individual variability about a mean population trend. Many of the most interesting and challenging problems in longitudinal analysis, however, have a qualitative dimension that allows for the possibility that there are meaningful subgroups within a population that follow distinctive developmental trajectories that are not identifiable ex ante on the basis of some measured set of individual characteristics such as gender or socioeconomic status. In psychology, for example, there is a long tradition of taxonomic theorizing about distinctive developmental progressions of these subcategories. For research problems with a taxonomic dimension, the aim is to chart out the distinctive trajectories, to understand what factors account for their distinctiveness, and to test whether individuals following the different trajectories also respond differently to a treatment such as a medical intervention or to a major life event such as the birth of a child.

Because traditional approaches to longitudinal analysis do not lend themselves to the identification and analysis of distinctive developmental trajectories, researchers have commonly resorted to creating the theorized groups using a blend of analysis and insight that is inevitably subjective. The use of subjective classification rules is fraught with statistical dangers, including, most prominently, the dual risks of creating groups that reflect only random variation and failing to identify important but unusual developmental patterns. Uncertainties about the reliability of the group assignments may also invalidate conventional statistical tests of differences across groups.

This book describes an alternative approach, based upon a formal statistical model, for conducting group-based analysis with time- and age-based data. Using real world research data, the book explains and applies a group-based statistical technique for analyzing processes that evolve over age or time. Rather than assuming the existence of developmental trajectories of a specific form before statistical data analysis begins, the method provides the capacity for testing whether the hypothesized trajectories emerge from the data itself. It also provides an exploratory capacity to identify previously unrecognized developmental patterns. As such, it can be thought of as a methodology for identifying meaningful groups in time-based data. It also provides the capacity for statistically identifying the factors that both predict and alter these distinctive time-based progressions.

Much research on human development aims to identify distinctive life trajectories and to understand the complex set of forces that propel people down these very different life paths. The methodology is designed to support this research by providing the statistical capacity for linking distinctive trajectories with characteristics of individuals and their environments that might account for qualitative differences across persons in their developmental course.

Life trajectories may seem to capture the continuity of behavioral patterns over time. Human behavior, however, is not immutable—trajectories of mental illness may be altered by medical treatments, trajectories of computer usage may be changed by new technologies, or trajectories of maternal drug abuse may be deflected by a turning-point event such as the birth of a child. The group-based method is also designed to provide a statistical basis for identifying the forces that alter life trajectories.

Across all application domains, this group-based statistical method lends itself to the presentation of findings in the form of easily understood graphical and tabular data summaries. In so doing, the method provides statistical researchers with a tool for figuratively painting a statistical portrait of the predictors and consequences of distinct trajectories of development. Data summaries of this form have the great advantage of being accessible to nontechnical audiences yet also quickly comprehensible to others who are technically sophisticated.

1.2 The Audience for This Book

This book is targeted at researchers from the social and behavioral sciences and medicine who investigate developmental processes. "Developmental processes" may be broadly understood to include any phenomenon, whether it be behavioral, biological, or physical, that evolves over age or time. Moreover, the unit of observation does not have to be an individual; it can be a community or an organization.

It is important to keep in mind this broad definition of a developmental process, because most of the real world examples used to demonstrate the methodology in this book involve the development of violent and antisocial behavior in people. But this is not a book about crime and violence. It is a book about a methodology that is broadly applicable to phenomena that evolve over age or time. The narrow focus of the applications used for demonstrative purposes here was motivated by several considerations. First, the developmental origin of crime and violence is one of my long-standing research interests. I thus have access to data for demonstrating the methodology with substantively rich examples. This is important, because one of the book's principal aims is to convince readers that the method can be fruitfully applied to more than toy examples. Second, the book also aims to demonstrate a style of statistical analysis that lends itself to the reporting of findings in the form of graphs and easily interpretable tables. Such forms of presentation are particularly important for effectively reporting statistical findings in a transparent fashion to less technically sophisticated audiences. To provide convincing examples, I draw on a substantive area with which I am familiar. Third, another goal of the book is to convince readers that there is much heterogeneity in developmental processes within most populations and that the group-based methodology is ideally suited to support a style of analysis that illuminates that heterogeneity rather than obscuring it in a welter of statistical jargon. Here again knowledge of the problem domain used in examples is helpful.

The use of examples that focus on crime and violence may reduce the likelihood that a demonstration will substantively overlap with a problem domain that is of specific interest to a reader. Such readers are encouraged to look beyond the specific problem domain and to ask whether the principle being demonstrated is applicable to a developmental process that is of personal substantive interest. This translation has already been made by others. The methodology has been applied to such diverse topics as Internet usage (Christ et al., 2002), the development of obesity (Mustillo et al., 2003), and trajectories of crime in geographic units (Weisburd et al., 2004).

The book assumes that the reader has the mathematical and statistical sophistication typical of graduates of Ph.D. programs in psychology, political science, and sociology. However, mathematical sophistication, either greater or lesser, should be no barrier. The mechanics of the calculations have generally been placed into dedicated chapter sections. These sections are targeted to individuals who are interested in mastering the analytic details and want assurance that they correctly understand how to perform required calculations. Those with especially strong technical backgrounds who do not require such assurance may want to skip these sections. Additionally, these sections can be safely skipped or skimmed by those who are primarily seeking to identify better ways of understanding their own data but who do not plan to perform the analyses themselves. Readers who are primarily interested in learning about possible applications should focus their attention on the demonstration sections within each chapter.

1.3 Group-Based Trajectory Modeling Contrasted with Standard Growth Curve Modeling

Hierarchical modeling (Bryk and Raudenbush, 1987, 1992; Goldstein, 1995), and latent curve analysis (McArdle and Epstein, 1987; Meredith and Tisak, 1990; Muthén, 1989; Willett and Sayer, 1994) are two important alternative approaches to the group-based methodology for modeling developmental processes. Like the group-based approach that is the subject of this book, these two alternatives are designed to provide a statistical tool for measuring and explaining differences across population members in their developmental course. Because all three approaches share the common goal of modeling individual-level heterogeneity in developmental trajectories, each must make technical assumptions about the distribution of trajectories in the population. It is these assumptions that distinguish the three approaches.

Although the assumptions underlying hierarchical modeling and latent curve analysis differ in important respects, they also have important commonalities (MacCallum et al., 1997; Raudenbush, 2001; Willett and Sayer, 1994). For the purposes of this book one commonality is crucial: both methodologies model the population distribution of trajectories based on *continuous* distribution functions. Unconditional models estimate two key features of the population distribution of trajectory parameters—their mean and their covariance structure. The former defines average growth within the population and the latter calibrates the variances of growth throughout the population. The conditional models are designed to explain this variability by relating trajectory parameters to one or more explanatory variables.

Modeling individual-level differences requires that assumptions be made about the distribution of trajectory parameters in the population. Both hierarchical modeling and latent curve analysis assume that the parameters are continuously distributed throughout the population according to the multivariate normal distribution. The methodology that is the subject of this book takes a qualitatively different approach to modeling individual differences. Rather than assuming that the population distribution of trajectories varies continuously across individuals and in a fashion that can ultimately be explained by a multivariate normal distribution of population parameters, it assumes that there may be clusters or groupings of distinctive developmental trajectories that themselves may reflect distinctive etiologies. In some applications, the groups may be literal entities. For example, the efficacy of some drugs depends on the users' genetic makeup. In many other application domains, however, the groups should not be thought of as literally distinct entities. Rather they serve as a statistical approximation to a more complex underlying reality. A key aim of this book is to demonstrate that trajectory groups are a powerful statistical device for summarizing and portraying complex patterns in longitudinal data sets. By identifying clusters of individuals with similar developmental trajectories, differences that may explain or at least predict individual-level heterogeneity can be expressed in terms of group differences. By contrast, a modeling strategy that assumes a continuous distribution of trajectories must explain individual-level heterogeneity in terms of that distribution function. As elaborated below, this difference has fundamental implications for the framing of the statistical analysis.

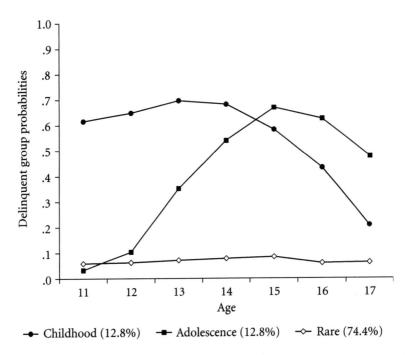

Figure 1.1   Trajectories of gang membership. Adapted from Lacourse et al. (2003).

An application of this group-based method is illustrated in Figure 1.1. The data, which are described in greater detail in section 1.6, were assembled as part of a Montreal-based study that tracked 1,037 males. Assessments were made on a wide range of factors. Among these were annual self-reports, made from ages 11 to 17, about involvement with a delinquent gang in the past year. Application of the group-based method to this gang involvement data identified the three highly distinct groups shown in the figure (Lacourse et al., 2003). The trajectory for each group is described by the probability of gang membership at each age. One trajectory, called the rare group, is estimated to include 74.4% of the population. This group's probability of gang membership was very small over all ages. The second group, called the childhood onset group, began at age 11 with a high probability of gang membership that modestly rises till age 13 and declines thereafter. The third group, called the adolescent onset group, had a near-zero probability of gang membership at age 11, but thereafter the probability rose to a rate that actually exceeded that of the childhood onset group. The latter two groups are each estimated to constitute 12.8% of the sampled population.

Had standard growth curve modeling methods been applied to these data, the product of the analysis would have been entirely different. The counterpart to the results in Figure 1.1 would have been the unconditional model, which would have described the average probability trajectory of gang involvement at each age from 11 to 17 and an associated set of variance parameters measuring the population variability about this mean trajectory. Thus the points of departure of the two modeling approaches for drawing inferences about the data are fundamentally different. The growth curve approach aims to identify the factors that account for individual variability about the population's mean trajectory of development. By contrast, the group-based approach frames questions of statistical inferences in terms of the trajectory group—what factors distinguish group membership and how do groups differ, if at all, in their response to events that might alter a trajectory.

For what types of problems is the group-based approach more appropriate than standard growth curve modeling and, conversely, for what types of problems is the standard approach a better fit? Although this is a question without a clear answer, some guidelines are possible. One guideline relates to the adjective "growth" that modifies "curve modeling." The prototypical application of standard growth curve modeling involves a process in which population members follow a common developmental pattern of either increase or decline. Raudenbush (2001:59) offers language acquisition as a quintessential example of such a process. Another good example is time spent with peers from childhood through adolescence (Warr, 2002). Standard growth curve methods are well suited for analyzing such developmental phenomena, because it is reasonable to assume that most individuals experience a common process of growth or decline, albeit at different rates. But there are large classes of developmental phenomena for which the conception of a common growth process does not naturally fit. Raudenbush describes the population differences for this class of problems as "multinomial," and for such problems he recommends a group-based approach as particularly appropriate. Raudenbush uses depression as an example. He observes: "It makes no sense to assume that everyone is increasing (or decreasing) in depression . . . many persons will never be high in depression, others will always be high, while others will become increasingly depressed."

The basis for Raudenbush's distinction between the developmental processes underlying language acquisition and those underlying depression is fundamental and cannot be overstressed. The former are appropriately analyzed by conventional analysis of variation; the latter are not. Because the vocabularies of all young children from normal populations increase with age, it is sensible to ask questions such as: What is the average growth curve of children's vocabulary over a specified age range? How large is the variation across children in their individual-level language acquisition growth curves? How do such "between-person" variations relate to factors such as the child's cognitive functioning and parental education? How are "within-person" changes in acquisition related to changes in interactions with primary caregivers due, for example, to parental conflict?

These questions are framed in the language of analysis of variance as reflected in the use of terms such as "within-person change" and "between-person change." This is only natural, because standard growth curve analysis has its roots in analysis of variance. Like analysis of variance, growth curve analysis is designed to sort out factors accounting for variation about a population mean.

To meaningfully frame an analysis in the conceptual apparatus of analysis of variance requires that it be sensible to characterize population differences in terms of variation about the population mean. For processes such as language acquisition the mean trend is, in fact, a sensible statistical anchor for describing individual variability. But for many processes evolving over time or age, it is not. For example, it makes no sense to frame a statistical analysis of population differences in the developmental progression of attention deficit disorder (ADD) in terms of variation about the mean trajectory of ADD, because ADD is the exception, not the norm, within the general population. Other examples of evolving behavioral phenomena that are not properly described in terms of variation about a population mean are most forms of psychopathology and abuse of both licit and illicit drugs. More generally, a group-based approach to analyzing longitudinal data is usefully applied to phenomena in which there may be qualitatively different trajectories of change over age or time across subpopulations that are not identifiable ex ante on the basis of measured characteristics such as gender or race.

The assumption that all individuals follow a process that increases or decreases regularly within the population may also be violated, because there may not be a single explanation for the differences in the developmental trajectories of subpopulations. For example, Nagin and Tremblay (2001a) found that a host of predictors involving the individual's psychological makeup and family circumstances distinguished individuals following low versus high trajectories of physical aggression in childhood. Yet a comparison of two distinct subpopulations of high childhood trajectories—those following a trajectory of chronic aggression versus those who started childhood with high aggression but later declined—revealed that only two maternal characteristics distinguished these groups. Using standard growth curve modeling methods, it would have been very difficult to identify this important difference in variables that distinguished among trajectories of childhood physical aggression. Identification of such differences is far easier with a methodology that clusters individuals with similar developmental trajectories.

A second guideline regarding the choice of approach concerns the motivation for the analysis. One common aim of analyses of longitudinal data is to uncover distinctive developmental trends in the outcome variable of interest. For example, do sizable numbers of youths follow a trajectory of adolescent-onset conduct disorder? The group-based approach is ideally suited for testing whether such distinctive patterns are present in the data. By contrast, another common aim of developmental studies is to test whether some identifiable characteristic or set of characteristics is associated with individual differences in trajectories of development. An example is whether trajectories of conduct disorder differ across the sexes. For this type of problem, standard growth curve modeling provides a natural starting point for framing the statistical analysis—a comparison of the mean trajectories for boys and girls. Thus according to this second guideline, the group-based approach lends itself to analyzing questions that are framed in terms of the shape of the developmental course of the outcome of interest, whereas standard growth curve modeling lends itself to analyzing questions framed in terms of predictors of the outcome's developmental course.[1]

A third guideline concerns the possibility of path dependencies in the response to turning-point events such as marriage or to treatments such as hospitalization for a psychiatric disorder. Path dependencies occur when the response to a turning-point event or treatment is contingent upon the individual's developmental history. For example, Nagin et al. (2003) find that the seeming impact of grade retention on physical aggression depended upon the child's trajectory of physical aggression. The subsequent physical aggression of children who had been following trajectories of little physical aggression or of chronic physical aggression appeared to be unaffected by the event of being held back in school. By contrast, the physical aggression of individuals who had been following trajectories of declining physical aggression seemed to be exacerbated. Such path dependencies are commonplace in the literature

---

1. I thank Steven Durlauf and Wayne Osgood for pointing out this important distinction.

on human development (Elder, 1985). Indeed the possibility of path dependencies is a key rationale for longitudinal studies. As will be developed in Chapter 7, the group-based trajectory model is well suited for identifying and testing whether the response to a turning-point event or treatment is contingent upon the individual's developmental trajectory

Laying out guidelines for the use of alternative statistical methods is a precarious exercise. Users naturally desire bright-line distinctions. Yet bright-line distinctions are generally not possible. The first guideline implies that developmental processes can be cleanly divided between those involving regular growth or decline and those that do not. The reality is that for many developmental processes it is not possible to confidently make this distinction. The second guideline implies that the objective of an analysis can be classified as either identifying distinctive developmental trajectories or testing predictors of developmental trajectories. The reality is that most analyses have both objectives. Still a further complication is that standard growth curve modeling can be used to identify distinctive developmental trajectories for *predefined* groups (for example, races or genders), and group-based modeling can be used to test theories about the underlying predictors and causes of population differences in developmental trajectories. The third guideline might be interpreted as implying that it is not possible to identify path dependencies with conventional growth curve models. This is not the case. Stated differently, both methods are designed to analyze change over time. The group-based method focuses on identification of different trajectory shapes and on examining how the prevalence of the shape and the shape itself relate to predictors. By contrast, standard growth curve modeling focuses on the population mean trajectory and how individual variation about that mean relates to predictors. Thus the alternative approaches are best thought of as complementary, not competing.

1.4 Other Rationales for a Group-Based Statistical Model

There is a long tradition in developmental psychology of group-based theorizing about both normal and pathological development. Examples include theories of personality development (Caspi, 1998), drug use (Kandel, 1975), learning (Holyoak and Spellman, 1993), language and conceptual development (Markman, 1989), depression (Kasen et al., 2001), eating disorders (Tyrka et al., 2000), alcoholism (Cloninger, 1987), anxiety (Cloninger, 1986), and the development of prosocial behaviors such as conscience (Kochanska,

1997) and of antisocial behaviors such as delinquency (Loeber, 1991; Moffitt, 1993; Patterson, DeBaryshe, and Ramsey, 1989).

Developmental researchers have commonly used assignment rules based on subjective categorization criteria to construct categories of developmental trajectories. For example, in their research on the developmental origins of violence Haapasalo and Tremblay (1994) propose a taxonomy comprising five groups—stable high fighters, desisting high fighters, late-onset high fighters, variable high fighters, and nonfighters. These groups were created from teacher ratings of a child's physical aggression in the previously described Montreal-based longitudinal study. Each child's physical aggression was rated at age 6 and annually from age 10 to age 12. Haapasalo and Tremblay labeled boys who scored high on this scale in any given period as "high fighters" for that period. They then defined rules for assigning individuals into their five-group taxonomy. These rules were based on the frequency and trend of each boy's classification as a high fighter. For example, "desisting high fighters" were boys who were high fighters in kindergarten but who were classified as high fighters in no more than one of the ensuing assessment periods.

Moffitt's (1993) well-known taxonomy is more parsimonious. She posits only two distinct developmental trajectories of problem behavior. One group follows what she calls a life-course-persistent (LCP) trajectory of antisocial behavior, and the other group is posited to follow an adolescent-limited (AL) trajectory. In empirical tests of her theory (Moffitt et al., 1996), she uses classification rules conceptually similar to those used by Haapasalo and Tremblay. LCPs are defined as individuals who score one or more standard deviations above the mean in three of four assessments of a conduct disorder index between the ages of 5 and 11 and who also score at least one standard deviation above the mean in self-reported delinquency at least once at either age 15 or age 18. The ALs are defined as individuals who do not meet the LCP criteria for childhood conduct problems but who do achieve the LCP threshold for adolescent delinquency (Moffitt et al., 1996).

Although such assignment rules are generally reasonable, there are limitations and pitfalls attendant on their use. One is that the existence of distinct developmental trajectories must be assumed a priori. Therefore the analysis cannot test for their presence, a fundamental shortcoming. A second and related pitfall is the risk of simultaneously "over- and under-fitting" the data by creating trajectory groups that reflect only random variation, and failing to identify unusual but still real developmental patterns. Third, ex ante specified rules provide no basis for calibrating the precision of individual classifications

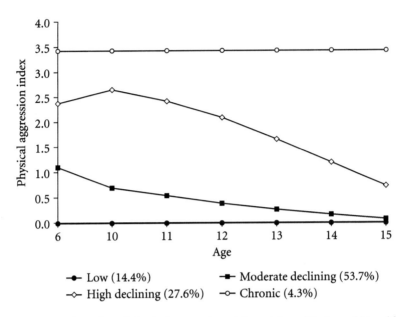

Figure 1.2   Trajectories of physical aggression. Adapted from Nagin and Tremblay (1999).

to the various groups that make up the taxonomy. Thus the uncertainty about an individual's group membership cannot be quantified in the form of probabilities.

The Haapasalo and Tremblay (1994) study illustrates these limitations. Figure 1.2 displays the results of an application of the group-based method to the physical aggression data used in that analysis. Specifically, the method was applied to annual assessments of physical aggression made at age 6 and again from ages 10 to 15.[2] Although Haapasalo and Tremblay (1994) originally proposed five taxonomic groups, the application of group-based trajectory analysis, which was first reported in Nagin and Tremblay (1999), found that a four-group model best fitted the data. A group called "lows" comprises individuals who display little or no physically aggressive behavior. This group is estimated to make up about 15% of the sample population. A second group, making up about 50% of the population, is best labeled "moderate declining."

---

2. At the time Haapasalo and Tremblay conducted their analysis, data on physical aggression were only available to age 12.

At age 6, boys in this group displayed a modest level of physical aggression, but by age 10 they had largely desisted. A third group, making up about 30% of the population, is labeled "high declining." This group starts off scoring high on physical aggression at age 6 but scores far lower by age 15. Notwithstanding this marked decline, at age 15 group members continue to display a modest level of physical aggression. Finally, there is a small group of "chronics," making up less than 5% of the population, who display high levels of physical aggression throughout the observation period.

The Nagin and Tremblay analysis provides formal statistical support for the presence of three of the groups hypothesized in the Haapasalo and Tremblay taxonomy: the stable high fighters (who correspond to the chronic trajectory group); the desisting high fighters (who correspond to the high declining trajectory group); and the nonfighters (who correspond to the low trajectory group). There is no evidence, however, of a trajectory corresponding to Haapasalo and Tremblay's late-onset high fighter group or of a variable high fighter group. These are examples of classifications that are likely to result from over-fitting the data, where random variation is confounded with real structural differences. There also seems to be evidence of the under-fitting problem, because the taxonomy fails to identify the moderate declining trajectory group. In Nagin and Tremblay (1999) and Nagin et al. (2003), the moderate declining group is found to be distinctive in some respects from the low physical aggression trajectory group.

Two other examples of the utility of the formal group-based trajectory method compared to ad hoc classification procedures are studies by Nagin, Farrington, and Moffitt (1995) and Lacourse et al. (2003). The former study was intended to test several predictions of Moffitt's two-group taxonomic theory, including testing for the very presence of the trajectories predicted by her taxonomy. On the basis of an analysis of a classic data set assembled by Farrington and West (1990), which includes data on convictions from ages 10 to 32 in a sample of over 400 males from a poor neighborhood in London, England, three offending trajectories were found.[3] These trajectories are shown in Figure 1.3. One trajectory, which peaks sharply in late adolescence, closely matches the adolescent-limited group predicted by Moffitt's theory. The high-hump-shaped trajectory, labeled high chronic, is similar in some respects to Moffitt's second group, the life-course persistents. This group is already

---

3. For further details on this data set, see section 1.6.

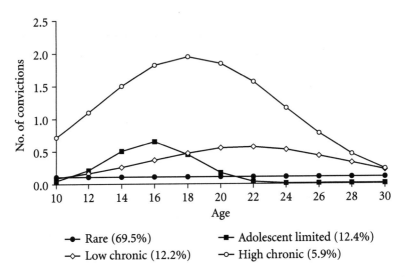

Figure 1.3   Trajectories of convictions. Adapted from Nagin, Farrington, and Moffitt (1995).

actively engaged in delinquency at age 10. However, group members' frequency of antisocial behavior, at least as measured by conviction, is very age dependent—a pattern that is not anticipated by Moffitt's theory. The trajectory rises until about age 18 and then begins a steady decline. By age 30 it has dropped below its starting point at age 10 and is about equal to the rate of a third group, called low-chronic offenders. This third group was not included in Moffitt's taxonomy. Thus the application of the group-based method provides basic confirmation of the presence of the AL and LCP trajectories that Moffitt predicts in her taxonomy, but also suggests that the LCP trajectory may be more age dependent than anticipated by the theory. Moreover, it identifies the low-chronic trajectory, which was not predicted by the taxonomy.

The gang membership trajectories from Lacourse et al. (2003) shown in Figure 1.1 illustrate two valuable properties of the group-based modeling approach compared with the use of classification rules. One is the capacity to identify qualitatively distinct developmental progressions that are not readily identifiable using ad hoc, ex ante classification rules. In principle the childhood-onset and adolescent-onset groups shown in Figure 1.1 are identifiable ex ante, but given the specific developmental course of each, it would be difficult to identify them without a formal statistical methodology. A second closely related advantage also stems from the use of a formal statistical structure. Because of this structure, the methodology has the capacity for distinguishing chance variation across individuals from real differences and for calibrating whether individual change is real or only random variation in behavior. Because the childhood- and adolescent-onset trajectories are the product of a formal statistical model, there is a firmer basis for their reality than if they had been constructed on the basis of subjective classification rules.

The formation of groups on the basis of the formal statistical model developed in this book, rather than on subjective classification rules, also has implications for the validity of statistical tests. Conventional statistical tests of differences across groups assume that group membership is known with certainty. As discussed in Chapter 6, conventional tests of cross-group differences are fortunately quite robust to classification error. However, they are not immune to classification error. One important shortcoming of the subjective classification approach is that it provides no basis for assessing the degree of classification error. By contrast, the group-based trajectory method does provide such a metric, the posterior probability of group membership (see Chapter 5). The method also provides a basis for conducting statistical tests that are not vulnerable to the problem of classification error.

The group-based methodology is also responsive to calls for the development of "person-based" approaches to analyzing development (Bergman, 1998; Magnusson, 1998). Such appeals are motivated by a desire for methods that can provide a statistical snapshot of the distinguishing characteristics and behaviors of individuals following distinctive developmental pathways. The group-based method lends itself to creating such profiles. This capacity is illustrated by the summary statistics reported in Table 1.1 that profile the characteristics of individuals following the four physical aggression trajectories shown in Figure 1.2. As developed in Chapter 5, the model's parameter estimates can be used to calculate the probability of an individual's belonging to each of the trajectory groups. To create the profiles reported in Table 1.1 individuals were assigned to the trajectory group to which they most likely belonged, on the basis of their measured history of physical aggression. The summary statistics reported in the table are simply the product of a cross-tabulation of group membership with the various individual characteristics and outcomes reported in the table.

The profiles conform to long-standing findings on the predictors and consequences of problem behaviors such as physical aggression. Individuals in the

Table 1.1   Physical aggression group profiles

	Group			
Variable	Low	Moderate declining	High declining	Chronic
Years of school (mother)	11.1	10.8	9.8	8.4
Years of school (father)	11.5	10.7	9.8	9.1
Low IQ (%)	21.6	26.8	44.5	46.4
Completed 8th grade on time (%)	80.3	64.6	31.8	6.5
Juvenile record (%)	0.0	2.0	6.0	13.3
Number of sexual partners at age 17 (past year)	1.2	1.7	2.2	3.5

Note: "Low IQ" distinguishes boys in the lower quartile of the sample's IQ distribution.

chronic aggression group tend to have the least-educated parents and most frequently score in the lowest quartile of the sample's IQ distribution. By contrast, individuals in the low aggression group are least likely to suffer from these risk factors. Further, 90% of the chronic aggression group fail to reach the eighth grade on schedule and 13% have a juvenile record by age 18. By comparison, only 19% of the low aggression group had fallen behind grade level by the eighth grade and none had a juvenile record. In between are the moderate- and high-declining groups.

Table 1.1 demonstrates that trajectory group membership varies systematically with the individual's psychosocial characteristics. An important generalization of the base model allows for joint estimation of both the shapes of the trajectory groups and the impact of psychosocial characteristics on the probability of trajectory group membership. For example, such an analysis shows that the probability of trajectory group membership is significantly predicted by low IQ, low paternal education, and being born to a mother who began childbearing as a teenager (Nagin and Tremblay, 2001a).

1.5 Focus on Methodology, Not Software

This book describes a methodology for analyzing developmental trajectories. It is not intended to be a tutorial on the use of any particular computer software package for estimating the models. At this time there are two excellent software alternatives for estimating group-based trajectories models.

One is a SAS-based procedure, called Proc Traj, developed by the author and colleagues. It is described in Jones, Nagin, and Roeder (2001) and in documentation available through the Web sites of the author and of Jones and at *http://www.ncovr.org/*. Proc Traj is designed to be inserted into the PC SAS software package. Once inserted, SAS treats it like any other standard SAS procedure. The other alternative is the widely used general latent variable software package M-Plus, developed by Bengt Muthén, Linda Muthén, and colleagues (Muthén and Muthén, 1998–2004). There are, of course, differences between these two software alternatives, but for the purposes of this book they are not material. With the exception of the Poisson modeling capability available in Proc Traj, the types of analyses described in this book generally can be conducted with either software package.

1.6 Data Sources

Two major longitudinal studies are the sources of the data for all but one of the examples used throughout this book.

Cambridge Study of Delinquent Development. The Cambridge Study of Delinquent Development (the London study) tracked a sample of 411 British males from a working-class area of London. Data collection began in 1961–62, when most of the boys were age 8. Criminal involvement is measured by the number of convictions for criminal offenses and is available for all individuals in the sample through age 32, with the exception of the eight individuals who died prior to this age. Between ages 10 and 32 a wealth of data were assembled on each individual's psychological makeup, family circumstances including parental behaviors, and performance in school and work. The demonstrations are based on the 403 individuals who survived to age 32. For a complete discussion of the data set, see Farrington and West (1990).

Montreal Longitudinal-Experimental Study of Boys. The subjects in the Montreal Longitudinal-Experimental Study of Boys (the Montreal study) were part of a longitudinal study started in the spring of 1984. All teachers of kindergarten classes in the 53 schools of the lowest socioeconomic areas in Montréal (Canada) were asked to rate the behavior of each boy in their classroom. The mean and median family income, when the boys were aged 10 years (1988), ranged between $25,000 and $30,000 Canadian dollars ($19,000 to $23,000 U.S. dollars). This is low compared with a median income of $44,000 (Canadian dollars) for couples with children in Canada in 1987. Eighty-seven percent (87%) of the kindergarten teachers agreed to participate, and a total of 1,161 boys were rated. To control for cultural effects, the boys were included in the longitudinal study only if both their biological parents were born in Canada and their biological parents' mother tongue was French. Thus a homogeneous white, French-speaking sample was created. The sample was reduced to 1,037 boys after applying these criteria and eliminating those who refused to participate and those who could not be traced. Informed consent was regularly obtained from mothers and the youths throughout the study. Assessments were made at age 6 and annually from ages 10 to 17. Wide-ranging measurements of social and psychological function were made on the basis of assessments by parents, teachers, and peers, the self-reports of the boy himself, and administrative records from schools and the juvenile court. See Tremblay et al. (1987) for further details on this study.

1.7 Chapter Overviews

Chapters 2, 3, 4, and 5 form Part I. These chapters develop the statistical foundation for group-based trajectory modeling. The results reported in Figures 1.1, 1.2, and 1.3 are the product of a statistical method called finite mixture modeling. Chapter 2 describes how mixture modeling can be used to capture heterogeneous groupings of developmental trajectories for a range of data types commonly found in longitudinal data sets. Chapter 3 discusses the use of trajectory groups as a statistical device for capturing the essential features of a more complex underlying reality. Chapter 4 provides detailed guidance on one of the most important modeling challenges attendant on the use of the group-based method—choosing the number of trajectory groups to be included in the model. Chapter 5 shows how the final model can be used to assign individuals to the trajectory group to which they most likely belong. The assignments, which are based on a quantity called the posterior probability of group membership, have many valuable uses that include creating a profile of each group's membership.

Chapters 6, 7, and 8, which form Part II, describe three important generalizations of the basic model. Chapter 6 develops a model extension that allows the probability of trajectory group membership to vary with characteristics of the individual. This model generalization creates the capacity for identifying and testing early predictors of long-run patterns of behavior. Another fundamental extension, which is the subject of Chapter 7, provides the capacity for obtaining trajectory group-specific estimates of whether and to what degree factors beyond time impact a group's trajectories. Such factors could include a turning-point event such as being held back in school, an intervention such as counseling, or an ecological factor such as changing neighborhood poverty. Chapter 8 describes a model extension that allows for the estimation of dual-trajectory models. This extension permits the investigator to study the unfolding of two distinct but related outcomes in a trajectory format. With this extension, trajectory modeling can be used to analyze two prominent themes in developmental psychopathology: comorbidity (the co-occurrence of two disorders) and heterotypic continuity (the manifestation over time of a latent individual trait in different but analogous behaviors).

Chapter 9 discusses potential pitfalls in the application of group-based trajectory modeling. It closes by returning to the central theme of this book—that trajectory groups are a powerful statistical device for summarizing complex longitudinal data sets and for drawing statistical inferences based on the resulting data summaries.

PART I

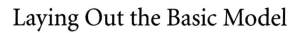

Laying Out the Basic Model

2

The Basic Model

2.1 Overview

This chapter lays out the basic structure of the group-based statistical model. The applications in Figures 1.1, 1.2, and 1.3 are examples of this structure, which has two defining features: (1) the predicted trajectory of each group, and (2) the probability that a randomly chosen individual from the sampled population is a member of each such group.

Technically, the group-based trajectory model is an application of a statistical method called "finite mixture modeling." Finite mixture models are an elaboration of the conventional maximum likelihood model that forms the statistical basis for many commonly used statistical methods, including Poisson, logit, and tobit regression. As will be formally developed in section 2.2, the elaboration involves combining a mixture of single-group models within a common multiple-group model structure.

Section 2.2 lays out the underlying structure of the likelihood function of the group-based trajectory model. An attractive feature of this structure is that it has the generality and flexibility to accommodate the wide variety of data types that are commonly present in longitudinal data sets. The specific form of the likelihood function is demonstrated for three types of data—censored data (for example, many psychometric scales measuring constructs such as altruism and depression), count data, and binary data. Figures 1.1, 1.2, and 1.3 are examples of trajectory models based on each of these types of data. Section 2.2 is necessarily technical. Sections 2.3 and 2.4 are directed at less technically oriented readers and provide guidance, illustrated with concrete examples, on the interpretation and use of the model's parameter estimates for each of the data types. Section 2.3 describes how the approach

used to specify the form of each group's trajectory provides the ability to identify distinctly different trajectory shapes across groups. Section 2.4 demonstrates the mechanics of using the model's parameter estimates to calculate
each group's predicted trajectory and also the probability of membership in
each such group.

2.2 The General Form of the Likelihood Function

Group-based trajectory models are a specialized application of finite mixture models. While the conceptual aim of the analysis is to identify clusters of individuals with similar trajectories, the model's estimated parameters are not the result of a cluster analysis. Rather they are the product
of maximum likelihood estimation. As such, they share the many desirable
characteristics of maximum likelihood parameter estimates—they are consistent and asymptotically normally distributed (Cramèr, 1946; Greene, 1990;
Thiel, 1971).

The specific form of the likelihood function to be maximized depends on
the type of data being analyzed, but all are a special form of the following underlying likelihood function: let $Y_i = \{y_{i1}, y_{i2}, \ldots, y_{iT}\}$ denote a longitudinal
sequence of measurements on individual i over T periods. For expositional
convenience, y_{it} will generally be described as the behavior of an individual.
However, the outcome of interest doesn't have to pertain to an individual or a
behavior—y_{it} can refer to an entity such as a community or an organization,
or it can measure a quantity such as a poverty rate, a mean salary level, or a
crime rate as in Weisburd et al. (2004).

Let $P(Y_i)$ denote the probability of Y_i. As will be developed below, for count
data $P(Y_i)$ is specified as the Poisson distribution, for censored data it is specified as the censored normal distribution, and for binary data it is specified as
the binary logit distribution. Whatever the probability distribution, the ulti-
mate objective is to estimate a set of parameters, Ω, that maximizes the probability of Y_i. The particular form of this parameter set is distribution specific.
However, across all distributions, these parameters perform the basic function
of defining the shapes of the trajectories and the probability of group membership. As will be developed in detail below, in both standard growth curve
modeling and group-based trajectory modeling, the shapes of the trajectories
are described by a polynomial function of age or time.

If the parameters of this polynomial function were constant across population members, the expected trajectory of all population members would be identical. Neither standard growth curve methods nor the group-based method assumes such homogeneity. Indeed the assumption of homogeneity is antithetical to the objective of either approach, because both aim to analyze the reason for individual differences in development. Standard growth curve modeling assumes that the parameters defining the polynomial describe only a population mean and that the trajectories of individual population members vary continuously about this mean, usually according to the multivariate normal distribution. The group-based method assumes that individual differences in trajectories can be summarized by a finite set of different polynomial functions of age or time. Each such set corresponds to a trajectory group which is hereafter indexed by j. Let $P^j(Y_i)$ denote the probability of Y_i given membership in group j, and π_j denote the probability of a randomly chosen population member belonging to group j.

If it were possible to observe group membership, the sampled individuals could be sorted by group membership and their trajectory parameters estimated with readily available Poisson, censored normal (tobit), and logit regression software packages. However, group membership is not observed. Indeed the proportion of the population making up each group j, π_j, is an important parameter of interest in its own right. Thus construction of the likelihood function requires the aggregation of the J conditional likelihood functions, $P^j(Y_i)$, to form the unconditional probability of the data, Y_i:

$$P(Y_i) = \sum_{j}^{J} \pi_j P^j(Y_i), \qquad (2.1)$$

where $P(Y_i)$ is the unconditional probability of observing individual i's longitudinal sequence of behavioral measurements, Y_i. It equals the sum across the J groups of the probability of Y_i given i's membership in group j weighted by the probability of membership in group j.

Equation 2.1 describes what is called a "finite mixture model," because it sums across a finite number of discrete groups that compose the population. The term "mixture" is included in the label because the statistical model specifies that the population is composed of a mixture of unobserved groups. Conventional growth curve models are also a type of mixture model. For this class of models, however, the mixing distribution is not finite. Instead it is defined by a continuous function, usually the multivariate normal distribution. Specifically, the model assumes that the parameters defining the mixture of individual-level trajectories in the population are drawn from a multivariate normal distribution.

For given j, conditional independence is assumed for the sequential realizations of the elements of Y_i, y_{it}, over the T periods of measurement. Thus

$$P^j(Y_i) = \prod_{}^{T} p^j(y_{it}), \qquad (2.2)$$

where $p^j(y_{it})$ is the probability distribution function of y_{it} given membership in group j.

The rationale for the conditional independence assumption deserves elaboration. This assumption implies that for each individual within a given trajectory group j the distribution of y_{it} for period t is independent of the realized level of the outcome in prior periods, y_{it-1}, y_{it-2}, ... Thus $p^j(y_{it})$ does not include prior values of y_{it} in its specification. This assumption greatly reduces the complexity of an already complex model. Because of this reduction in complexity, most applications of finite mixture modeling with longitudinal data assume conditional independence for the sake of tractability.

On its face, the conditional independence assumption may seem implausible, because it would seem to imply that current behavioral outcomes are uncorrelated with past outcomes. At the level of the group, which is not observed, this is indeed the case. For individuals within a given group j, behavioral outcomes over time are assumed not to be serially correlated in the sense that individual-level deviations from the group trend are uncorrelated. Even with the assumption of conditional independence at the level of the latent group, however, there will still be serial dependence over time at the level of the population. Specifically, past outcomes will be correlated with current outcomes (for example, across individuals, body mass indices at period t will be correlated with their values in subsequent periods). Such serial dependence results from the group-specific specification of $p^j(y_{it})$. Difference in this specification across groups allows for persistent differences of the outcome variable across population members.

The conditional independence assumption is also invoked in the standard random effect model that underlies conventional growth curve models. The random effect model assumes that the sequential realizations of y_{it} are independent, conditional upon the individual's random effect. Thus, in the group-based model the conditional independence assumption is made at the level of the group, whereas in the random effect model it is invoked at the level of the individual. In this sense, the conditional independence assumption is stronger in the group-based model than in the standard random effect model. Balanced against this disadvantage is the advantage that the group-based model does not make the strong assumption that the random effect is independently and identically distributed according to the normal distribution.

The likelihood for the entire sample of N individuals is simply the product of the individual likelihood functions of the N individuals who make up the sample, equation 2.1:

$$L = \prod_{i}^{N} P(Y_i).$$

The specific form of the likelihood for each data type is derived in sections 2.2.1–2.2.3, but intuitively, the estimation procedure for all data types identifies distinctive trajectory groups as follows. Suppose a population is composed of two distinct groups: (1) youth offenders (making up 50% of the population) who up to age 18 have an expected offending rate, λ, of 5 and who after age 18 have a λ of 1; and (2) adult offenders (the other 50% of the population) whose offending trajectory is the reverse of that of the youth offenders—through age 18 their $\lambda = 1$ and after age 18 their λ increases to 5. Longitudinal data on the recorded offenses of a sample of individuals from this population would reveal two distinct groups: a clustering of about 50% of the sample who have had many offenses prior to age 18 and relatively few offenses after 18, and another 50% clustering with the reverse pattern.

If these data were analyzed under the assumption that the relationship between age and λ was identical across all individuals, the estimated value of λ would be a "compromise" estimate of about 3 for all ages. From this one might mistakenly conclude that the rate of offending is invariant with age in this population. If the data were instead analyzed using the group-based approach, which specifies the likelihood function as a mixing distribution, no such mathematical "compromise" would be necessary. The parameters of one component of the mixture would effectively be used to accommodate (that is, match) the youth-offending portion of the data whose offending declines with age and another component of the mixing distribution would be available to accommodate the adult offender data whose offending increases with age.

2.2.1 Specification of the Likelihood for the Censored Normal Distribution

This section demonstrates the adaptation of the general form of the model (equation 2.1) to estimate trajectory models in which y_{it} is a censored variable, such as a psychometric scale in which there are clusters of data at the scale minimum or maximum. For example, consider the teacher ratings of physical aggression used to estimate the trajectories reported in Figure 1.1. The minimum and maximum of this scale were, respectively, 0 and 6. Teacher ratings of physical aggression decline, on average, over the 7 assessment periods. At age 6, 46.8% of the boys were rated at the scale minimum. By age 15, the percentage at the scale minimum had increased to 79.6%. Conversely, the percentage of boys at the scale maximum declines from 5.0% to 0.6% over the same time period.

Other examples of data with censoring are grade point averages and annual household expenditures on durable goods. The censoring in grade-point-average data arises from the clustering of top students at the highest possible grade point. In the case of durable purchases the censoring is caused by a substantial fraction of sampled households that will make no purchase in any given year.

The model developed in this section can also be used for data which is measured on a continuous scale without censoring, such as the body mass index or pollution discharge levels.

Adaptation of the general model to censored data requires two key modeling assumptions: (1) the choice of an appropriate form of $p^j(y_{it})$ for characterizing the distributional properties of censored data, and (2) specification of a link function that connects the course of the behavior or outcome with age or time. The censored normal distribution, also called the tobit model in econometrics,[1] is used to define $p^j(y_{it})$, and the linkage between age and behavior is established via a latent variable, y_{it}^*. This latent variable can be thought of as measuring individual i's potential for engaging in the behavior of interest at age t. For the applications considered in this book, the model allows for up to a cubic relationship between y_{it}^* and age,

$$y_{it}^* = \beta_0^j + \beta_1^j Age_{it} + \beta_2^j Age_{it}^2 + \beta_3^j Age_{it}^3 + \varepsilon_{it}, \qquad (2.3)$$

---

1. In the econometric literature censored normal regression is generally called "tobit regression" after its originator, James Tobin (Tobin, 1958).

where Age_{it}, Age_{it}^2, and Age_{it}^3 are individual i's age, age squared, and age cubed at time t, ε_{it} is a disturbance assumed to be normally distributed with a zero mean and a constant standard deviation σ, and β_0^j, β_1^j, β_2^j, and β_3^j are parameters that determine the shape of the polynomial.[2]

An important note: a trajectory can also be defined in terms of elapsed time from a specified anchoring date. For such applications, equation 2.3 could be recast as a function of t, t^2, and t^3. For example, Christ et al. (2002) analyzed trajectories of Internet usage in a sample of individuals who were provided free computers and Internet connections. In that study the trajectories were defined in terms of the time elapsed following provision of the computer and Internet connection. Similarly, Jones (2001) analyzed trajectories of depression as a function of elapsed time following completion of initial treatment. For expositional convenience, trajectories will generally be defined in terms of age, but elapsed time is always an appropriate alternative.

In the censored normal model the latent variable, y_{it}^*, is linked to its observed but censored counterpart, y_{it}, as follows. Let S_{min} and S_{max}, respectively, denote the minimum and maximum possible score on the measurement scale. The model assumes:

$$y_{it} = S_{min} \quad \text{if } y_{it}^* < S_{min},$$
$$y_{it} = y_{it}^* \quad \text{if } S_{min} \leq y_{it}^* \leq S_{max}, \quad \text{and}$$
$$y_{it} = S_{max} \quad \text{if } y_{it}^* > S_{max}.$$

In words, if the latent variable, y_{it}^*, is less than S_{min}, it is assumed that the measured behavior, y_{it}, equals this minimum. Likewise, if the latent variable, y_{it}^*, is greater than S_{max}, it is assumed that the measured behavior equals this maximum. Only if y_{it}^* is within the scale minimum and maximum does $y_{it} = y_{it}^*$. Figure 2.1 provides a graphical depiction of the relationship between y_{it} and y_{it}^*.[3]

---

2. See section 2.3 for a discussion of how a polynomial equation such as equation 2.3 can model a great variety of potential trajectory shapes.

3. In the context of this model the term *latent variable* is used to describe y_{it} because it is not fully observed. This use of the term "latent" is different from that in the psychometric literature, where the term *latent factor* refers to an unobservable construct that is assumed to give rise to multiple manifest variables.

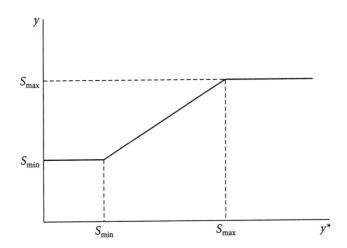

Figure 2.1   The relationship between y^* and y in the censored normal model.

Uncensored data is a specific case of the censored model where there is no scale minimum or maximum or where as a practical matter all data are less than S_{max} and greater than S_{min}.[4]

For notational convenience, let $\beta^j X_{it}$ denote $\beta_0^j + \beta_1^j Age_{it} + \beta_2^j Age_{it}^2 + \beta_3^j Age_{it}^3$. Thus equation 2.3 can be restated as $y_{it}^* = \beta X_{it} + \varepsilon_{it}$. Because ε_{it} is assumed to be normally distributed with a zero mean and a standard deviation σ, it follows that y_{it}^* is normally distributed with mean $\beta^j X_{it}$ and conditional on age with a standard deviation σ. The model is referred to as the "censored normal" model because the distribution of its fully observed but censored counterpart, y_{it}, is also defined in terms of the normal distribution. Specifically, $p^j(y_{it})$ equals:

$$p^j(y_{it} = S_{min}) = \Phi\left(\frac{S_{min} - \beta^j x_{it}}{\sigma}\right), \qquad (2.4.1)$$

$$p^j(y_{it}) = \frac{1}{\sigma}\phi\left(\frac{y_{it} - \beta^j x_{it}}{\sigma}\right) \quad \text{for} \quad S_{min} \leq y_{it} \leq S_{max}, \quad \text{and}, \qquad (2.4.2)$$

$$p^j(y_{it} = S_{max}) = 1 - \Phi\left(\frac{S_{max} - \beta^j x_{it}}{\sigma}\right), \qquad (2.4.3)$$

---

4. Models for uncensored data can be estimated with the trajectory software, Proc Traj, by setting the scale minimum and maximum at values that are, respectively, smaller than and larger than any data value.

where ϕ and Φ are, respectively, the density function and cumulative distribution function of a normal random variable with mean $\beta^j X_{it}$ and standard deviation σ.

Equation 2.4.1 measures the probability of censoring at the scale minimum. It equals the cumulative standardized normal distribution evaluated at $(S_{min} - \beta^j x_{it})/\sigma$. This probability is inversely related to $\beta^j x_{it}$. Consequently, and in accord with intuition, as the propensity index, $\beta^j x_{it}$, increases, the probability of y_{it} equaling S_{min} declines. Conversely, the probability of y_{it}'s being censored at the scale maximum (equation 2.4.3) is an increasing function of $\beta^j x_{it}$. Again this accords with intuition—the higher an individual's potential for a behavior, the greater the likelihood that measured behavior will be at the scale maximum. Finally, equation 2.4.2 states that both y_{it}^* and y_{it} follow the same normal density function for values between the scale minimum and maximum.

For the censored normal case, a complete specification of the likelihood simply entails substituting equations 2.4.1, 2.4.2, or 2.4.3 into equation 2.2 for values of y_{it} that are, respectively, equal to S_{min}, between S_{min} and S_{max}, and equal to S_{max}.

The importance of accounting for the clustering of data at the scale minimum and maximum is not specific to group-based models and can be illustrated with a conventional single group model. Suppose the latent propensity, y_{it}^*, is a positive linear function of age. In this case $E(y_{it}^*) = \beta_0 + \beta_1 Age_{it}$. If censoring is ignored and ordinary least-squares regression is used to estimate the rate of increase with age in latent propensity, β_1, the resulting regression will provide an attenuated estimate of this parameter. At younger ages when y_{it}^* is low, individuals will tend to be at the scale minimum. As a result, the measured behavior, y_{it}, will be greater, on average, than the latent propensity, y_{it}^*. Such downside censoring will decline with age because the age-related increase in latent propensity will reduce the proportion of individuals at the scale minimum. On the other hand, as individuals in the population age, the proportion of the population at the scale maximum will increase. Because y_{it}^* is greater than y_{it} once the scale maximum is reached, on average, y_{it} will tend to be less than y_{it}^* at older ages. As a result of this compression of data between the scale minimum and maximum, a regression of y_{it} on age will provide an estimate of β_1 with an expected value that underestimates the true rate of change.

By formally accounting for the censoring of y_{it} in the specification of the likelihood function, the censored normal model provides consistent estimates of the parameters of the polynomial relationship that describes the trajectory of y_{it}^* for each trajectory group j. With these estimates in hand, for each group j the expected value of y_{it}^*, $E(y_{it}^*)$, can be estimated by $\hat{\beta}^j x_{it}$, where $\hat{\beta}^j$ denotes the maximum likelihood estimate of β^j. For each group j the expected value of the measured quantity, $E(y_{it}^j)$, can also be estimated by:

$$E(Y_{it}^j) = \Phi_{min}^j S_{min} + \hat{\beta}^j x_t (\Phi_{max}^j - \Phi_{min}^j)$$
$$+ \sigma(\phi_{min}^j - \phi_{max}^j) + (1 - \Phi_{max}^j) S_{max}, \qquad (2.4)$$

where Φ_{min} and Φ_{max}, respectively, denote $\Phi^j[(S_{min} - \hat{\beta}x_{it}^j)/\sigma]$ and $\Phi^j[(S_{max} - \hat{\beta}x_{it}^j)/\sigma]$ with corresponding definitions for the normal densities ϕ_{min} and ϕ_{max}.

In section 2.4.2 these calculations are illustrated with an example.

2.2.2 Specification of the Likelihood for the Poisson Distribution

Figure 1.3 illustrates the application of the base model to a common form of data in criminological research—counts of the number of times that an individual is convicted. Examples of count data from other fields are number of physician visits in medical research and number of purchases of a specific type of product in marketing research.

This section demonstrates the adaptation of the base model for estimating trajectories for count data. This adaptation uses the most common probability distribution for modeling count data, the Poisson distribution. Specifically, for each group j:

$$p^j(y_{it}) = \frac{\lambda_{jt}^{y_{it}} e^{-\lambda_{jit}}}{y_{it}!} \qquad (y_{it} = 0, 1, 2, \ldots). \qquad (2.5)$$

In words, equation 2.5 specifies the probability of y_{it} equaling any nonnegative integer value; for example, the probability of an individual's having 0, 1, 2, ... convictions in any given year. The probability assigned to each possible outcome depends upon the mean rate of occurrence of the event for all individuals in a given group j at each time t. This rate is denoted by λ_{jt}. In the case of conviction data, λ_{ji} measures the expected number of convictions per annum for all individuals belonging to group j at time t.

Figure 2.2 shows four examples of the Poisson distribution for $\lambda = 0.5, 1.0, 2.0,$ and 5.0. The probability of larger values of y is an increasing function of

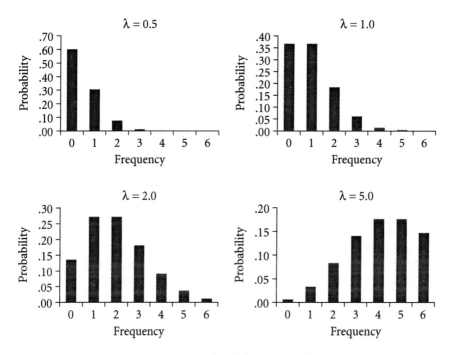

Figure 2.2 Four examples of the Poisson distribution.

λ while the probability of smaller values of y correspondingly decreases. For example, for λ = .5 the probability of 0 occurrences (for example, no convictions) is about .6 and the probability of 3 occurrences is .01. By contrast, for λ = 2 the probability of 0 occurrences drops to less than .15 and the probability of 3 occurrences increases to .18.

Also, observe that as λ increases the Poisson distribution begins to resemble the normal distribution. The convergence of the Poisson and normal distributions as λ increases implies that in applications where the mean rate is thought to be large across all groups, analyses based on the censored normal and Poisson models will yield similar results.

As with the censored normal model, specification of the Poisson model requires the specification of a link function that connects the behavioral trajectory with age. This linkage is accomplished by assuming that λ_{jt} varies with age as follows:

$$\ln(\lambda_t^j) = \beta_0^j + \beta_1^j Age_{it} + \beta_2^j Age_{it}^2 + \beta_3^j Age_{it}^3. \tag{2.6}$$

The link function is specified in terms of the natural logarithm of λ_t^j, rather than in terms of λ_{jt}, for computational reasons only. Because λ_t^j measures the mean rate of occurrence, it is theoretically impossible to have a negative value. If equation 2.6 were specified in terms of λ_t^j rather than $\ln(\lambda_t^j)$, the algorithm used to search for the maximum likelihood estimates of $\beta_0^j, \beta_1^j, \beta_2^j$, and β_3^j might select interim estimates that would result in negative values of λ_{jt}. Such estimates would cause the estimation process to fail. By specifying equation 2.6 in terms of $\ln(\lambda_t^j)$, the possibility of a negative value for λ_t^j is precluded, because $e^{\ln(\lambda_t^j)}$ is always greater than 0.

An even more general version of the Poisson-based model was first proposed in Nagin and Land (1993; see also Land, McCall, and Nagin, 1996, and Land and Nagin, 1996). This generalization used what Lambert (1993) called the zero-inflated Poisson (ZIP) distribution. The Poisson distribution assigns a probability to all possible non-negative integer values including 0. Lambert observed that in some problem applications, the Poisson distribution provides a good fit to the probability distribution of the data, but underestimates the probability of 0 occurrences.[5] The ZIP model is an elegant elaboration of the Poisson model to accommodate this problem. In parallel, an analytically equivalent extension was proposed in Nagin and Land (1993) for the purpose of studying a phenomenon called intermittency in criminal careers research.

The concept of intermittency refers to episodes of inactivity in a criminal career, which Nagin and Land modeled as follows. Suppose that in each period t some members of group j are inactive in the sense that their mean occurrence rate, λ_{ji}, equals 0. Let α_i^j denote the probability that a member of j will be inactive. Under this generalization zero occurrences can occur for two reasons. One is that the individual is inactive in the sense that $\lambda_{jt} = 0$. The second is that the person is active in the sense that $\lambda_{jt} > 0$, but, by chance, experiences no occurrences. In the study of criminal behavior this might occur if an individual is actively seeking out criminal opportunities but in a given period identifies no attractive opportunities for crime. For $\lambda_{jt} = 0$, the probability of

---

5. Examples include symptom counts for diseases that periodically go into remission or counts of defects in industrial processes that go into and out of periods of perfect running order. In the first example, patients may be symptom free because the disease is in remission or because it has yet to produce symptoms even though it is in its active state. In the second example, a period of zero defects may reflect that the process is operating perfectly or only that a process imperfection has yet to yield a defect.

zero occurrences is $e^{-\lambda_{jt}}$. Thus across these two sources of zero occurrences the total probability of $y_{it} = 0$ is

$$p^j(y_{it} = 0) = \alpha_t^j + (1 - \alpha_t^j)e^{-\lambda_{jt}}, \tag{2.7}$$

where the first term of equation 2.7 is the probability of inactivity and the second term is the probability of the combined event's being active $1 - \alpha_t^j$ and the probability of zero occurrences given $\lambda_{jt} > 0$.

Also, for $y > 0$:

$$p^j(y_{it}) = (1 - \alpha_t^j)\frac{\lambda_{jt}^{y_{it}}e^{-\lambda_{jit}}}{y_{it}!} \qquad (y_{it} = 1, 2, \ldots). \tag{2.8}$$

2.2.3 Specification of the Likelihood for the Binary Logit Distribution

This section demonstrates the adaptation of the general model to a form that is suitable for the analysis of longitudinal data in which the outcome at each assessment period is binary. Figure 1.1 illustrates the application of the binary model to annual assessments from ages 11 to 17 on whether or not the subject belonged to a gang in the prior year. Other examples of binary longitudinal data are whether an individual has been hospitalized in each of t assessment periods or whether a firm has experienced a labor stoppage in each of t years.

This form of the basic model again utilizes the concept of a latent variable $y_{it}^* = \beta_0^j + \beta_1^j Age_{it} + \beta_2^j Age_{it}^2 + \beta_3^j Age_{it}^3 + \varepsilon_{it}$. Under this formulation, it is assumed that the observed binary outcome $y_{it} = 1$ (for example, individual i is hospitalized in period t) if $y_{it}^* > 0$, whereas $y_{it} = 0$ (for example, individual i is not hospitalized in period t) if $y_{it}^* \leq 0$. Let α_{it}^j denote the probability of $y_{it} = 1$ given membership in group j, $p^j(y_{it} = 1)$. If ε_{it} is assumed to be normally distributed, α_{it}^j is described by the probit function (Greene, 1995; Maddala, 1983). Alternatively, if ε_{it} follows the extreme value distribution, α_{it}^j follows the binary logit distribution:

$$\alpha_{it}^j = \frac{e^{\beta_0^j + \beta_1^j Age_{it} + \beta_2^j Age_{it}^2 + \beta_3^j Age_{it}^3}}{1 + e^{\beta_0^j + \beta_1^j Age_{it} + \beta_2^j Age_{it}^2 + \beta_3^j Age_{it}^3}}. \tag{2.9}$$

The logit and probit distribution are nearly identical "S-shaped" distributions. Thus there is no substantive basis for choosing between them. The binary logit distribution is used, because unlike the probit function, it is described by a closed-form equation.

For each trajectory group j, the model yields an estimate of α_{it}^{j} for each assessment period. Thus in the application reported in Figure 1.1, the trajectory for each group member is defined by the probability of gang membership from ages 11 to 17. In the case of the adolescent-onset group, this probability starts at nearly 0 at age 11, but thereafter rises to a peak of about .7 by age 15.

Note that α_{it}^{j} is determined by the value of y_{it}^{*}. As was the case for the censored normal model, y_{it}^{*} can be interpreted as an index of latent potential. As this potential increases, α_{it}^{j} also increases. This general point is illustrated in section 2.4.

2.2.4 Missing Data

An endemic problem in longitudinal research studies is incomplete assessment histories for study participants. Gaps in assessment histories occur for a myriad of reasons, including the death or disappearance of participants or their simple refusal to continue to participate in or respond to specific aspects of the assessment. Gaps in the assessment history are an example of missing data.

Missing data is commonly regarded as nothing more than a statistical nuisance that at worst reduces sample size and thus statistical power (that is, reliability). In the context of longitudinal research, however, the impact of missing assessments can be far more pernicious if the missing assessments are not random but instead are systematically related to the response variable of interest (Schafer and Graham, 2002). For example, in the study of antisocial behavior, individuals with the worst outcomes also tend to be the subjects who have the highest missing-value rates. A common practice in longitudinal research is to exclude from analysis those individuals who have incomplete assessment histories. For individuals with very incomplete histories this may be a practical necessity. At the same time, exclusion of subjects because of missing data may inject serious, albeit underappreciated, biases into the analysis.

Little and Rubin (1987) lay out a useful taxonomy of missing data. The taxonomy is meant to span the statistical importance and complexity of accommodating missing data. The simplest form of missing data in their taxonomy is data that is missing completely at random. The base model as specified by equations 2.1 and 2.2 is easily adapted to accommodate such data. Mechanically, this is accomplished by setting $p^j(y_{it})$ equal to 1 if y_{it} is missing and also adjusting the sample count so as not to include this missing observation in the sample size, N.

Ideally, it would be desirable to accommodate the more complex forms of missing data. This is not practically feasible, however, because there is no general model form that can accommodate these more complex forms. Still, the extension of the base model to accommodate data that is missing completely at random is a great advance over the option of expunging individuals with incomplete assessment histories from the sample.

2.2.5 Model Estimation

The models used in creating the illustrative applications throughout this book were estimated with a SAS-based procedure called Proc Traj. As is the case with most maximum likelihood–based statistical models, it is not possible to derive closed-form equations for calculating parameter estimates and their associated variances and covariances. Instead a search routine must be used to locate empirically the parameter estimates that maximize the likelihood function. The Proc Traj estimation software uses a general quasi-Newton procedure to perform this search. The variance-covariance matrix for the parameter estimates is obtained from the inverse observed information matrix evaluated at the maximum likelihood parameter estimates.

2.3 Determination of Trajectory Shape

While the specific form of the link function differs in the Poisson, censored normal, and binary logit formulations, in each case it is specified in terms of a polynomial function of age that is defined by the parameters β_0^j, β_1^j, β_2^j, and β_3^j. These parameters determine the shape of the trajectory for each trajectory group j. In this regard, it is important to emphasize that a separate set of parameters is estimated for each group j. As a consequence, the model allows the shapes of trajectories to vary freely across groups. This flexibility is a key feature of the model. It provides the capacity for identification of

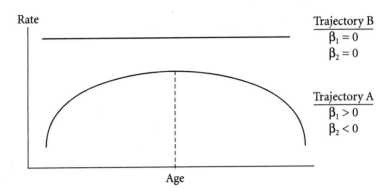

Figure 2.3   Two hypothetical trajectories for $\beta_0 + \beta_1 Age + \beta_2 Age^2$. Adapted from
Nagin (1999).

distinctly different developmental trajectories across groups, not only in the
level of behavior at a given age but also in the behavior's developmental course
over age.

Figure 2.3 illustrates two hypothetical forms of a quadratic trajectory. A
single peaked trajectory—labeled "A" in the figure—is implied if $\beta_1 > 0$ and
$\beta_2 < 0$. Thus if data collection began at age 1 and ended at age 12, the
trajectory implies that for this group the occurrence of the behavior rose
steadily until age 6 and then began a steady decline. Changes in the method
of data collection can affect the interpretation of the shape of the trajectory.
For example, if data collection began at age 6, as was the case in the Montreal study, it would be inappropriate to extrapolate backward to younger ages
outside the period of measurement. Consequently, the model implies a declining trajectory in which the rate of decline was quickening with age. Such a
trajectory would typify cessation from the behavior. Conversely, if data collection began at age 1 and ended at age 6, the model would imply an increasing
trajectory in which the rate of increase was tapering off with age. The second
trajectory—labeled "B" in Figure 2.3—has no curvature. Rather it remains
constant over age. This trajectory is implied if $\beta_1 = 0$ and $\beta_2 = 0$. If the behavior under examination is consistently high, this trajectory would typify a
group that chronically engages in the behavior.

Other interesting possibilities include trajectories in which growth is either
steadily accelerating or decelerating over all ages. The former is characterized
by a trajectory in which both β_1 and β_2 are positive, and the latter by both

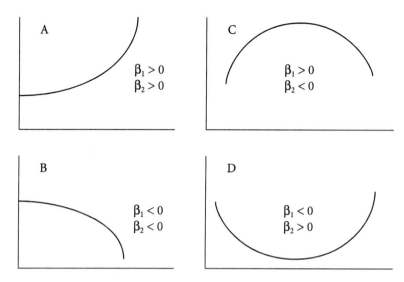

A $\quad \beta_1 > 0$
$\quad \beta_2 > 0$

C $\quad \beta_1 > 0$
$\quad \beta_2 < 0$

B $\quad \beta_1 < 0$
$\quad \beta_2 < 0$

D $\quad \beta_1 < 0$
$\quad \beta_2 > 0$

Figure 2.4 Four types of quadratic equations.

being negative. Still another possibility is the case where $\beta_1 < 0$ and $\beta_2 > 0$. Figure 2.4 demonstrates all of the possibilities. As illustrated by panels C and D, if β_1 and β_2 have different signs, it is not possible to determine the actual form of the trajectory over the range of ages in the data solely on the basis of the signs of β_1 and β_2. To make this determination it is necessary to inspect the predicted values of the trajectory at each such age. The predicted values can be calculated from estimates of β_1, β_2, and β_0.

Table 2.1 uses the Montreal data to illustrate the importance of inspecting predicted values. The results pertain to an analysis of data on self-reported violent delinquency between ages 11 and 17. Using these data, a five-group model was estimated with the Poisson-based model. In this model all trajectories were quadratic. The table reports the estimates of β_1 and β_2 and the predicted mean offending rate, λ, from age 8 to age 20 for four of these trajectories. In bold are the predicted values of λ from ages 11 to 17, the ages that provide the actual support in the data for the estimates. Observe that for trajectories A, B, and C, $\beta_1 > 0$ and $\beta_2 < 0$. Consequently each trajectory is described by a downward-facing parabola. However, C is the only trajectory that actually follows the complete rising and then falling pattern from ages 11 to 17. Trajectory A follows only the declining portion of the

Table 2.1   Predicted value of λ_{it} for trajectories of violent delinquency using data from ages 11 to 17

Age	A $\beta_1 = 10.6$ $\beta_2 = -4.5$	B $\beta_1 = 18.2$ $\beta_2 = -5.4$	C $\beta_1 = 9.3$ $\beta_2 = -3.6$	D $\beta_1 = -11.8$ $\beta_2 = 3.7$
8	.93	.05	1.79	2.44
9	1.25	.11	2.47	1.40
10	1.55	.25	3.18	.87
11	1.75	.50	3.81	.58
12	1.83	.90	4.26	.41
13	1.73	1.44	4.43	.32
14	1.50	2.08	4.29	.26
15	1.19	2.70	3.87	.23
16	.86	3.14	3.25	.22
17	.57	3.29	2.54	.23
18	.35	3.08	1.85	.25
19	.19	2.60	1.26	.30
20	.10	1.97	.79	.39

parabola, whereas B follows only the rising portion. While trajectory D is described by an upward-facing parabola in which $\beta_1 < 0$ and $\beta_2 > 0$, observe that only the declining portion of the parabola is reflected in the trajectory from ages 11 to 17.

As demonstrated in Figures 2.3 and 2.4, the quadratic form is quite flexible in its capacity to capture alternative trajectories of change—it can capture trajectories that rise or fall without interruption, rise and then fall, or fall and then rise. For the latter two cases, however, the quadratic functional form does impose two potentially important constraints. One is that the rising portion of the trajectory must be the mirror image of the falling portion. Thus if a theory predicted a steep rise followed by a steady but gradual decline, the quadratic relationship could not capture this asymmetry. The second important constraint is that the quadratic relationship only allows a single turning point in which the trajectory shifts from rising to falling or falling to rising. Therefore the trajectory can only have a single peak in the case of $\beta_1 > 0$ and $\beta_2 < 0$ or a single minimum point in the case of $\beta_1 < 0$ and $\beta_2 > 0$. The addition of a cubic term to the trajectory provides the capacity to avoid both these constraints. Note, however, that asymmetry in the arc of a trajectory and multiple maximums or minimums may represent theoretical features that are difficult to actually extract from the data.

2.4 Calculation of Trajectories and Group Membership Probabilities from Model Parameter Estimates

Group-based trajectory models are highly nonlinear. Complicated mathematical relationships link the model's parameters to the two key components of the model—the predicted trajectory for each group, and the probability of group membership. This section demonstrates the calculations that link parameter estimates to these quantities. It begins with a demonstration of the calculation of group membership probabilities, because this calculation is the same for the Poisson, logit, and censored normal models.

2.4.1 Calculation of Group Membership Probabilities

In principle, the probability of membership in group j, π_j, could be estimated directly. In practice this is not done for two reasons. First, π_j must be between 0 and 1. As a practical matter, it is difficult to force this constraint in model estimation. Second, Chapter 6 develops an important generalization of the basic model that allows group membership probabilities to depend on characteristics of the individuals. This generalization requires a specification of π_j that lends itself to this purpose. For these reasons π_j is linked to a set of parameters θ_j, $j = 1, 2, \ldots, J$, by:

$$\pi_j = \frac{e^{\theta_j}}{\sum\limits_{j=1}^{j} e^{\theta_j}}. \tag{2.10}$$

In this formulation the parameters to be estimated θ_j, $j = 1, 2, \ldots, J$, can take on any value—positive or negative—without violating the constraint that each π_j is between 0 and 1. It also conforms to the requirement that across all J groups the values of π_j sum to 1. The latter requirement also implies that only $J - 1$ estimates of θ_j are required, because the probability of one group can be computed as one minus the sum of the probabilities of the $J - 1$ other groups. By convention, for $j = 1$, θ_1 is set equal to 0.

To illustrate the mechanics of the calculation, consider the estimates of θ_j that determine the group membership probabilities for four trajectories of delinquency based on the London data shown in Figure 1.3. For $j = 2$, which corresponds to the adolescent-limited group, the estimate of θ_2 is -1.723. For $j = 3$, corresponding to the low chronic group, $\hat{\theta}_3 = -1.740$, and for $j = 4$, corresponding to the high chronic group, $\hat{\theta}_4 = -2.463$. Substituting these estimates into equation 2.9 along with $\theta_1 = 0$, which corresponds to the rare group, yields:

$$\pi_1 = \frac{e^0}{e^0 + e^{-1.723} + e^{-1.740} + e^{-2.463}} = .695$$

$$\pi_2 = \frac{e^{-1.723}}{e^0 + e^{-1.723} + e^{-1.740} + e^{-2.463}} = .124$$

$$\pi_3 = \frac{e^{-1.740}}{e^0 + e^{-1.723} + e^{-1.740} + e^{-2.463}} = .122$$

$$\pi_4 = \frac{e^{-2.463}}{e^0 + e^{-1.723} + e^{-1.740} + e^{-2.463}} = .059$$

Observe that all the estimates of θ_j are outside the interval from 0 to 1, yet the form of the calculation ensures that all of the probability estimates lie within this range. In addition, the form of the model guarantees that they sum to 1.

2.4.2 Calculations of Trajectories for the Censored Normal, Poisson, and Binary Logit Models

This section illustrates the calculation of trajectories for each of the three model types based on the model's maximum likelihood parameter estimates. Each illustration involves a quadratic trajectory.[6]

Table 2.2 demonstrates the calculation of the predicted trajectory for the censored normal model based on equation 2.4. The calculation is illustrated for the high declining trajectory of physical aggression shown in Figure 1.2. For these data the scale minimum and maximum are, respectively, 0 and 6. This is a complicated calculation that first requires five quantities be computed: (1) $\beta_0^j + \beta_1^j Age_{it} + \beta_2^j Age_{it}^2 + \beta_3^j Age_{it}^3$; (2) Φ_{min}^j; (3) Φ_{max}^j; (4) ϕ_{min}^j;

---

6. Note, however, that the SAS-based procedure Proc Traj calculates these trajectories. So as a general rule, users do not have to undertake these tedious calculations themselves.

Table 2.2 Calculation of trajectories for censored normal model for $\beta_0 = 2.92$, $\beta_1 = 12.94$, $\beta_2 = -7.521$, $\sigma = 2.35$, $S_{min} = 0$, and $S_{max} = 6$

Age/10	$\beta x = \beta_0 + \beta_1 Age/10 + \beta_2(Age/10)^2$	Φ_{min}	Φ_{max}	ϕ_{min}	ϕ_{max}	$E(y) =$ eq. 2.4
.6	2.14	.182	.950	.264	.103	2.32
1.0	2.50	.144	.932	.227	.132	2.60
1.1	2.21	.173	.946	.256	.109	2.38
1.2	1.78	.225	.963	.300	.080	2.05
1.3	1.19	.306	.980	.351	.049	1.63
1.4	.46	.423	.991	.391	.025	1.18
1.5	−.43	.573	.997	.932	.009	.74

Table 2.3 Calculation of trajectories for Poisson and binary logit model

	Poisson model $\beta_0 = -5.73$ $\beta_1 = 10.64$ $\beta_2 = -4.47$		Binary logit $\beta_0 = -55.19$ $\beta_1 = 72.94$ $\beta_2 = 23.83$	
Age/10	$\ln(\lambda) = \beta_0^j + \beta_1^j Age/10$ $+ \beta_2^j(Age/10)^2$	$\lambda = e^{\ln(\lambda)}$	$y^* = \beta_0 + \beta_1 Age/10$ $+ \beta^2(Age/10)^2$	$P(gang = 1) = \frac{e^{y^*}}{1+e^{y^*}}$
1.1	.565	1.76	−3.79	.022
1.2	.601	1.82	−1.98	.122
1.3	.548	1.75	−.641	.345
1.4	.405	1.50	.219	.555
1.5	.173	1.19	.603	.646
1.6	−.149	.86	.509	.625
1.7	−.560	.57	−.061	.485

and (5) ϕ_{max}^j. Each of these intermediate calculations, as well as the final calculation of the predicted trajectory, is reported in the table.

Consider next the Poisson model. Recall from 2.2.2 that λ_{jt} is linked to age by equation 2.6: $\ln(\lambda_t^j) = \beta_0^j + \beta_1^j Age_{it} + \beta_2^j Age_{it}^2 + \beta_3^j Age_{it}^3$. Thus λ_t^j is calculated by $\lambda_t^j = e^{\beta_0^j + \beta_1^j Age_{it} + \beta_2^j Age_{it}^2 + \beta_3^j Age_{it}^3}$. Table 2.3 illustrates the calculation of both these quantities for the violent delinquency trajectory A from Table 2.1.

Table 2.3 also illustrates the calculation of the adolescent-onset gang membership trajectory shown in Figure 1.1. This trajectory is the product of the binary logit model. The probabilities of gang membership over age that define the trajectory are calculated on the basis of equation 2.9. This calculation first requires that $\beta_0^j + \beta_1^j Age_{it} + \beta_2^j Age_{it}^2$ be computed at each age. This quantity is then substituted into equation 2.8 to calculate the probability of gang membership at each age.

Observe that age is divided by 10 in all of these illustrations. This is done for computational reasons only, but it is imperative. The maximum likelihood parameter estimates are identified by a complex computer search. The computational accuracy of the calculations required by this search is often greatly improved by scaling the age or time variable so that the successively higher terms in the polynomial defining the trajectory are all of about the same scale (that is, age, age squared, and age cubed are within the same order of magnitude).

This chapter has laid out the basic structure of the statistical model that underlies all of the analyses described in this book. Chapter 3 has a more conceptual objective. It discusses the use of the trajectory groups as a statistical device for modeling a more complex reality.

3

Groups as an Approximation

3.1 Overview

This book describes the construction and application of a group-based statistical model for analyzing developmental trajectories. Although there may be populations made up of groups that are literally distinct, they are not the norm. Most populations are composed of a collection of individual-level developmental trajectories that are continuously distributed across population members. The statistical question is how to best model the population heterogeneity of individual-level trajectories. Chapter 1 discussed circumstances under which a group-based approximation has important advantages over another form of approximation—the conventional growth curve model. But neither model of the heterogeneity of individual-level trajectories is entirely correct. No population is comprised of literally distinct groups; nor are the parameters describing the population variation normally distributed. Both models are just approximations of a more complex reality. As William Baumol (1992:55) observes, "A well-designed model is, after all, a judiciously chosen set of lies, or perhaps more accurately put, partial truths about reality, which have been chosen so as to permit us to reason more effectively about some issue than we otherwise could. The model must be an oversimplification if it is to be tractable analytically. Optimality in model constructions must be based on the trade-off between these two desiderata—accuracy of representation of reality and usability in analysis."

This chapter discusses the statistical implications of using trajectory groups as constructs for approximating a more complex underlying structure. Section 3.2 describes the use of groups as a device for approximating an unknown distribution. Section 3.3 reports simulation evidence on the capacity of the group-based trajectory model to reveal the essential features of a highly irregular population distribution of trajectories. Section 3.4 discusses an alternative conception of a trajectory group from the structural equation modeling tradition. Section 3.5 reports an extension of the simulation reported in section 3.3 that is designed to demonstrate that the group-based trajectory framework can be used to draw valid statistical inferences even when it is explicitly viewed as an approximation of a more complex underlying structure.

3.2 Using Groups to Approximate a Continuous Distribution

One use of finite mixture models is to approximate a continuous distribution function (Everitt and Hand, 1981; Heckman and Singer, 1984; McLachlan and Peel, 2000; Titterington, Smith, and Makov, 1985). For example, Everitt and Hand (1981) describe the use of a mixture of univariate normal distributions to approximate any unspecified univariate distribution function. McLachlan and Peel (2000:8) describe such use of finite mixture modeling as a "niche between parametric and nonparametric approaches to statistical estimation . . . [M]ixture model-based approaches are parametric in that parametric forms [of $p^j(y_{it})$] are specified for the component density functions, but that they can also be regarded as nonparametric by allowing the number of components [j] to grow." For this reason, my previous writings on the group-based trajectory method often describe it as a semiparametric method (for example, Nagin, 1999).

Heckman and Singer (1984) built upon the approximating capability of finite mixture models to construct a nonparametric maximum likelihood estimator for the distribution of unobservables in duration models. The motivation for this seminal innovation was their observation that social science theory rarely provides theoretical guidance on the population of the distribution of unobserved individual differences, yet statistical models of duration data have often been sensitive to the assumed form of the distribution of such differences. Their proposed estimator finessed the problem of having to specify a distribution of unobserved individual difference by approximating the distribution with a finite mixture model.

The idea of using a finite number of groups to approximate a continuous distribution is most easily illustrated with an example. Suppose that panel A in Figure 3.1 depicts the population distribution of some behavior z. In panel B, this same distribution is replicated and overlaid with a histogram that ap-

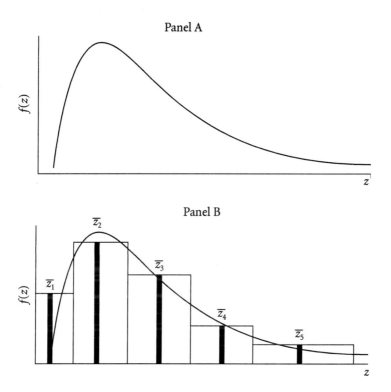

Figure 3.1 Using groups to approximate an unknown distribution. Adapted from Nagin and Land (1993).

proximates its shape. Panel B illustrates that any continuous distribution with finite end points can be approximated by a discrete distribution (that is, a histogram) or alternatively by a finite number of "points of support" (that is, the dark-shaded "pillars"). A higher number of support points yields a discrete distribution that more closely approximates the true continuous distribution.

Why use groups to approximate a continuous population distribution of developmental trajectories? This brings us back to the key distinction, highlighted in Chapter 1, between standard growth curve modeling and the approach developed in this book. Both approaches model individual trajectories with a polynomial relationship that links age to behavior. The approaches differ in their modeling strategy for incorporating population heterogeneity in the growth curve parameters (that is, β_0, β_1, β_2, and β_3). In conventional growth curve modeling, the parameters describing individual-level trajectories are assumed to be distributed according to a specific function, usually the multivariate normal distribution. In the semiparametric group-based trajectory model, the distribution is approximated by a finite number of trajectory groups, also known as points of support.

Although users of conventional growth curve modeling have demonstrated great ingenuity is adapting the basic model to accommodate longitudinal data that is clearly not normally distributed (for example, binary data or highly skewed data), these adaptations of the basic model do not resolve the more fundamental problem described by Raudenbush (2001): the standard growth curve modeling structure is not well adapted for modeling complex mixtures of developmental trajectories within a population. Instead, a multinomial statistical framework such as that provided by the group-based trajectory model is recommended. As McLachlan and Peel (2000:xix) observe: "Because of their flexibility, [finite] mixture models are being increasingly exploited as a convenient, semiparametric way in which to model unknown distributional shapes."

3.3 Using Group-Based Modeling to Explore Complex Distributions of Developmental Trajectories

The hallmark of a multinomial problem is that the population distribution of trajectories follows a highly irregular function. Using simulated data in which the true model is known, this section explores the capability of the group-based trajectory model to identify the distinctive features of a highly irregular but still continuous population distribution of trajectories.

The demonstration is based on the application of the Poisson-based trajectory model to a simulated longitudinal data set. The data set comprises 100,000 cases. Nine periods of count data were generated for all cases as follows. Each case, i, was assigned a random draw, z_i, from a normal distribution with a mean of 0 and standard deviation of 1. The random variable z_i was then converted into a Poisson rate parameter for each period t (λ_{it}) by the model described in Table 3.1. In period 1, $\lambda_{i1} = e^{z_i}$. Thus larger values of z_i correspond to larger initial period values of λ_{it}. In periods 2 through 5, λ_{it} either increases or decreases linearly with z_i. The direction of change depends upon the sign of z_i. For cases in which $z_i > 0$, λ_{it} decreases linearly, and for cases

Table 3.1   The specification of individual-level trajectories of λ_{it} as a function of z_i

Period	λ_{it}
1	e^{z_i}
2	$e^{z_i - .1z_i}$
3	$e^{z_i - .2z_i}$
4	$e^{z_i - .3z_i}$
5	$e^{z_i - .4z_i}$
6	$e^{z_i - .3z_i}$
7	$e^{z_i - .2z_i}$
8	$e^{z_i - .1z_i}$
9	e^{z_i}

in which $z_i < 0$, λ_{it} increases linearly. For periods 6 through 9, the direction of change is reversed. For cases in which $z_i > 0$, λ_{it} increases linearly, and for cases in which $z_i < 0$, λ_{it} decreases linearly. By period 9 for all cases, λ_{i9} has returned to its value in period 1, λ_{i1}.

Figure 3.2 provides a graphical depiction of the resulting trajectories of λ_{it} for representative values of z_i. Panel A shows the trajectories for z_i equal to -2, -1, and 0, and panel B shows the trajectories for z_i equal to 1 and 2. For z_i equal to -2 or -1, the time path of λ_{it} linearly rises and then linearly falls back to its period 1 value. However, the steepness of the rise and fall depends on z_i. It is larger for $z_i = -2$ than for $z_i = -1$. For $z_i = 0$, λ_{it} has no time trend and is a constant 1.0. Panel B illustrates the trajectories of λ_{it} associated with positive values of z_i. For $z_i > 0$, the trajectories of λ_{it} fall until period 5 and rise thereafter. By period 9, λ_{it} has returned to its value in period 1. The steepness of the rise and fall becomes ever shallower as z_i approaches 0.[1] Note also that because z_i is exponentiated to compute λ_{it}, the resulting trajectories are skewed rightward, with a concentration of low-valued λ trajectories followed by a rightward tail of high-valued λ trajectories.

Having generated 100,000 trajectories of λ according to this model, the resulting values of λ_{it} were used to generate 900,000 ($= 100,000 * 9$) random

---

1. Compared with the difference in the rate of rise and fall between $z = 2$ and $z = 1$ (panel B), the difference for $z = -2$ and $z = -1$ (panel A) is less pronounced but still real. For $z = -2$, λ increases by 122% from period 1 to 5, whereas for $\lambda = -1$ the increase is only 49%.

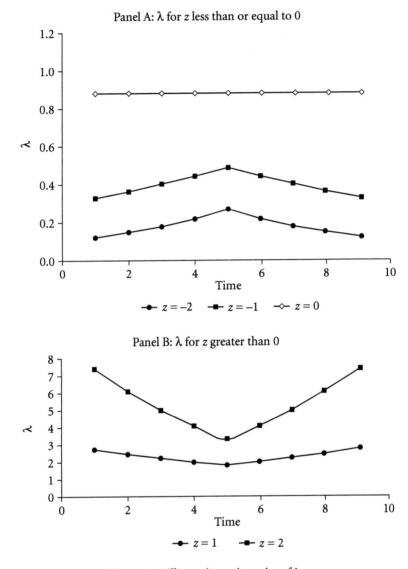

Figure 3.2   Illustrative trajectories of λ_{it}.

draws from a Poisson distribution. Each such draw can be thought of as the number of events for case i in period t (for example, number of outpatient visits). Table 3.2 reports the mean number of events by period ($\overline{y}_t$) in this simulated data set. There is a modest decline in $\overline{y}_t$ from period 1 to period 5,

Table 3.2 A comparison of the mean ($\bar{y}_t$) and variance (S_t^2) of the number of events by period in the simulated data set

Period	Entire data set		Group 4 only	
	$\bar{y}_t$	S_t^2	$\bar{y}_t$	S_t^2
1	1.64	6.20	5.30	5.24
2	1.49	4.20	4.49	4.49
3	1.37	3.03	3.78	3.88
4	1.27	2.28	3.22	3.24
5	1.19	1.82	2.72	2.76
6	1.27	2.28	3.22	3.17
7	1.38	3.03	3.76	3.65
8	1.49	4.24	4.49	4.45
9	1.64	6.20	5.33	5.43

1.64 to 1.19, which is followed by a steady rise back to the period 1 average. However, the trend in $\bar{y}_t$ conceals a great deal of population heterogeneity in the underlying individual-level trajectories. Some trajectories are rising and then falling with varying levels of steepness, whereas others are falling and then rising.

We now examine the capability of a group-based trajectory model to capture the essential features of this irregular distribution. Figure 3.3 reports the actual and predicted trajectories for a six-group model fitted to these data. All of the trajectories are quadratic. In interpreting this figure it is important to keep in mind two salient characteristics of this simulated data. First, individual-level trajectories are distributed continuously throughout this population, meaning there are no actual groups. Second, while the population distribution of trajectories is continuous, the distribution has very distinctive features. Thus the key test of the model is whether the groups (that is, points of support) capture these features.

Inspection of Figure 3.3 suggests that the model does do a good job of revealing the distinctive features of the λ-trajectories for this distribution. Panel A displays two trajectories; one trajectory rises and then falls, and the other is basically flat. The remaining four trajectories displayed in panels A and B follow a pattern of progressively steeper falls followed by progressively steeper increases. For all groups there is a close correspondence between the actual and predicted trajectories despite the specification error in modeling

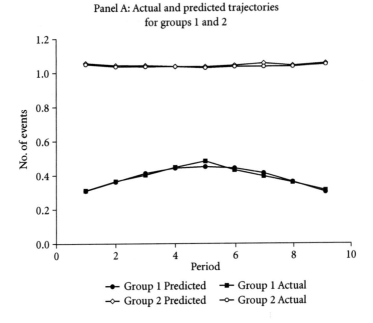

Panel A: Actual and predicted trajectories
for groups 1 and 2

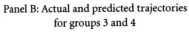

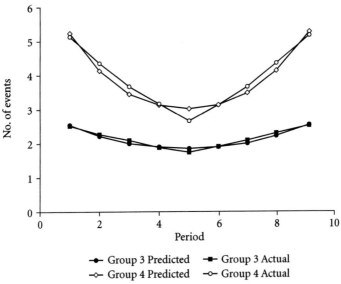

Panel B: Actual and predicted trajectories
for groups 3 and 4

Figure 3.3 Actual and predicted trajectories for a six-group model fitted to the simulated data.

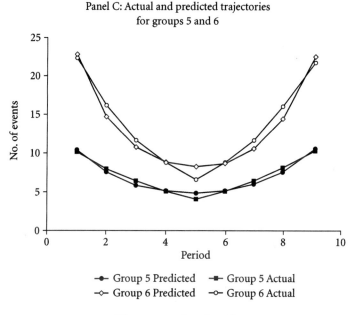

Panel C: Actual and predicted trajectories
for groups 5 and 6

─●─ Group 5 Predicted   ─■─ Group 5 Actual
─◇─ Group 6 Predicted   ─○─ Group 6 Actual

Figure 3.3 *(continued)*

the shape of the trajectories. Specifically, the model assumes that the trajectories of λ follow a quadratic function of time, even though the actual trajectory is a triangular function of time.

The sizes of the trajectories also closely approximate the true distribution of shapes. For z-scores between $-.5$ and $.5$ the trajectories are basically flat. The flat trajectory group (group 2) is estimated to comprise 39.8% of the population, which almost exactly equals the probability of a z-score between $-.5$ and $.5$—$\Phi(-.5 < z < .5) = .393$. The probability of membership in the rising and then falling group (group 1) is .309, which exactly equals $\Phi(z < -.5) = .309$. Finally, the combined probability of membership in the four falling and the rising groups, .293, very closely corresponds to $\Phi(z > .5) = .309$. It is also noteworthy that the probability of membership in these four trajectories becomes progressively smaller with the steepness of their rise and fall. Again, this pattern corresponds to the distribution of the normal random variable that underlies the generation of the trajectories.

Table 3.2 reports another test of the adequacy of the group-based approximation. The Poisson distribution assumes that at any given time all population members have identical mean rates, λ_t (that is, λ_{it} is identical across population members). By the construction of this model, this assumption is violated because the value of λ_{it} for each case i is determined by z_i. One test of the degree of failure of the homogeneity of the λ_t assumption is to compare the mean and variance of the number of events by period for the entire sample of 100,000 cases. In a sample where the homogeneity assumption holds, the mean and variance of the number of events will be approximately equal. A comparison of the means and variances by period shows that in some periods the variance is three to four times larger than the mean. Thus across all 100,000 cases the homogeneity assumption is very substantially violated. Also reported in Table 3.2 are the means and variances by period for members of trajectory group 4. Cases were assigned to this group on the basis of the maximum posterior probability assignment rule that is described in Chapter 5. Observe that once cases are combined into approximately homogeneous groups, the means and variance by period are very similar. This close correspondence is also found for the other five groups, and is another indication that the groups are indeed made up of relatively homogeneous cases, and that the differences across the groups are doing an effective job of approximating the heterogeneity in the population.

3.4 An Alternative Conception of a Group from the Structural Equation Modeling Tradition

Section 2.2.1 points out that a specific case of a censored normal model is a standard normal model without censoring in which y_{it} is distributed according to the normal distribution, with mean $\beta^j x_{it}$ and standard deviation σ. Muthén and Shedden (1999) develop an elegant and technically demanding extension of the uncensored normal model which adds random effects to the parameters, β^j, that define a group's mean trajectory.

This extension allows the trajectories of individual-level group members to vary about the group's mean trajectory that is defined by $\beta^j x_{it}$. The model for each group can be interpreted in a manner that is equivalent to that for the conventional normal-based growth curve model described in Chapter 1. The estimate of β^j defines the mean trajectory for the group and the estimate of the covariance matrix of the random effects characterizes the variation of group members' trajectories about this mean. The fundamental difference between the Muthén and Shedden model and the conventional growth curve model is that the former comprises multiple latent groups whereas the latter is defined by a single group.

Muthén (2001) uses the term "generalized growth mixture modeling" (GGMM) to label this modeling extension. The principal advantage of GGMM compared with the models described in Chapter 2 and used throughout this book is that by allowing variation about the group mean, fewer groups are generally required to specify a satisfactory model. Balanced against this benefit are a number of disadvantages. One is that the complexity of the model makes it difficult to extend it to model forms suitable for other types of data, such as count data.

Another disadvantage is that a group is defined by a far more complex set of parameters—those defining the group's mean trajectory plus those defining the variability of group members about this mean. The addition of the parameters measuring group variability not only makes the model much more complicated but also raises fundamental conceptual issues about what constitutes a group. For the purposes of this book, a group is thought of as a collection of individuals who follow approximately the same developmental trajectory. In terms of the technical discussion in sections 3.2 and 3.3, the groups are points of support on the population distribution of trajectories. Population variability is captured principally by differences across groups in the shape and level of their trajectories. GGMM adds an additional source of variability—individual differences in the expected trajectory of group members. The addition of this source of individual-level variability fundamentally alters the conception of group. It implies that an individual belonging to group A might actually have a trajectory that more closely corresponds to the mean trajectory of group B. Such "group cross-overs" reflect a fundamental indeterminancy in the conception of a group.

In the GGMM schema, a latent group is a population of *heterogeneous* individuals that can nonetheless be described by a single probability distribution. The population at large is only made up of multiple latent groups when more than one probability distribution is required to model individual differences within the population. Stated differently, the GGMM describes population heterogeneity with multiple layers of heterogeneity. This layering of heterogeneity may serve to improve model fit, but it is also the source of the group cross-over problem alluded to above. In addition, the layering of heterogeneity raises difficult issues of model identification.

The challenge of identification is reflected in the work of Bauer and Curran (2003a; 2004). Their analyses show that under the GGMM definition of a group, relatively modest errors in the specification of the group's probability distribution can result in mistaken inferences about the number of groups making up the population. Specifically, one might conclude that multiple groups are required to model the population, when, in fact, the population can be described by a single correctly specified probability distribution. Thus Bauer and Curran conclude that GGMM is vulnerable to creating the illusion of groups when, in fact, there are none.[2]

It is important to understand what is and is not implied by the Bauer and Curran caution about illusory groups. What is implied is that seemingly sensible extensions of a model can sometimes have unforeseen traps. What is not implied is that the models described in their article suffer from this same vulnerability. In all applications of group-based modeling I know of, the researchers are attempting to identify whether there are distinctive clusters of trajectories and, if so, whether individuals following such trajectories are distinctive in some respects. In this context a group bears no relationship to the definition of a group analyzed by Bauer and Curran. Specifically, it is not a subpopulation of heterogeneous individuals that can be described by a single probability distribution. Instead it is a cluster of approximately homogeneous individuals, in the sense that they are following about the same developmental course, who may have distinctive characteristics from other clusters of individuals following different developmental courses.[3] In statistical terms the groups are points of support on the unknown distribution of trajectories.

3.5 Statistical Inference

Titterington, Smith, and Makov (1985) distinguish between direct and indirect applications of finite mixture models. In a direct application, it is assumed that there really are physically distinct groups, and the goal of the analysis is

---

2. Structural equation mixture modeling is their term for group-based modeling.

3. For example, when Moffitt uses the terms "life-course-persistent offenders" and "adolescent-limited offenders," she is using these labels to describe two distinct clusters of developmental trajectories. Even if it were possible to pose a single distribution function that describes both clusters of individuals, this would not vitiate her theoretical conception of them as distinct groups.

to recover these groups. The latent classes (mixing components) of the model directly represent these groups, and the estimates obtained for each class are estimates of true population parameters. In indirect applications, the goal is to approximate a complex distribution. In the parlance of Titterington and his colleagues, the approximation conception of groups that underlies this book is an indirect application of finite mixture modeling.

Bauer and Curran acknowledge that their caution about the extraction of illusory groups applies only to direct applications of finite mixture, not to indirect applications. However, they do indicate that if the trajectory groups are regarded as a statistical device for approximating an unknown distribution of trajectories, statistical inference about the population may be problematic (Bauer and Curran, 2003b). The source of the problem is that if the model is explicitly regarded as an approximation, the model's parameters do not correspond exactly to the true population parameters. Thus, according to this argument, the parameter estimates cannot properly be used to draw inferences about the population parameters. We next turn to a set of simulations that are intended to show that it is possible to use the model to make statistical inferences, even though it is expressly an approximation.

The simulation exercise examines the correspondence between parameter estimates from the group-based model and their true counterparts from the underlying continuous distribution. It is designed to address two crucial questions concerning the inferential validity of statistical inferences about the true population parameters when using parameter estimates from the group-based approximation. The first is whether, except for sampling variability, the parameter estimates for each group accurately approximate the true parameters in the region of the continuous distribution that the group is approximating. The second is whether the standard errors of the group-based parameter estimates produced in model estimation accurately measure the true sampling variability of parameter estimates. If the answer to both these questions is affirmative, the group-based parameter estimates provide a valid basis for drawing statistical inferences about the true population parameters.

Table 3.3 describes an elaboration of the model laid out in section 3.3 that is designed to address these two questions. The elaboration adds a time-varying covariate to the individual-level trajectories. This variable, which is binary, is denoted by $treat_{it}$. For each period t and case i, $treat_{it}$'s value was randomly assigned to 0 and 1 with probability .5. Like the time trend in λ_{it}, the magnitude and sign of $treat_{it}$'s impact on λ_{it} depended on z_i. Specifically, the impact of $treat_{it}$ on λ_{it} equaled $.1 * z_i$. Thus for $z_i > 0$, the impact was

Table 3.3 The specification of individual-level trajectories of λ_{it} as a function of z_i and treat$_{it}$

Period	λ_{it}
1	$e^{z_i + .1z_i Treat_{i1}}$
2	$e^{z_i - .1z_i + .1z_i Treat_{i1}}$
3	$e^{z_i - .2z_i + .1z_i Treat_{i1}}$
4	$e^{z_i - .3z_i + .1z_i Treat_{i1}}$
5	$e^{z_i - .4z_i + .1z_i Treat_{i1}}$
6	$e^{z_i - .3z_i + .1z_i Treat_{i1}}$
7	$e^{z_i - .2z_i + .1z_i Treat_{i1}}$
8	$e^{z_i - .1z_i + .1z_i Treat_{i1}}$
9	$e^{z_i + .1z_i Treat_{i1}}$

positive and linearly increasing in z_i. For $z_i < 0$, the impact was negative, with the magnitude of the negative impact again growing linearly in z_i. Thus for $z = -2, -1, 0, 1, 2$, the corresponding treatment effects for treat$_{it} = 1$ were $-.2, -.1, 0, .1$, and $.2$, respectively.

Twenty data sets were generated for this specification of the population distribution of λ trajectories. Each such data set comprised 2,000 cases. Twenty models, each with five groups, were estimated with these data. All trajectories were quadratic in time and included treat$_{it}$ as a time-varying covariate. (See Chapter 7 for a discussion of adding time-varying covariates to the model.)

Let $\hat{\alpha}_j^n$ denote the estimated effect of treat$_{it}$ for trajectory group j for simulated data set n. Because the sign and magnitude of treat$_{it}$'s impact varies continuously with z_i, in reality there is no true α_j. Instead $\hat{\alpha}_j^n$ approximates the average impact of treat$_{it}$ for individuals clustered in trajectory group j. Because treat$_{it}$'s true impact equaled $.1 * z_i$, the average effect for group j can be directly estimated with the quantity $.1 * \bar{z}_j^n$, where $\bar{z}_j^n$ is the average value of z_i in sample n for cases assigned to trajectory group j according to the maximum probability assignment rule. Thus the correspondence between $.1 * \bar{z}_j^n$ and $\hat{\alpha}_j^n$ provides a test of the validity of using $\hat{\alpha}_j^n$ as an estimator of the group's average response to the treat$_{it}$ variable. For each of the five trajectory groups, Table 3.4 reports $\hat{\alpha}_j$ and $.1 * \bar{z}_j$, the average values respectively of $\hat{\alpha}_j^n$ and $.1 * \bar{z}_j^n$. For groups 1, 2, and 4, the values of $\hat{\alpha}_j$ and $.1 * \bar{z}_j$ are very

Table 3.4 The statistical properties of group-based estimates of treatment effects

Group	Average α_j^n	Average $.1 * z_j^n$	SV_j	ASE_j
1	−.113	−.111	.046	.047
2	.008	.004	.024	.027
3	.094	.083	.027	.024
4	.169	.161	.027	.026
5	.299	.257	.072	.039

close. For groups 3 and 5, there is a modest difference in these two quantities but the divergence is less than 20% of $.1 * \bar{z}_j$. Therefore, for this simulation, the five-group model's estimates of the treatment effects of $treat_{it}$ do a good job of approximating the continuous distribution of treatment effects in the population.

We turn now to the second question of whether the estimated standard errors accurately measured the sampling variability of $\hat{\alpha}_j^n$. Across the twenty trials, the sampling variability of $\hat{\alpha}_j^n$ for group j (SV_j) was measured by:

$$SV_j = \left[1/20 \sum_n (\hat{\alpha}_j^n - .1\bar{z}_j^n)^2 \right]^{1/2} . \tag{3.1}$$

Equation 3.1 follows the usual form for computing a standard deviation. Its one unusual feature is that the quantity $.1 * \bar{z}_j^n$ is subtracted from $\hat{\alpha}_j^n$ instead of the average of $\hat{\alpha}_j^n$ over the twenty trials, $\hat{\alpha}_j$. The quantity $.1 * \bar{z}_j^n$ is substituted for $\hat{\alpha}_j$ because the precise location of the groups changes from trial to trial. Thus $\hat{\alpha}_j^n$ is measuring a slightly different group average effect from trial to trial. This suggests that $.1 * \bar{z}_j^n$ gives a better estimate of the true treatment effect in group j for a given trial n than $\hat{\alpha}_j$.

Table 3.4 reports SV_j and the average standard error estimate of $\hat{\alpha}_j^n$ across the twenty trials, ASE_j. For groups 1, 2, 3, and 4, the two quantities are nearly identical. This implies that the maximum likelihood estimates of the standard errors of $\hat{\alpha}_j^n$ accurately measure the sampling variability of this quantity. However, for group 5, ASE_j is nearly 50% smaller than SV_j. This implies that the estimated standard error of $\hat{\alpha}_j^n$ for group 5 is substantially too small. The result would be a false sense of security about the precision of $\hat{\alpha}_j^n$ for group 5.[4] Overall, however, the simulation suggests that the standard errors accurately capture the true sampling variability of group-based parameter estimates.

The simulation exercises reported in this section and in section 3.3 are intended to make two important points about group-based trajectory modeling. The first is to demonstrate its capability to identify the distinctive features of highly irregular, albeit continuous, population distributions of trajectories. The second is to show that even if group-based modeling is explicitly treated as an exercise in approximation, it can still be used to draw valid statistical inferences. The demonstration of both of these points has been based on a simulation exercise, not on a general proof. Thus the analysis does not establish the boundary conditions under which group-based trajectory modeling will begin to fail in achieving the approximation objective. All models will fail once pushed past their boundaries of applicability. Establishing those boundaries is an issue for future research. The aim of this section has been to establish that the group-based method can be used to approximate and draw valid inferences about a complex population distribution of trajectories and treatment effects. This goal is less ambitious than establishing boundary conditions for the model's applicability, but establishing the goal's feasibility achieves an important end.

---

4. There are at least two possible explanations for this underestimate. One is that group 5 was very small, typically including less than 50 of the 2,000 cases. The other is that the group had the most heterogeneity in the magnitude of the treatment effect across group members, because it was made up of individuals with the largest values of z_i.

4

Model Selection

4.1 Overview

The objective of group-based trajectory modeling is the identification of groups of individuals with distinctive individual-level trajectories. This chapter investigates the interplay of formal statistical criteria and subjective judgment that is required for making a well-founded decision on the number of groups to include in the model. It also addresses the secondary issue of the specification of the order of the polynomial equation used to represent the shape of each group's trajectory.

Because modeling choices on the number and shapes of trajectories are normally made at the outset of an analysis, the outcome of this selection process has important ramifications for all analyses that follow. Thus both the character of the judgments involved and their influence on the final model choice are issues that deserve close attention. The aim of this chapter is to provide the reader with a working knowledge of the use of one specific test statistic for model selection, the Bayesian Information Criterion (BIC). Application of a formal statistical criterion such as BIC to the model selection process disciplines subjective judgments and guides the search through the labyrinth of model possibilities. However, model selection based on the mechanical and rigid application of a formal statistical criterion may lead to an inferior choice. Good judgment and real world domain knowledge are also required in the model selection process. Thus another goal of this chapter is to provide insight into the subjective considerations based on domain knowledge that must also enter into a well-considered decision on the number of groups to include in the model.

Section 4.2 formalizes the model selection problem and discusses why the conventional χ^2-based goodness-of-fit test is not appropriate for this model selection problem. Section 4.3 describes an alternative model selection test statistic, the Bayesian Information Criterion. Section 4.4 reports an actual application of BIC for model selection. Section 4.5 elaborates further on the interpretation of BIC, and section 4.6 reports an application of this elaboration. Section 4.7 summarizes the findings of a study of the performance of BIC and two alternative criteria, the Akaike Information Criterion (AIC) and the Integrated Classification Likelihood-BIC, in identifying the correct model in simulated data. Sections 4.8 and 4.9 move beyond the use and interpretation of formal statistical criteria for model selection and discuss the necessity for using real world domain knowledge in choosing the final form of a model.

4.2 The Model Selection Problem

As developed in Chapter 2, the group-based trajectory model is an application of the finite mixture modeling framework. The term "finite mixture" refers to the modeling assumption that the population comprises a mixture of a finite number of unobserved groups. Technically, the choice of the number of such groups to include in the model reduces to the specification of the number of components, J, to include in the finite mixture modeling framework, $P(Y_i) = \sum_j^J \pi_j P^j(Y_i)$.

A subsidiary decision of model selection concerns the shape of each group's trajectory. Technically, this choice involves the specification of the appropriate order of the polynomial equation of age or time that is used to model each group's trajectory. As discussed in section 2.3, a third-order polynomial defines a cubic trajectory (that is, $\beta_0^j + \beta_1^j Age_{it} + \beta_2^j Age_{it}^2 + \beta_3^j Age_{it}^3$), a second-order polynomial defines a quadratic trajectory in which β_3 is set equal to zero, a first-order polynomial defines a linear equation in which β_3 and β_2 are set equal to zero, and a zero-order polynomial defines a flat line in which β_3, β_2, and β_1 are set equal to zero.

The problem of how many components to include in a finite mixture model is among the most challenging in statistics. Conceptually, if the groups are seen as a statistical device for approximating an unknown but continuous population distribution of trajectories, the question of what constitutes an optimum number of such groups is ill-posed. It is ill-posed because the groups are intended only as an approximation of a cluster of individuals with similar trajectories. As such, they are not real identities. I return to this issue at the close of this chapter.

However, even under the assumption that the population is literally composed of J discrete groups, there are still formidable technical challenges to making a valid statistical inference about the value of J. At first blush, the standard χ^2 goodness-of-fit statistic would seem appropriate for making this inference. But it is not. A concrete example illustrates the problem with its use. Suppose the χ^2 statistic was used to test whether the addition of a quadratic trajectory group to a J group model added significant explanatory power. The test statistic, which is computed as -2 times the log of the likelihood of the $J + 1$ group model less the log of the likelihood of the J group model, is asymptotically χ^2 distributed with degrees of freedom equal to the difference in number of parameters between the two models.

For this application of the χ^2 test, the degrees of freedom are indeterminate, because the additional quadratic group in the $J + 1$ group model may reveal itself as superfluous in two ways. One is by the proportion of the population in that group, π_j, approaching zero. The other is by the three parameters defining the trajectory of the new group collapsing onto those for an existing group. The result is a new trajectory that is virtually identical to, rather than distinctive from, another group. What then are the appropriate degrees of freedom—one or three? From a technical perspective, this indeterminacy is a reflection of the fact that the classical asymptotic results that underlie the χ^2-based test do not hold for applications involving tests of the proper number of components, J, in a finite mixture model (Ghosh and Sen, 1985; Titterington, Smith, and Makov, 1985).

4.3 The Bayesian Information Criterion

The question of what criterion should be used to infer the correct number of components in a finite mixture is not a settled issue. One widely recommended option is the Bayesian Information Criterion. Kass and Raftery (1995), Raftery (1995), and Schwarz (1978) argue that BIC can be used for model selection in a wide range of circumstances, including the selection of the number of groups in the mixture model that underlie the group-based trajectory method. They recommend the selection of the model with the largest BIC score.

In the context of group-based trajectory modeling, application of this selection rule requires the estimation of models with varying numbers of groups and selection of the model with the largest BIC score. For a given model, BIC is calculated as:

$$\text{BIC} = \log(L) - 0.5k \log(N), \tag{4.1}$$

where L is the value of the model's maximized likelihood, N is the sample size, and k is the number of parameters in the model. The number of parameters is determined by the order of the polynomial used to model each trajectory and the number of groups. For example, a three-group model in which all of the trajectories are specified to follow a quadratic form uses eleven parameters. Nine of the parameters are required to model the three trajectories—β_0^j (intercept), β_1^j (age), and β_2^j (age²)—for each of the three quadratic trajectories. The remaining two parameters are required to measure the probabilities of membership in the three-trajectory groups, π_1, π_2, and π_3. Only two parameters are required for this purpose, because, by definition, the probability for one of the groups is 1 minus the sum of the probabilities for the other two groups.

For insight into the usefulness of BIC as a criterion for model selection, consider its calculation for discrete data. The first term of equation 4.1 is the natural logarithm of the value of the model's likelihood function. For discrete data the value of the likelihood function equals the probability of the actual data used in model estimations based on the model's estimated parameters. By definition, these parameter estimates maximize this probability for a model with a given number of groups, J.[1] For a model that predicts the data perfectly, the likelihood equals one and its corresponding natural logarithm is zero.[2] As the quality of the model's fit with the data declines, the log of the likelihood decreases (that is, becomes more negative).

One way to improve fit and thereby increase the likelihood is to add another group. The additional group may improve the likelihood of the actual data

---

1. Maximum likelihood estimation assumes that the actual data is the outcome of a random process that follows the probability distribution specified by the likelihood function. The objective of maximum likelihood estimation is to estimate the parameter values of the likelihood function that maximize the probability of the actual data's being the outcome of this random process.

2. For continuous data the likelihood measures its density, not its probability. Nonetheless, the conceptual points being made in this discussion of the interpretation of BIC apply to continuous data as well.

used in estimation by very little, but it cannot reduce this likelihood. There is a close analogy to this important point from the standard regression model. Adding more variables to the model can only increase r^2, even if only by very little. Thus the first term of equation 4.1 always increases as more groups are added to the model.

The second term acts as a counterbalance to adding more groups, because it extracts a penalty for their addition. Specifically, the addition of a group requires an increase in the number of parameters, k, defining the model. For example, the addition of a fourth quadratic trajectory group to the above example increases k from 11 to 15—three parameters are required to define the group's trajectory and one parameter is required to measure its probability. Because of this penalty for adding more parameters, Kass and Raftery (1995) observe that the BIC rewards parsimony.

Note also that the size of the penalty for adding more parameters to the model is proportional to the natural logarithm of the sample size. Thus the larger the sample size the larger the penalty.[3]

To summarize, the first component of BIC measures the improvement in model fit that is gained by generalizing the model to include more parameters. The second component acts as a counterforce to increasing model complexity by extracting a penalty for the addition of more parameters. If we follow the BIC criterion, expansion of a group-based trajectory model by the addition of another trajectory group is only desirable if the resulting increase in fit, as measured by the change in the natural logarithm of the maximized likelihood function, is larger than the penalty for adding more parameters. For example, suppose that $N = 1,000$, $k = 5$, and $\log(L) = -150$. For this model, $\text{BIC} = -167.27 (= -150 - .5 * 5 * \log(1,000))$. Now suppose that k was increased to 9 and $\log(L)$ increased to -110. For this value of k, $\text{BIC} = -141.09 (= -110 - .5 * 9 * \log(1,000))$. For this example, the increase in the $\log(L)$ from -150 to -110 exceeds the increase in the penalty from $17.27 (= .5 * 5 * \log(N))$ for $k = 5$ to $31.08 (= .5 * 9 * \log(N))$ for $k = 9$. Thus, according to BIC, the model with nine parameters is preferred to the model with five parameters. The strength of that preference is related to the absolute increase in the BIC score. Section 4.5 describes an interpretable

---

3. By scaling the size of the penalty by sample size, BIC tends to avoid a problem that plagues conventional hypothesis testing—always rejecting the null hypothesis in very large samples.

standard for judging whether a change in BIC is substantively important or not.

Model selection requires that the best model be selected from a predetermined range of model options that form the model choice set. The decision on what models to include in the choice set is of fundamental importance, because models outside of this set will never be considered. One possible approach to constructing this choice set is to exhaustively search all the possibilities. This strategy is impossible to implement, however, because the upper limit on the number of possible groups, J, is N, the number of individuals in the sample. A more limited version of an exhaustive search begins by placing an upper limit on J, and then exploring all the model possibilities within that limitation on number of groups.

For any reasonable upper limit on J (for example, 20 in most applications) even this option is impractical. The reason is that there are far more than J model choices. For any given number of groups there are large numbers of modeling possibilities for specifying the order of each of the individual trajectory groups. For example, for a five-group model, there are 243 ($= 3^5$) possible combinations of trajectories from order 0 (that is, flat) to 2 (that is, quadratic). For a search that was expanded to include cubic trajectory models, the number of possibilities for the five-group model alone is 1,024 ($= 4^5$). A full search requires estimating models over varying numbers of groups.

A more practical alternative to the exhaustive approach to constructing the model choice set involves a two-stage model selection process. The focus of the first stage is the choice of the number of groups to include in the model. The first-stage search involves estimation of one model for each value of J from one group to a preset maximum number of groups. The order of the polynomial defining each group's trajectories is determined by a preset rule, for example, all are trajectories that are quadratic. The number of groups in the final model is set at the value of J for the model with the maximum BIC score. In the second stage, the focus turns to determining the preferred order of the polynomial specifying the shape of each trajectory given the first-stage decision on number of groups. The specific process for making this determination is illustrated by an example in the next section.

This approach is not only more practical than the exhaustive strategy, it also focuses attention on the key modeling decision of how many groups to include in the model. As will be discussed below, with a few important exceptions, the choice of the order of the trajectory for each group is of less importance than the choice of the number of such groups.

4.4 Illustrative Application of BIC for Model Selection

The application of BIC to model selection is illustrated for the childhood physical aggression trajectories from the Montreal study that are reported in Figure 1.2. This model is a four-group model in which two of the trajectories are specified to follow a quadratic equation and the remaining two are specified as constant over time (that is, a zero-order polynomial).

In the context of the physical aggression model, a small but nontrivial minority of individuals were rated as engaging in little or no physical aggression over the entire observation period. To accommodate this group, all of the models in the first-stage search included one group that was specified to follow a zero-order trajectory. The trajectories for the remaining groups were all quadratic. Thus, for example, the three-group model was defined by one group following a zero-order trajectory and two groups following a quadratic trajectory. In the four-group model one group again followed a zero-order trajectory and the remaining three were quadratic.

Note that the genesis of the rule "one group is 0-order and the others are 2nd-order" to structure the first-stage search was based on substantive knowledge of the phenomenon under investigation, in this case physical aggression, not on purely statistical considerations. Thus the basis for its construction illustrates the importance of using domain knowledge in structuring the model search process. In other problem settings a different rule for structuring the first-stage search might be more appropriate.

Table 4.1 reports BIC scores for models made up of two to seven groups. Two BIC scores are reported: one for a sample size of 939 and another for a sample size of 6,010. Also reported is a statistic labeled "probability correct model," which is described in section 4.5. Recall that in the Montreal study over the period from age 6 to age 15, seven assessments were conducted, one at age 6 and another six annually from ages 10 to 15. For this application individuals with more than three missing assessments were not included in the estimation sample. The smaller N pertains to the number of individuals in the estimation sample after the deletion of such individuals. The larger sample size counts the total number of assessments used in model estimation across persons and time.

Table 4.1   Using BIC to select the number of groups to include in the model

No. of groups	BIC ($N = 939$)	BIC ($N = 6{,}010$)	Probability correct model
2	−7460.99	−7466.56	.00
3	−7276.69	−7285.97	.03
4	−7269.63	−7282.63	.97
5	−7274.83	−7291.53	.00
6	−7271.98	−7292.40	.00
7	−7278.08	−7302.21	.00

In theory N is meant to measure the number of independent observations that make up the sample. Because the intra-individual observations are not totally independent, the N across individual and time overstates the theoretically correct N. On the other hand, N measured by the number of individuals understates the true N, because intra-individual variation across assessments is to some degree independent. If there were not some degree of independence, there would be no point in collecting longitudinal data. Thus the two BIC scores actually bracket the theoretically correct BIC.

For this application both BIC calculations select the four-group model as best. Specifically, for either N, BIC rises steadily (that is, becomes less negative) as the number of groups increases from two to four groups and thereafter begins a steady decline.[4] However, without a concrete standard for calibrating the magnitude of the change in BIC, it is difficult to judge whether the four-group model is clearly better. We now pause from this illustration to describe two concrete standards for interpreting BIC.

4.5 Interpreting BIC

A construct from Bayesian statistics called the Bayes factor provides a useful statistic for calibrating the substantive importance of a difference in the BIC scores of two models. Suppose that one of these two models is the correct model. The Bayes factor, which is denoted by B_{ij}, measures the posterior odds of i being the correct model given the data. In the context of group-based modeling, model i might be a two-group model and j a three-group model.

---

4. For $N = 939$, BIC is larger for $J = 6$ than $J = 5$ but still smaller than for $J = 4$.

Table 4.2 Jeffreys's scale of evidence for Bayes factors

Bayes factor	Interpretation
$B_{ij} < 1/10$	Strong evidence for model j
$1/10 < B_{ij} < 1/3$	Moderate evidence for model j
$1/3 < B_{ij} < 1$	Weak evidence for model j
$1 < B_{ij} < 3$	Weak evidence for model i
$3 < B_{ij} < 10$	Moderate evidence for model i
$B_{ij} > 10$	Strong evidence for model i

B_{ij} is computed as the ratio of the probability of i being the correct model to j being the correct model. Thus a Bayes factor of 1 implies that the models are equally likely (that is, $1 = .5/.5$), whereas a Bayes factor of 10 implies that model i is 10 times more likely than j, which is to say that the probability of model i being correct is .909 and the probability of model j being correct is .091.

Table 4.2 shows Jeffreys's scale of evidence for Bayes factors as reported in Wasserman (2000). Jeffreys was an early and very prominent contributor to Bayesian statistics. His scale ranges from the evidence strongly favoring model i to that strongly favoring model j. In between is weak and moderate support for the two model alternatives. The point of neutrality between the models is defined by a Bayes factor of 1 in which the two models are equally likely. A value of $B_{ij} > 1$ favors model i, and conversely, a value of $B_{ij} < 1$ favors model j. In Jeffreys's view, if one model is at least ten times more likely than another model, it is strong evidence for that model. Thus if $B_{ij} > 10$, model i is strongly supported, and alternatively, if $B_{ij} < 0.1$, model j is strongly supported. This seems a reasonable standard.

Computation of the Bayes factor is in general very difficult and indeed commonly impossible. Schwarz (1978) and Kass and Wasserman (1995), however, show that $e^{BIC_i - BIC_j}$ is a good approximation of the Bayes factor for problems in which models i and j are ex ante judged equally likely. On the basis of this approximation, the odds of the four-group model compared with the three- or five-group model far exceed 10 to 1, regardless of whether BIC is calculated for $N = 939$ or $N = 6,010$. For example, consider the comparison of the four- versus the three-group model. For $N = 939$, the estimate of $B_{ij} = e^{-7269.63 - (-7276.690)} = 1,164$ and for $N = 6,010$, its estimate equals $e^{-7282.63 - (-7285.97)} = 28.2$. Thus, according to Jeffreys's scale, this is very strong evidence in favor of the four-group model.

Schwarz (1978) and Kass and Wasserman (1995) also provide a related metric for comparing more than two models. Let p_j denote the probability that a model with j groups is the correct model from a set of J different models. They show that p_j is reasonably approximated by:

$$\frac{e^{BIC_j - BIC_{max}}}{\sum_j e^{BIC_j - BIC_{max}}}, \tag{4.2}$$

where BIC_{max} is the maximum BIC score of the J different models under consideration. Also reported in Table 4.1 are the probabilities, as computed by equation 4.2, that the models with varying numbers of groups are the true model. With this BIC-based probability approximation ($N = 6{,}010$), the probability of the four-group model being the correct model is nearly .97.

4.6 Example of Model Selection Continued

In the model search illustration described in section 4.4, the model search space was restricted to models composed of quadratic trajectories, with the exception of a single zero-order trajectory to accommodate nonaggressive boys. Recall that a four-group model emerged as the preferred alternative. The actual and predicted physical aggression of the zero-order group, which is estimated to make up about 18% of the sampled population, is 0. If this four-group model is estimated with all trajectories quadratic, the predicted trajectories and group membership probabilities are virtually identical. The only change is that according to Jeffreys's scale of evidence the BIC score declines substantially, from −7,282.6 to −7,289.3 ($N = 6{,}010$). The deterioration in BIC reflects the reality that two parameters are being "wasted" because a quadratic equation is not required to predict a trajectory of no physical aggression. All that is required is a zero-order polynomial defined by a negative intercept.

Stated in terms of the calculation of BIC, the expansion of the low-group trajectory from a zero-order polynomial to a second-order polynomial resulted in only a minute increase in the first term of BIC, the log likelihood. However, by increasing k (the number of parameters) by two, the BIC's second term (the penalty for more parameters) swamped the small improvement in model fit.

We move now to the optional second stage of the model search process, in which the model is refined by altering the orders of the trajectories. As was shown in Figure 2.3, a zero-order polynomial can be used to model a stable chronic trajectory. In some cases the need for such refinement may be apparent from inspection of the statistical output. For example, in the four-group, all-quadratic physical aggression model, the parameter estimates for the low trajectory had very large standard errors. This is a statistical symptom of the prior observation that three parameters are not required to describe a trajectory of no physical aggression.

In some applications the raison d'être for specifying alternative trajectory forms may be based on substantive theory rather than on the straightforward observation that it is unnecessary to model a no-aggression trajectory with a quadratic equation. For instance, the theories of Moffitt (1993) and Patterson et al. (1998) predict the presence of a small group following a high-level trajectory of chronic physical aggression. This suggests that a further refinement of the four-group model includes two zero-order trajectories, one to accommodate the low group and the other to accommodate a high-level chronic trajectory.

Table 4.3 compares the (0,2,2,2) model (that is, one zero-order trajectory and three quadratic trajectories) with the (0,2,2,0) model. Following Jeffreys's scale of evidence, the improvement in BIC for $N = 6,010$ strongly favors the (0,2,2,0) model over the (0,2,2,2) model—$e^{-7280.1-(-7282.6)} = 12.2$. For the

Table 4.3   Comparing the (0,2,2,2) and (0,2,2,0) models of physical aggression

	(0,2,2,2) Model	(0,2,2,0) Model
BIC ($N = 939$)	−7269.6	−7269.0
BIC ($N = 6,010$)	−7282.6	−7280.1
Prob. of group 4 (π_4)	.090	.043
Group 4's average aggression by age:		
6	3.0	3.2
10	3.7	3.8
11	3.6	3.7
12	2.7	2.8
13	3.1	3.5
14	2.6	3.5
15	2.0	2.8

$N = 939$ BIC calculation, support for the (0,2,2,0) model is only in the weak support range.

Also reported in Table 4.3 are the size of this fourth group and its average actual physical aggression. For the (0,2,2,0) model, the chronic group represents only 4.3% of population, compared with 9% for the (0,2,2,2) model. Because the fourth group of the (0,2,2,0) model is made up of a more extreme group than its counterpart in the (0,2,2,2) model, it is not surprising that at each age the former has higher average physical aggression than the latter. The two alternative group 4 trajectories also have different trends over age. For the (0,2,2,0) model there is no apparent trend, whereas for the (0,2,2,2) model, the fourth group's average physical aggression increases from age 6 to age 10 and thereafter generally begins to decline. The pattern of increase and then decline for the fourth group in the (0,2,2,2) model is also reflected in the statistical significance of the age and age-squared trajectory coefficients for this group.

Does the statistical significance of the age-trend coefficients for group 4 in the (0,2,2,2) model cast doubt on the superiority of the (0,2,2,0) model based on the BIC criterion? No, because the two groups are not actually comparable. The fourth group in the (0,2,2,2) model is more than twice the size of that in the (0,2,2,0). It can be demonstrated with the classification procedure described in Chapter 5 that all of the group 4 members in the (0,2,2,0) belong to group 4 in the (0,2,2,2). The remaining group 4 members from the (0,2,2,2) model are drawn from group 3 members of the (0,2,2,0) model. This trajectory is referred to as the high-declining group in Figure 1.2. Contrariwise less than half of the group 4 members in the (0,2,2,2) model belong to group 4 in the (0,2,2,0) model. The apparent age trend in the behavior of the group 4 members in the (0,2,2,2) model does not pertain to the smaller group of even more physically aggressive boys making up group 4 in the (0,2,2,0) model. Rather it reflects the declining physical aggression of the (0,2,2,0) model's third group. Indeed the improvement in the BIC score for the (0,2,2,0) model provides strong support for the contention that this group's physical aggression was not declining.

4.7 An Evaluation of BIC's Performance in Simulated Data

As previously indicated, the question of how best to determine the number of groups comprising a finite mixture model is not a settled issue. Although there is agreement that the standard χ^2 goodness-of-fit statistic is an inappro-

Table 4.4 Simulation specifications: Three-group Poisson model

Simulation	λ_1	λ_2	λ_3	π_1	π_2	π_3
A	1	3	5	.60	.30	.10
B	1	3	5	.33	.33	.33
C	1	3	10	.60	.30	.10
D	1	3	10	.33	.33	.33

priate statistical criterion, there is far from unanimous agreement that the BIC should be the preferred alternative. Two other commonly suggested alternatives are the Akaike Information Criterion (Akaike, 1974) and the Integrated Classification Likelihood–BIC (McLachlan and Peel, 2000).

In response to the lack of consensus on the appropriateness of BIC for the selection of number in groups in finite mixture models, Brame, Nagin, and Wasserman (2004) examine the performance of BIC in identifying the correct number of groups in simulated data for which the true model is known. For this analysis count data were generated from three versions of a simulation based on a three-group Poisson process. The key features of models are summarized in Table 4.4. In simulation A, λ for group 1 was 1, for group 2 was 3, and for group 3 was 5. Groups 1, 2 and 3, respectively, make up 60%, 30%, and 10% of the simulated data. These percentages correspond to the probability of group membership, π_j. In simulation B, the group λ values were the same as in A, but the group membership probabilities were set equal at $\frac{1}{3}$. In simulation C, the probabilities reverted to those in simulation A, but λ for group 3 was increased to 10. In simulation D, λ for group 3 was again 10, but the group probabilities were equal as in simulation B. This 2×2 design was intended to test BIC's accuracy in model selection under alternative values of λ_j and π_j.

The analysis was conducted as follows. For each simulation model, A–D, 10,000 samples of sizes 500, 2,500, and 10,000 were randomly generated. Thus, for example, 10,000 samples each of size 500 were generated according to the specifications of simulation A. For each of these samples, models with one to five groups were estimated. A key summary statistic was the percentage of samples for which the maximum BIC score was obtained for the true three-group model.

There are four key findings of the analysis. First, BIC is a conservative criterion for model selection. It never selected a preferred model with more than three groups. However, its use commonly resulted in the selection of a two-group model instead of the true three-group model. Second, as sample size increased, BIC converged on selection of the true three-group model in 100% of the simulated data sets. Third, in simulations C and D, where the values of λ are more distinct than in simulations A and B, the rate of selection of the three-group model over the two-group model was higher for all sample sizes. Fourth, the difference in group membership probabilities in simulations A and C versus B and D had no material impact on the number of groups selected.

We also examined the performance of the AIC and ICL-BIC in identifying the correct number of groups. The AIC is very similar to BIC but does not vary with sample size. It is calculated by $\log(L) - 0.5k$. The ICL-BIC adds a so-called entropy component to BIC. A model's entropy score is calculated by $\sum_i \sum_j pp_{ij} \ln(pp_{ij})$, where pp_{ij} is case i's posterior probability membership in group j. ICL-BIC performed very poorly. It nearly always picked the two-group model as the preferred alternative. AIC identified the three-group model as preferred at a higher rate than BIC, particularly in small samples. However, unlike BIC, in some cases it selected a model comprising more than three groups. In so doing, the AIC is more vulnerable to selecting a model that includes an illusory group.

4.8 When BIC Is Not Useful in Identifying the Best Model

The physical aggression data from the Montreal study provide a good illustration of the utility of BIC as a model selection criterion. In that application BIC increased steadily to its maximum at four groups and then began a steady decline. However, BIC does not always cleanly identify a preferred number of groups. Instead, in some applications the BIC score continues to increase as more groups are added. In such instances, more subjective criteria based on domain knowledge and the objectives of the analysis must be used to select the number of groups to include in the model. Selection must balance the objective of model parsimony with the objective of reporting the distinctive developmental patterns in the data.

This situation is illustrated with another important measurement series from the Montreal study, annual self-reports of violent delinquency from ages 11 to 17. In these data there are very few individuals who consistently report absolutely no violent delinquency over the entire period. An occasional fist fight, one of the items in the index, is the norm in these data. Thus in the search for the preferred number of groups, all trajectories were specified as following a quadratic polynomial in age. Unlike the analyses of physical aggression, BIC continued to improve for this measurement series as more groups were added.

Table 4.5 reports the predicted trajectories for the four-, five-, and six-group models. For the four-group model, the trajectories are either declining or follow the classic hump-shaped rise and fall that is predicted by many classic theories in criminology (Farrington, 1986; Hirschi and Gottfredson, 1983). In the five-group model, this pattern is broken with the addition of the group designated as 3 in that model. This group engages in only a negligible level of violence at age 11 but thereafter the trajectory steadily rises. By age 17 this group's level of violence is second only to group 5. Its trajectory is a classic example of what developmental criminologists call late-onset or adolescent-onset delinquency (Loeber and Stouthamer-Loeber, 1998). The six-group model reproduces trajectories very similar to those in the five-group model, including the adolescent-onset trajectory. The sixth trajectory is an amalgam of characteristics of trajectories 1 and 3 in the five-group model. Like trajectory 1 in the five-group model, the delinquency level of the sixth trajectory is low throughout the observation period. But unlike the five-group model's trajectory 1, trajectory 6 follows the rising pattern with age of the five-group model's trajectory 3. Thus it seems that group 6 was carved from the elements of groups 1 and 3 in the five-group model. Indeed, using the method for classifying individuals into their most likely trajectory groups described in Chapter 5, this can be demonstrated to be the case.

In instances such as this, when BIC is not a useful criterion for choosing a model, how should model selection proceed? For reasons of parsimony and comprehensibility, the fewer the groups the better. Yet limiting the model to too few groups may conceal features of the data that are theoretically or empirically important. In the violent delinquency example, the four-group model conceals the presence of the adolescent-onset group which, while relatively small (about 13% of the population), is substantively important. The adolescent-onset group first reveals itself in the five-group model. Thereafter, the addition of further groups does not reveal any other important features in these data. For this reason, Nagin and Tremblay (2002) used the five-group model in an analysis that examined the relationship of these five trajectories of adolescent violence with counterpart trajectories of childhood physical aggression.

Model selection must balance the sometimes competing objectives of model parsimony and capturing the distinctive features of the data. When BIC is

Table 4.5   Comparison of predicted trajectories for the four-, five-, and six-group models of violent delinquency

	Four-group model: Predicted trajectory			
Age	Group 1	Group 2	Group 3	Group 4
11	.73	1.26	3.29	5.47
12	.49	1.44	3.71	7.08
13	.35	1.56	3.94	8.39
14	.26	1.58	3.97	9.10
15	.21	1.51	3.78	9.00
16	.18	1.35	3.41	8.15
17	.17	1.14	2.90	6.75

	Five-group model: Predicted trajectory				
Age	Group 1	Group 2	Group 3	Group 4	Group 5
11	.59	1.75	.52	3.79	5.37
12	.42	1.83	.91	4.25	7.06
13	.32	1.74	1.45	4.43	8.48
14	.26	1.51	2.08	4.30	9.32
15	.23	1.20	2.69	3.88	9.36
16	.22	.87	3.14	3.25	8.60
17	.23	.57	3.31	2.53	7.22

	Six-group model: Predicted trajectory					
Age	Group 1	Group 2	Group 3	Group 4	Group 5	Group 6
11	.68	2.03	1.48	4.06	5.37	.19
12	.43	1.99	1.87	4.75	6.99	.44
13	.29	1.80	2.32	4.96	8.33	.81
14	.20	1.50	2.82	4.62	9.10	1.23
15	.15	1.16	3.35	3.84	9.12	1.52
16	.11	.82	3.89	2.85	8.37	1.54
17	.09	.53	4.43	1.89	7.04	1.28

not useful in identifying a preferred model, the recommendation is to select a model with no more groups than is necessary to communicate the distinct features of the data. What constitutes a distinct feature depends principally on the substantive goal of the analysis. Therefore, the concept of distinctiveness can not be generically defined in methodological terms.

4.9 Concluding Comments on Model Selection

This discussion has focused on the use of the BIC for model selection. As already discussed, another widely used statistic for model selection is AIC. More recently Lo, Mendell, and Rubin (2001) have suggested another statistic for testing the number of components in a normal mixture. The question of which criterion is best is not a settled issue. See, for example, the exchange among Weakland (1999), Gelman and Rubin (1999), and Raftery (1999) over the technical merits of BIC as a basis for model selection.

Such debate is important for advancing the theoretical foundations of model selection. However, disagreement about the technical merits of alternative criteria may obscure a fundamental point—there is no correct model. Statistical models are just approximations. The strengths and weaknesses of alternative model specifications depend upon the substantive questions being asked and the data available for addressing these questions. Thus the choice of the best model specification cannot be reduced to the application of a single test statistic. To be sure, the application of formal statistical criteria to the model selection process serves to discipline and constrain subjective judgment with objective measures and standards. However, there is no escaping the need for judgment; otherwise insight and discovery will fall victim to the mechanical application of method. In the end the objective of the model selection is not the maximization of some statistic of model fit. Rather it is to summarize the distinctive features of the data in as parsimonious a fashion as possible.

5

❖

Posterior Group-Membership Probabilities

5.1 Overview

This chapter describes the calculation and use of a set of probabilities that are known as the "posterior probabilities of group membership." These probabilities collectively measure a specific individual's likelihood of belonging to each of the model's J trajectory groups. They are referred to as *posterior* probabilities because they are computed postmodel estimations using the model's estimated coefficients.

The posterior probabilities can be used to create profiles of the trajectory group members and to assess the quality of the model's fit to the data. They can also be used as sampling weights in making various important calculations such as computing the expected outcomes of trajectory group members. Because they provide a way to relate concrete individuals to the statistical abstractions of the model, the posterior probabilities are among the most useful products of the group-based modeling approach.

The *posterior probability* of group membership is distinct from the *probability* of group membership, π_j. The probability of group membership, which was a key topic of Chapter 2, measures the proportion of the population that belongs to group j. This probability can also be thought of as the probability that a randomly chosen individual follows group j's trajectory. Its analytic purpose is to measure the size of each trajectory group. The *posterior* probability of group membership, by contrast, measures the probability that an *individual with a specific behavioral profile* belongs to a specific trajectory group j. For example, consider the four physical aggression trajectories from the Montreal study that are shown in Figure 1.2. The estimated probability of group membership for the chronic group is .04, which concretely means that an estimated 4% of the population follow the chronic trajectory. Now consider a specific individual from the Montreal study who had a sustained history of high physical aggression. Because of this history, the posterior probability calculations would assign a much higher probability to his membership in the chronic group than the group's population rate of 4%. Conversely, the posterior probability calculations would assign a much lower probability of membership in the low trajectory than this group's overall population membership rate of 14%. Thus, whereas π_j measures the aggregate size of each trajectory group, the posterior probability takes into account the observed outcomes of the specific individual over the t assessment periods.

Section 5.2 lays out the calculation of the posterior probability of group membership. Section 5.3 demonstrates the use of the posterior probabilities to assign individuals to trajectory groups, and section 5.4 shows how these assignments can be used to create profiles of trajectory group members. These two sections should be of particular interest to practitioners. Section 5.5 has a more technical orientation and discusses the use of posterior probabilities to assess model adequacy. Section 5.6 describes the use of the posterior probabilities in calculating weighted averages. Section 5.7 provides a summary of Part I to set the stage for Part II.

5.2 Calculation of the Posterior Probabilities of Group Membership

The posterior probability of individual i's membership in group j is denoted by $\hat{P}(j|Y_i)$, where as in prior chapters Y_i is a vector comprising i's measured behavior in each assessment period t, y_{it}. Formally, the posterior probability of group membership measures individual i's probability of membership in group j given his measured behavior in each of the t assessment periods.

$\hat{P}(j|Y_i)$ cannot be calculated directly from the model's parameter estimates, but a related probability—the probability of Y_i assuming membership in group j, $\hat{P}(Y_i|j)$—can be directly calculated. Conceptually $\hat{P}(Y_i|j)$ measures the probability that individual i would have behaved as he did given that he was a member of group j. Our interest, however, is in making an inference about group membership in light of behavior, not the reverse. $\hat{P}(j|Y_i)$ rather than $\hat{P}(Y_i|j)$ is the relevant quantity for making the desired inference.

Bayes's Theorem provides the analytical basis for calculating $\hat{P}(j|Y_i)$ from $\hat{P}(Y_i|j)$ as follows:

$$\hat{P}(j|Y_i) = \frac{\hat{P}(Y_i|j)\hat{\pi}_j}{\sum\limits_{j}^{J} \hat{P}(Y_i|j)\hat{\pi}_j}, \tag{5.1}$$

One aspect of the mechanics of this calculation deserves special attention. Observe that for each j, $\hat{P}(Y_i|j)$ is always weighted by its counterpart $\hat{\pi}_j$. Consequently, bigger groups, as measured by $\hat{\pi}_j$, will, on average, have larger posterior probability estimates. As a consequence, even if $\hat{P}(Y_i|j)$ is larger for a small group than for a big group, the posterior probability estimate, $\hat{P}(j|Y_i)$, for the big group may still be larger. This tendency means that a large posterior probability estimate for a small group requires that Y_i be so strongly consistent with the small group that $\hat{P}(Y_i|j)$ for that group is very large in comparison to its companion probabilities for the big groups.

Contrary to intuition, weighting for group size as a matter of method, independent of actual evidence supporting a particular individual's membership in each group, does *not* inject bias into the posterior probability calculation. Bayesian-based calculations are always weighted by the size of the group. This weighting by population size helps to ensure that anomalous events, which might otherwise seem to suggest membership in an unusual group, are not over-weighted post hoc. On rare occasions a member of a large group may experience an event that is unusual for the group. The bigger the group, the more likely that such an event will actually be observed post hoc. Weighting by $\hat{\pi}_j$ adjusts for this tendency.

5.3 Use of Posterior Probabilities for Group Assignment

The posterior probability calculations provide the researcher with an objective basis for assigning individuals to the trajectory group that best matches their behavior. A maximum-probability assignment rule places individuals into the group to which their posterior membership probability is largest.

Table 5.1 illustrates the assignment process for the four trajectory groups identified in the London data that are shown in Figure 1.3. The table reports the posterior probabilities of group membership for four selected individuals from this data set. Individual A had twelve convictions from ages 10 to 19 and four additional convictions as an adult. The posterior probability calculations assigned him to the high-chronic group with probability 1.00.[1] Similarly, individual B was assigned with probability 1.00 to the low-chronic group. This individual had two convictions in both the adolescent and the adult

---

1. Posterior probability calculations always assign a nonzero probability to all groups. For this individual the probability of membership in all other groups was minute but still nonzero.

Table 5.1 Group assignment based on the posterior probabilities of group membership: Illustrative examples from the London sample

	Number of convictions			Posterior probability		
Individual	Ages 10–19	Ages 20–32	Rare	Adolescent limited	Low chronic	High chronic
A	12	4	.00	.00	.00	1.00
B	2	2	.00	.00	1.00	.00
C	2	0	.01	.95	.04	.00
D	1	1	.34	.00	.66	.00

periods. B's pattern was indicative of chronic offending but not at a high enough level to count as a high chronic. Individual C's conviction history was limited to two convictions in his adolescence. The posterior probability calculations assigned him to the adolescent-limited group with probability .95. A small probability of .04 was attached to the low-chronic group because of the possibility that C was actually a low chronic who had zero convictions during his adulthood.

For C the model also assigned a .01 probability to membership in the rare group, despite his having had two adolescent convictions. The reason for this seeming anomaly is most clearly illustrated by individual D, who had 1 conviction in the age 10–19 period and another in the age 20–32 period. This individual was most likely a low chronic, but the model still assigned a .34 probability to the rare group. The reasons are twofold. First, the rare group has a small but still nonzero offending rate (λ) in all periods. Thus there were individuals assigned to this group with a single conviction, an unusual but not utterly anomalous event for a member of the rare group. Second, the rare group is the biggest group—an estimated 70% of the sampled population belong to this group. As explained above, the posterior probability calculation tends to assign higher probabilities to the larger groups, such as, in this instance, the rare group.

5.4 Using Group Assignments to Create Profiles of Group Membership

Once distinctive trajectory groups are identified, a host of questions follow. One of the most important is whether there are shared characteristics of trajectory group members that distinguish them from their counterparts in other

Table 5.2   Group profiles

	London data by group			
Variable	Rare	Adolescent limited	Low chronic	High chronic
Low IQ (%)	16.3	23.5	34.8	43.5
Poor parenting (%)	18.4	29.4	30.4	47.8
High risk taking (%)	21.2	47.1	37.0	69.5
Parents with criminal record (%)	18.0	43.5	33.3	60.9

	Montreal data by group			
Variable	Low	Low declining	High declining	Chronic
Years of school (mother)	11.1	10.8	9.8	8.4
Years of school (father)	11.5	10.7	9.8	9.1
Mother began childbearing as a teenager	12.6	20.7	28.9	53.3
Low IQ (%)	21.6	26.8	44.5	46.4
Completed 8th grade on time (%)	80.3	64.6	31.8	6.5
Juvenile record (%)	0.0	2.0	6.0	13.3
No. of sexual partners at age 17 (past year)	1.2	1.7	2.2	3.5

trajectory groups. A natural first step in answering this question is the creation of profiles of trajectory group members that characterize their life circumstances. The posterior probability–based classifications provide a straightforward basis for producing such profiles; all that is required is a cross tabulation of individual-level trajectory group assignments with individual-level characteristics that might be associated with trajectory group membership.

To illustrate the utility of such profiles, Table 5.2 reports summary statistics on individual characteristics and behaviors for the groups identified in the London conviction data and Montreal physical aggression data (see Figures 1.2 and 1.3). The profiles are intended to illustrate their utility in two important functions that transcend specific subject matter: (1) communication of research findings in an easily interpretable format and (2) identification of subtle but significant variations in the phenomenon being studied.

In the London data, the high chronics, on average, were most likely to have a low IQ, to have had at least one parent with a criminal record, to have had poor parenting, and to have engaged in risky activities. Conversely, the rare group was lowest on these risk factors. The contrasting characteristics of the high-chronic and rare groups are strongly consistent with much prior research. The adolescent-limited and low-chronic groups fall in between, but the differences between these two groups form a more complex pattern. The low chronics have a higher incidence of the low IQ risk factor than the adolescent-limited group but have a lower incidence of parental criminality and risk-taking behavior. This suggests the possibility of a difference in the etiology that underlies the criminality of these two groups.[2]

For the physical aggression trajectory groups in the Montreal data, the chronics have the least well educated parents, are more likely to have a mother who began childbearing as a teenager, and most frequently score in the lowest quartile of the measured IQ distribution of the sample, whereas the low group is lowest on these risk factors. Further, 93% of the chronics fail to reach the eighth grade on schedule, and 13% have a juvenile record by age 18. Only 19% of the low group have fallen behind grade level by the eighth grade and none have a juvenile record. The differences in the academic performance and juvenile records between the two groups imply that teachers' observations of physical aggression predict outcomes far more serious than only schoolyard rough-housing.

Consider now the comparison of the high-level declining group with the chronic group. In Nagin and Tremblay (2001a), it was shown that among the psychosocial risk factors established at age 6 or before, only two maternal characteristics—low education and teen onset of childbearing—distinguished these two groups. Indications of this finding are reflected in the profiles. There is almost no difference in the incidence of low IQ scores between the chronic (44.5%) and the high-declining (46.4%) groups, whereas there is a large difference in the teen childbearing risk factor: 28.9% for the high-declining group versus 53.3% for the chronic group.

The creation of these profiles is only possible because group-based trajectory modeling allows for the calculation of posterior probabilities. The profiles are a valuable tool for easy and transparent communication of findings on the distinctive characteristics and outcomes of individuals following different trajectories.

---

2. Chapters 6 and 7 discuss tests for making a formal statistical determination of whether such differences are statistically significant.

5.5 Judging Model Adequacy

The posterior probabilities of group membership are also a source of valuable information for an important technical function—judging the model's correspondence with the data. On the basis of the maximum probability assignment rule, 283, 51, 46, and 23 individuals from the London data were assigned, respectively, to the rare, adolescent-limited, low-chronic, and high-chronic groups. Table 5.3 reports the average posterior probability of membership in each of these groups for those individuals that were assigned to it. Henceforth this average will be referred to as the average posterior probability (AvePP) of assignment. Ideally, the assignment probability for each individual should be 1. Under this ideal condition, AvePP equals 1. For persons assigned to the rare and high-chronic groups, the ideal is close to being achieved. In both cases, the AvePP of assignment was .95. For the adolescent-limited and the low-chronic groups these averages are, respectively, .76 and .89. These AvePPs of assignment are still high, but how close to 1 is good enough?

Although no definitive answer to this question can be provided, this section aims to provide some useful guidance on the more general issue of judging the adequacy of the model that is ultimately selected via the search process described in Chapter 4. The goal is to provide guidance in answering the question: is this a model that one can have confidence in or is it only the best from a poor set of choices?

To ground this advice in concrete evidence on model performance, a series of models were estimated on the basis of simulated data. All simulations involved two groups, each making up 50% of the total population. For each group, simulated data were generated for 500 cases over two periods. The data for the two groups were then combined into a single data set of 1,000 cases

Table 5.3   Average assignment probabilities based on maximum posterior probability rule for the London data

		Group				
Assigned group	Number assigned	Rare	Adolescent limited	Low chronic	High chronic	Range
Rare	283	.954	.032	.014	.000	.62–.97
Adolescent limited	51	.162	.759	.077	.002	.49–.98
Low chronic	46	.036	.038	.887	.039	.51–1.00
High chronic	23	.000	.025	.020	.955	.58–1.00

with two periods of data for each case. The simulated data were the product of a Poisson process. In all simulations, $\lambda = 3$ for one group. The only variation across simulations is λ for the second group (λ_H), which was alternatively set at 4, 5, 6, and 9.

The values of λ for the second group were set to create a gradient of difficulty both in empirically estimating the true λ for each group and in assigning individual cases to their correct group on the basis of the posterior probability of group membership. It was anticipated that performance on these two dimensions would be best for the simulations in which $\lambda_H = 9$, where the separation between λ for the low and high group is largest, and poorest for $\lambda_H = 4$, where the separation is least.

A concrete demonstration of the anticipated difficulty of separation for $\lambda_H = 4$ versus $\lambda_H = 9$ may help to illustrate this prediction. For $\lambda = 3$, the probability of 3 or fewer events is .65, which is only modestly larger than the counterpart probability of .43 for $\lambda = 4$. Consequently, there was considerable overlap in the simulated data for the low and high λ groups. By contrast, the probability of 3 or fewer events for $\lambda = 9$ is only .02. Thus in the simulation where $\lambda_H = 9$, there was little data overlap between the high and low groups.

Table 5.4 reports the estimates of λ and π for each of the four simulations. Each of the simulations has reasonably good success at estimating λ_L and λ_H. However, the accuracy of the estimates of the proportion of population belonging to the two groups is clearly sensitive to the value of λ_H. For $\lambda_H = 4$, the estimates of π_L and π_H are, respectively, .33 and .67. These estimates are relatively far from the true values of .5. By comparison, the estimated split between the low and high population for $\lambda_H = 9$, 51% for λ_L and 49% for λ_H, is nearly correct.

Table 5.4 Model performance for simulated data

High group λ_H ($\lambda_L = 3$ in all)	$\hat{\pi}_L$	$\hat{\pi}_H$	$\hat{\lambda}_L$	$\hat{\lambda}_H$	% Correctly classified	Overall performance
4	.33	.67	2.91	3.81	59.3	Poor
5	.63	.37	3.16	5.43	72.3	Fair
6	.52	.48	3.08	6.09	85.5	Good
9	.51	.49	3.05	9.04	99.6	Excellent

Also reported in Table 5.4 is the percentage of cases that were correctly classified as belonging to the low and high λ groups. This statistic was computed by comparing each case's true group identity, which is known, with its classification based on the maximum probability rule. For example in the simulation for $\lambda_H = 4$, 137 of the 500 cases in which $\lambda = 3$ were correctly classified into the low λ group. Classification success for the $\lambda = 4$ group was better; 456 of 500 cases were correctly classified. Thus in the combined sample of 1,000 cases, 593 were correctly classified for an overall success rate of 59%. Such a comparison is only possible with simulated data such as this in which, by construction, the true group membership of each case can be known.

The results of the classification exercise demonstrate that for $\lambda_H = 4$ the model's classification accuracy is poor, with only 59.3% of the cases being correctly classified. If individuals were assigned randomly to the low or high groups on the basis of the estimated probabilities of group membership, .33 and .67, respectively, the expected rate of correct classification was almost as high, $.56(= .33 * .33 + .67 * .67)$. Classification accuracy increases steadily as λ_H increases. For $\lambda_H = 6$, classification accuracy is a respectable 85.5%. As anticipated, for $\lambda_H = 9$ it is nearly perfect.

The summary statistics on model performance reported in Table 5.4 are not directly applicable to real world data, because interpretation of the statistics requires knowledge of the true group membership of individual cases and the actual values of the model's parameters. In simulated data both are knowable. In real world data they are not. Table 5.5 reports another set of summary statistics that can be used to construct diagnostics on model performance that do not require knowledge of true group membership or of the model's true parameters. The four diagnostics constructed from this table are intended to provide concrete guidance for judging a model's capacity to identify distinct groups of trajectories. Combined with the guidelines for model selection developed in Chapter 4, the diagnostics are intended to provide a practical framework for model selection and evaluation in real world applications.

The first two diagnostics focus on the accuracy of the group membership classifications based on the maximum posterior probability assignment rule. Because the simulations suggest that the model's estimates of the probabilities of group membership carry valuable information on the model's capacity to identify distinctive groups, the focus of diagnostics three and four is the accuracy of the estimates of π_j.

Table 5.5 Diagnostics of model performance

High group λ	$\pi_{\lambda=3}$					$\pi_{\lambda=High(H)}$				
	Model estimate $\hat\pi_{\lambda=3}$	98% C.I. for $\pi_{\lambda=3}$	P_L (proportion classified as $\pi_{\lambda=3}$)	Ave. PP	Odds correct classification	Model estimate $\pi_{\lambda=H}$	98% C.I. for $\hat\pi_{\lambda=H}$	P_H (proportion classified as $\pi_{\lambda=H}$)	Ave. PP	Odds correct classification
4	.33	(.00, 1.00)	.18	.55	2.5	.67	(.01, 1.00)	.82	.72	1.3
5	.63	(.48, .77)	.70	.81	2.5	.37	(.23, .52)	.30	.78	6.0
6	.52	(.43, .60)	.50	.86	5.7	.48	(.57, .40)	.50	.82	4.9
9	.51	(.47, .55)	.52	.95	18.3	.49	(.45, .53)	.48	.97	33.7

5.5.1 Average Posterior Probability of Assignment (diagnostic 1)

The first diagnostic is based on AvePP for each trajectory group. As previously explained, the ideal is that the assignment probability for each individual equals 1 with the result that AvePP also equals 1. As the certainty of the group assignments based on the posterior probability assignment rule declines, AvePP also declines. My personal minimum rule-of-thumb is that AvePP should be at least .7 for *all* groups. This threshold is not achieved for the low group in the $\lambda_H = 4$ scenario (AvePP = .55), but for all other scenarios the .7 minimum is achieved for both the low and high groups.

5.5.2 Odds of Correct Classification (diagnostic 2)

Table 5.5 also reports a second diagnostic statistic which is based on AvePP for group j and π_j. It measures the odds of correct classification for group j (OCC_j). The statistic is computed by:

$$OCC_j = \frac{AvePP_j / 1 - AvePP_j}{\hat{\pi}_j / 1 - \hat{\pi}_j}. \qquad (5.2)$$

The numerator of this ratio is the odds of a correct classification into group j on the basis of the maximum probability classification rule. Suppose $AvePP_j$ equaled .9. This implies 90% of individuals are correctly classified into group j and 10% are incorrectly classified into the group. Thus the odds of correct classification are 9 to 1. The denominator is the odds of correct classification based on random assignment, with the probability of assignment to group j equal to its estimated population base rate, $\hat{\pi}_j$. Suppose $\hat{\pi}_j$ equaled .25. For this probability estimate, random assignment of individuals into group j would correctly classify 25% of individuals and incorrectly classify the other 75%. The odds of correct classification based on random assignment are thus only 1 in 3. For this example $OCC_j = [9/1]/[1/3] = 27$. Alternatively, had $\hat{\pi}_j$ equaled .90 the odds of correct classification based on random assignment would also equal 9 to 1, and OCC_j would equal 1. If the maximum probability assignment rule has no predictive capacity beyond random chance, $OCC_j = 1$. As $AvePP_j$ approaches its ideal value of 1, OCC_j increases. Larger values for OCC_j indicate better assignment accuracy.[3]

Inspection of Table 5.5 shows that for $\lambda_H = 6$ and $\lambda_H = 9$, OCC_j is nearly 5 or greater. Recall that in these two simulations assignment accuracy was high, 85% or greater. For $\lambda_H = 4$, OCC_H is particularly bad for the high group, only 1.3. OCC_L is higher, but still only 2.5. For $\lambda_H = 5$, OCC_H is a respectable 6.0, but OCC_L is only 2.5. On the basis of these results, my conclusion is that in a real world application, an OCC_j greater than 5.0 for all groups is indicative that the model has high assignment accuracy.

5.5.3 Estimated Group Probabilities versus the Proportion of the Sample Assigned to the Group (diagnostic 3)

The results of model estimation provide two alternative estimates of the probability of group membership. One is $\hat{\pi}_j$, as estimated by equation 2.10. The second is the proportion of the sample assigned to group j on the basis of the maximum posterior assignment rule. Let P_j denote the proportion assigned to group j. This proportion equals N_j/N, where N_j is the number assigned to group j and N is the total sample size. If individuals were assigned to groups with perfect certainty (that is, their AvePP of assignment equaled 1), π_j and P_j would be identical. As assignment error increases, the correspondence between $\hat{\pi}_j$ and P_j may deteriorate.

Table 5.5 reports the estimates of π_L and π_H, denoted by $\hat{\pi}_L$ and $\hat{\pi}_H$, and P_L and P_H. Observe that the correspondence of $\hat{\pi}_L$ and $\hat{\pi}_H$ with their counterparts P_L and P_H improves as the true λ_H increases. For example in the $\lambda_H = 4$ simulation, $\hat{\pi}_L = .33$, but P_L is nearly 50% smaller, .18. By contrast, for $\lambda_H = 9$, $\hat{\pi}_L$ and P_L are nearly identical, .51 and .52, respectively. Thus an easily applied diagnostic of model adequacy is whether there is a reasonably close correspondence between a group's estimated probability, $\hat{\pi}_j$, and the proportion of individuals classified to the group on the basis of the maximum posterior probability assignment rule, P_j.

---

3. A simpler measure of predictive capacity is $\text{AvgPP}_j/\hat{\pi}_j$. This measure, however, suffers from the critical deficiency that its upper bound depends upon $\hat{\pi}_j$. For example, for $\hat{\pi}_j = .5$ the upper bound is 2, whereas for $\hat{\pi}_j = .25$ it is 4.

5.5.4 Confidence Intervals for Group Membership Probabilities (diagnostic 4)

A related diagnostic of the precision with which the π_j's are estimated is the breadth of the confidence intervals of their estimate, $\hat{\pi}_j$. A narrow confidence interval implies that the probability is accurately estimated. Table 5.5 reports 98% confidence intervals (C.I.) for the estimates of $\hat{\pi}_L$ and $\hat{\pi}_H$ under the alternative values of λ_H.[4] Observe that for the model in which $\lambda_H = 4$, the intervals for both probabilities nearly span the entire allowable range, 0 to 1. This reflects the difficulty of distinguishing groups with very similar λ's. As λ_H increases, the breadth of all of the intervals narrows. There are no formal criteria for determining when a confidence interval is sufficiently narrow that its point estimate can be considered accurate. However, by $\lambda_H = 6$ the group membership probabilities seem quite accurately measured. In terms of absolute magnitude, the breadth of the interval above and below the point estimate is only about .08, or about one-sixth the estimates of π_L and π_H. For $\lambda_H = 9$ the breadths are still smaller, about .04 plus or minus the point estimate.

5.5.5 Application of the Model Accuracy Diagnostics to the London Data

Table 5.6 reports the four diagnostics for the model based on the London data. The diagnostics suggest that the capacity of the model to estimate accurately group membership probabilities and to sort cases among the groups is very good. For each group there is a close correspondence between $\hat{\pi}_j$ and the proportion assigned to the group on the basis of the maximum posterior assignment probability rule (diagnostic 3). The 98% confidence intervals are also relatively narrow for each group, less than .08 plus or minus $\hat{\pi}_j$ (diagnostic 4). The AvePP is .95 for the rare and high chronics and a very respectable .89 for the low-chronic group. Only for the adolescent-limited group does it come close to the .7 minimum threshold (diagnostic 1). Finally, the OCC is well above 5 for all groups (diagnostic 2).

---

4. For reasons discussed in Chapter 6, these confidence intervals cannot be computed directly from the model's parameter estimates. Instead they must be simulated, using a procedure described in that chapter. The confidence intervals that result from this procedure are not necessarily symmetrical like those from the conventional approach, which are not valid in this problem context. As developed in Chapter 6, the asymmetry of the interval is a reflection of the boundedness of probabilities between 0 and 1.

Table 5.6 Diagnostics of assignment accuracy applied to London data

Group	$\hat{\pi}$	98% C.I. for $\hat{\pi}$	P_j (proportion classified in group j)	Ave. PP	Odds correct classification
Rare	.70	(.61, .76)	.70	.95	8.1
Adolescent limited	.12	(.073, .20)	.13	.76	23.2
Low chronic	.12	(.078, .18)	.11	.89	59.3
High chronic	.059	(.035, .14)	.057	.95	303.0

5.6 Using the Posterior Probabilities to Compute Weighted Averages

Section 5.4 illustrated the use of trajectory group classifications based on the posterior probabilities to create profiles of trajectory group members. A significant technical criticism of these profiles is that they do not take into account the uncertainty about an individual's trajectory group membership. All of the summary statistics in Table 5.2 are computed as an unweighted average over all individuals assigned to a particular trajectory group. Should the same weight be put on the characteristics of an individual who was assigned to a trajectory group with probability .99 as an individual who was assigned to the group with probability .75? How about individuals who are not assigned to a specific trajectory group on the basis of the maximum posterior probability rule, but who still have a non-negligible chance of membership in the group? Should not their characteristics be taken into account in constructing the profile of group members?

The posterior probabilities of group membership provide a solution to this technical dilemma. They can be used as weights in calculating a group-specific weighted average, $\bar{x}_j$, for some characteristic or outcome. This weighted average is calculated by:

$$\bar{x}^j = (1/(N * \hat{\pi}_j)) \sum_{i=1}^{N} P(j|Y_i)x_i, \tag{5.3}$$

where the term $(1/N * \hat{\pi}_j)$ in equation 5.3 is a scale factor to account for the size of the group and x_i measures a characteristic of the ith individual in the sample. Its denominator equals the expected number of group j members in the total sample of N individuals.

A couple of observations about the calculation of equation 5.3 may clarify its interpretation. First, the calculation of $\bar{x}^j$ uses the data for all N individuals in the sample, regardless of whether the individual is assigned to group j by the maximum probability rule or not. However, each individual's contribution to the calculation of $\bar{x}^j$ depends upon the posterior probability of group membership, $P(j \mid Y_i)$. If this probability for group j is small, an individual i's contribution is correspondingly small. Conversely, if $P(j \mid Y_i)$ is large, the contribution is correspondingly large. Consider, for example, the individuals in Table 5.1. Individual A would only make a material contribution to the computation of $\bar{x}^j$ for the high chronics, because $P(j \mid Y_i)$ is near 0 for all other groups. Alternatively, individual D would make a material contribution to the calculation of $\bar{x}^j$ for both the rare and the low-chronic groups, where his posterior probability of group membership is .34 and .66, respectively. Second, equation 5.3 may also be used to calculate the group profiles reported in Table 5.2. Indeed, from a purely statistical perspective, this is the preferred approach, because it accounts for the uncertainty in group membership in the calculation of the profiles. However, experience shows that for well-fitting models, such as those that form the basis for Table 5.2, the profiles that emerge from these alternative calculation methods are nearly identical.

Equation 5.3 can also be used to compute weighted averages of the response variable, y_{it}, over which the trajectories themselves are defined. The weighted average of y_{it} for trajectory j, $\bar{y}_t^j$, can then be compared with the predicted value of y_t^j, which is calculated on the basis of the estimates of the β parameters. This comparison allows an assessment of how closely the model's predicted values match the weighted averages for each trajectory using the actual data.

5.7 Summary of Part I and Overview of Part II

Part I has laid out the basic structure of the group-based trajectory model, described the key outputs of the basic model, and discussed the challenges of determining how many groups should be included in the model. I now turn in Part II to three important elaborations of the basic structure: allowing group membership probability to vary with individual characteristics (Chapter 6), introducing variables beyond age or time into the specification of the trajectory itself (Chapter 7), and modeling the trajectories of two distinct but related measurement series in the form of a dual trajectory model (Chapter 8).

PART II

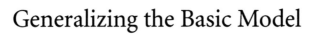

Generalizing the Basic Model

6

$$\diamondsuit$$

Statistically Linking Group Membership
to Covariates

6.1 Overview

Thus far our focus has been on the identification of distinctive trajectory groups within the population. In this chapter the focus shifts to a model generalization that links characteristics of individuals, measuring their psychological and biological makeup and life circumstances, to the probability of trajectory group membership. The aim is to create the statistical capacity to address two related issues. One concerns hypotheses testing. A central theme of the human development literature is the enduring impact of an individual's psychological profile and circumstances early in life on his or her subsequent trajectories of development. As Alexander Pope observed, "Just as the twig is bent, so the tree's inclined."[1] More generally, individual-level characteristics, whether they be characteristics of individuals themselves or characteristics of their life circumstances, may profoundly influence outcome trajectories for an immense diversity of social, economic, or biological phenomenon (for example, wages, computer usage, physical health status). The model extension allows the statistical testing of hypotheses about whether such individual-level characteristics distinguish trajectory group membership. The other issue concerns risk assessment. Here the aim is to provide a capability to predict the probability of group membership for specific values of individual-level characteristics. The purpose is to provide an objective portrayal of the degree to which membership in a specific trajectory group can be predicted with high probability. As part of such a portrayal, it is important to report estimates of

---

1. Alexander Pope (1688–1744), *Moral Essays*, Epis. I, line 149.

the reliability of the prediction. Thus a procedure for computing confidence intervals for the predicted probabilities is also described.

Because the trajectories themselves describe the long-term course of a behavior or outcome, the possible predictors of group membership should be established by the time of the initial period of the trajectories. By contrast, in Chapter 7 the focus shifts to a model generalization, which is designed to analyze whether events that occur *during* the course of a trajectory might alter the trajectory itself.

Section 6.2 develops the extension of the basic model that permits probability of trajectory group membership to vary with individual-level characteristics. Section 6.3 reports an application of this extension, and section 6.4 describes a generalized approach for statistically testing whether one or more individual-level characteristics distinguish the probabilities of membership across selected trajectory groups. Sections 6.5 and 6.6 shift to the topic of prediction. The former describes how the model's parameter estimates can be used to predict the probability of trajectory group membership for individuals with a specific set of characteristics. The latter describes a procedure for computing confidence intervals for these predicted probabilities. These two sections should be of particular interest to readers interested in risk assessment. Section 6.7 returns to Chapter 4's topic of model selection, but in the context of a model with predictors of trajectory group membership. Section 6.8 concludes with several cautionary observations about the interpretation and application of the model extension demonstrated in this chapter.

6.2 Expanding the Basic Model to Include Predictors of Trajectory Group Membership

The group-based trajectory model comprises two basic components: (1) expected trajectories for each group j, and (2) probabilities of group membership in each such group, π_j. Prior chapters have focused primarily on the former component. In this chapter the discussion shifts to the latter.

Chapter 5 demonstrated a procedure for constructing profiles of trajectory group membership. Such profiles are a first step in addressing questions about the predictors of trajectory group membership, but for three reasons they are only a beginning. First, while the profiles provide insight into how group membership probability may vary with each of the profile characteristics, they do not specify an exact mathematical relationship between π_j and each of these characteristics. Second, the profiles are only a collection of univariate contrasts. For the purpose of constructing a more parsimonious list of predictors and for causal inference, a multivariate model is required to sort out redundant predictors and to control for correlations among the predictors. Third, the profiles rely on group identifications based on the maximum posterior probability classification rule. Because the classifications are probabilistic and are not certain, some are erroneous. Conventional statistical methods to test for cross-group differences, such as F- and χ^2-based tests, assume no classification error in group identification (Roeder, Lynch, and Nagin, 1999). Thus in general they are technically inappropriate for making inferences about characteristics that distinguish trajectory group membership in circumstances in which class membership is not known with certainty (but see the discussion in section 6.7).

The solution to these problems is to specify a functional relationship between π_j and multiple individual-level characteristics and to estimate the association of each of these characteristics with π_j simultaneously with the estimation of the trajectories themselves. The specification of the linkage between π_j and multiple potential predictors makes it possible to test whether, and by how much, a specific characteristic affects the probability of group membership, controlling for other characteristics that are also posited to predict π_j. Because the relationship of individual-level characteristics to trajectory group membership is estimated jointly with the trajectories themselves, individuals are never categorized as belonging to a specific trajectory group. Thus the problem of classification error is finessed.

Let x_i denote a vector of variables measuring individual i's individual, familial, or environmental factors that are potentially associated with group membership. Then let $\pi_j(x_i)$ denote the probability of individual i's membership in group j given x_i. As already noted, because the variables making up x_i are possible predictors of trajectory group membership, these variables should be established by the time of the initial period of the trajectories.

For a two-group model, the binary logit function is a natural candidate for modeling group membership probability as a function of x_i. Specifically, the binary logit function relates the probability of membership in one of the two groups, say, 1, to x_i by:

$$\pi_1(x_i) = \frac{e^{x_i\theta}}{1 + e^{x_i\theta}}. \tag{6.1}$$

For a two-group model, it is only necessary to specify $\pi_1(x_i)$. By definition $\pi_2(x_i) = 1 - \pi_1(x_i)$, which implies that for the logit model $\pi_2(x_i) = \frac{1}{1+e^{x_i\theta}}$.

Equation 2.1 specifies the basic trajectory model without predictors of trajectory group membership. For the binary case it can be generalized to allow π_1 to vary with x_i by substituting 6.1 for π_1 in equation 2.1. The resulting individual-level likelihood function is:

$$P(Y_i) = \pi_1(x_i)P^1(Y_i) + (1 - \pi_1(x_i))P^2(Y_i)$$
$$= \left[\frac{e^{x_i\theta}}{1+e^{x_i\theta}}\right]P^1(Y_i) + \left[\frac{1}{1+e^{x_i\theta}}\right]P^2(Y_i). \tag{6.2}$$

For the more general case, in which there are more than the two groups, the logit model generalizes to the multinomial logit model (Maddala, 1983):

$$\pi_j(x_i) = \frac{e^{x_i\theta_j}}{\sum_j e^{x_i\theta_j}}, \tag{6.3}$$

where the parameters of the multinomial logit model, θ_j, capture the effect of x_i on the probability of group membership across the J groups. Without a loss of generality, θ_j for one "contrast" group can be set equal to zero. As developed below, the coefficient estimates for the remaining groups measure impacts relative to the contrast group. For this more general case, equation 6.3 is substituted into equation 2.1, which yields the individual-level likelihood function:

$$P(Y_i) = \sum_j^J \pi_j(x_i)P^j(Y_i)$$
$$= \sum_j^J \left[\frac{e^{x_i\theta_j}}{\sum_j e^{x_i\theta_j}}\right]P^j(Y_i). \tag{6.4}$$

Equations 6.2 and 6.4 are not actually different formulations of the likelihood function. It can easily be shown that equation 6.4 reduces to equation 6.2 for the specific case of $J = 2$. For either formulation, it is important to reiterate that model estimation is not a two-stage process in which the trajectories are first estimated and then in a second stage related to x_i. The parameter vectors, θ_j, measuring the impact of x_i on each π_j, are estimated simultaneously with the β parameters that describe the form of each group's trajectory.

6.3 Examples in Which Probability of Trajectory Group Membership Varies with Individual Characteristics

Table 6.1 reports the results of an analysis based on application of the binary logit-based likelihood function, equation 6.2. This form of the likelihood function applies only to model specifications involving two trajectory groups. The two-group model reported in the table was estimated using the London data. The model examines the relationship of the probability of group membership to four classic risk factors for criminal behavior: low IQ, having a parent with a criminal record, high risk-taking behavior, and poor parenting.

Both groups were specified to follow a quadratic trajectory. The resulting two-group version of the four-group model reported in Figure 1.3 results in

Table 6.1 Two-group London model with predictors of trajectory group membership

Variable	Coefficient estimate	z-score
Group 1 (Low crime)		
Intercept	−8.69	−6.53
Age/10	6.36	4.38
$(Age/10)^2$	−1.73	−4.52
Group 2 (High crime)		
Intercept	−4.57	−7.86
Age/10	4.99	8.10
$(Age/10)^2$	−1.33	−8.47
Probability of group 2		
Intercept	−3.16	−9.94
Low IQ	1.07	3.09
Criminal parents	1.36	4.18
High risk taking	1.17	3.57
Poor child rearing	.80	2.31

a "low" and "high" trajectory group. The parameter estimates for the low-crime group defines a trajectory of negligible criminal involvement, at least as measured by conviction. The group's peak rate, which is achieved at age 18, is less than 0.1 convictions per year, on average. The parameter estimates for the high-crime group define a trajectory of high criminal involvement that reaches a peak rate of more than 1.5 convictions per year. Coincidentally, this peak is also reached at age 18.

In a model that specifies group membership probability as a function of individual-level characteristics, no single base-rate probability is estimated for each group. Instead the parameter vector θ_j, which relates group membership probability to each such characteristic, is estimated. For this analysis, the estimated coefficients measure how the probability of membership in the high-crime group varies as a function of each of the four crime risk factors. All of the coefficient estimates are positive and also significant at the .05 significance level or better. Thus we can conclude that each risk factor, controlling for the presence or absence of the other risk factors, significantly increases the probability of membership in the high-crime trajectory group. Accordingly, they each also decrease the probability of membership in the low-crime trajectory group.

Table 6.2 reports the results of a companion analysis for the four-group London model. For this analysis the probability of trajectory group membership varies according to the multinomial logit model (equation 6.3) and the model in its entirety was estimated according to the individual-level likelihood function specified by equation 6.4. The parameter estimates describing the shapes of the four trajectories are not reported. They predict trajectories that are virtually identical to those reported in Figure 1.3 that were estimated according to the base model without predictors of trajectory group membership.

The coefficient estimates reported in the table correspond to the parameters θ_j in equation 6.3. For each trajectory group, the estimate of θ_j has four elements in addition to the intercept estimate—one for each of the four risk factors. Each such coefficient estimate measures how the risk factor influences the probability of membership in the particular trajectory group relative to membership in a specified comparison group. For this model the rare trajectory group serves as the comparison group. The table can be thought of as reporting three separate binary logistic regression analyses that contrast the adolescent-limited, low-chronic, and high-chronic groups with the rare

Table 6.2 Predictors of trajectory group membership in the four-group London model (rare trajectory is comparison group)

Variable	Coefficient estimate	z-score
Adolescent limited		
Intercept	−2.986	−6.31
Low IQ	.735	1.50
Criminal parents	1.011	2.19
High risk taking	1.438	3.29
Poor child rearing	.793	1.68
Low chronic		
Intercept	−2.787	−7.48
Low IQ	1.154	2.86
Criminal parents	1.380	3.46
High risk taking	.715	1.71
Poor child rearing	.563	1.28
High chronic		
Intercept	−4.970	−8.22
Low IQ	1.333	2.50
Criminal parents	2.078	3.98
High risk taking	2.207	4.03
Poor child rearing	1.160	2.22

group. A positive coefficient estimate for a specific trajectory group implies that the associated variable increases the probability of membership in that group relative to the rare group. Conversely, a negative coefficient implies a decreased relative probability. For every trajectory group, all coefficient estimates are positive. This implies that each of these psychosocial characteristics is a risk factor for following a trajectory of heightened delinquency. Not all, however, are statistically significant. For the low-chronic group the poor-child-rearing risk factor has a z-score of only 1.28, which falls short of statistical significance at conventional levels. Still the results provide strong support for the hypothesis that each of these individual-level characteristics is a significant risk factor for membership in a trajectory of heightened criminal involvement.

Though informative, these statistical tests leave unanswered other important questions about whether these same individual characteristics distinguish among the noncontrast trajectory groups that involve some substantial degree of criminal involvement. For example, an interesting question is, What risk factors distinguish membership in the high- and low-chronic trajectory groups? Observe that the magnitudes of the low IQ coefficients for these two groups are virtually identical, 1.15 for the low chronics and 1.33 for the high chronics. Is the difference between these two coefficient estimates statistically insignificant? In contrast, the magnitudes of the coefficient estimates for the risk-taking variable do seem to differ materially: 0.72 for low chronics versus 2.21 for the high chronics. Is this difference statistically significant? These statistical tests involve tests of differences between two coefficient estimates, whereas the tests reported in Tables 6.1 and 6.2 only involve a test of whether a single coefficient estimate is different than zero.[2] The next section demonstrates how these and other more general tests of differences across trajectory groups can be conducted.

6.4 Expanded Statistical Testing of Predictors of Trajectory Group Membership

This section describes two procedures for testing whether θ_j varies among the "noncontrast" trajectory groups. The first is a conventional z-score-based procedure for testing whether two coefficients are significantly different. The second test, called the Wald Test (Wald, 1943), is more general. It is appropriate for testing whether any number of coefficients is significantly different. Neither test is unique to group-based trajectory modeling. Statistical texts which describe the tests in detail include Greene (1990) and Wooldridge (2002).

6.4.1 Testing the Equality of Two Coefficients

Consider a test of whether a specific predictor denoted as z (for example, low IQ) differentially affects the probability of membership in trajectory group j (for example, low chronics) versus group k (for example, high chronics).

---

2. Specifically, the z-scores reported in tables 6.1 and 6.2 are computed as the ratio of the coefficient estimate to its standard error.

Denote the multinomial logit coefficients for z in groups j and k by θ_j^z and θ_k^z. In the context of the multinomial logit formulation of group membership probability, this amounts to testing the following hypothesis:

Null hypothesis: $\theta_j^z = \theta_k^z$, or equivalently $\theta_j^z - \theta_k^z = 0$

Alternative hypothesis: $\theta_j^z \neq \theta_k^z$ or $\theta_j^z - \theta_k^z \neq 0$

The test statistic for conducting this test is:

$$z = \frac{\hat{\theta}_j^z - \hat{\theta}_k^z}{\sqrt{v(\hat{\theta}_j^z - \hat{\theta}_k^z)}}, \tag{6.5}$$

where $\hat{\theta}_j^z$ and $\hat{\theta}_k^z$ are the maximum likelihood estimates of θ_j^z and θ_k^z, respectively, and $v(\hat{\theta}_j^z - \hat{\theta}_k^z)$ is the variance of their difference. This variance is calculated by $v(\hat{\theta}_j^z - \hat{\theta}_k^z) = v(\hat{\theta}_j^z) + v(\hat{\theta}_k^z) - 2\,\text{cov}(\hat{\theta}_j^z, \hat{\theta}_k^z)$, where $\text{cov}(\hat{\theta}_j^z, \hat{\theta}_k^z)$ is the covariance of $\hat{\theta}_j^z$ and $\hat{\theta}_k^z$. Note that $\text{cov}(\hat{\theta}_j^z, \hat{\theta}_k^z)$, $v(\hat{\theta}_j^z)$, and $v(\hat{\theta}_k^z)$ are each products of model estimation.

The z-score for the test of whether low IQ differentiates the probability of membership in the high- and low-chronic groups is only .30, which is insignificant for even $\alpha = .10$. However, the z-score for the counterpart test for the high-risk-taking variable equals 2.40, which is significant for $\alpha = .05$.[3] This series of tests implies that while the high- and low-chronic groups are not distinguished by low IQ, they are distinguished by their propensity for risk taking. Specifically, high risk-taking increases the probability of membership in the high-chronic group relative to the low-chronic group.

6.4.2 Testing the Equality of More than Two Coefficients

An even more general test of the equality of effects across groups involves contrasts of more than two groups. For example, one might want to test whether (1) low IQ predicts membership in one of the three delinquent trajectories, but (2) does not distinguish membership among the three alternative developmental courses of delinquency. An affirmative answer to (1) is provided

---

3. For the reader who is interested in replicating this calculation, the necessary quantities are as follows: $\hat{\theta}_j^z = 2.21$, $\hat{\theta}_k^z = .715$, $v(\hat{\theta}_j^z) = .299$, $v(\hat{\theta}_k^z) = .174$, and $\text{cov}(\hat{\theta}_j^z, \hat{\theta}_k^z) = .043$.

directly by the results reported in Table 6.2. A test of (2) could be accomplished by using equation 6.5 to conduct two pair-wise comparison tests to test whether low IQ distinguishes the high- versus low-chronic groups and also distinguishes the low-chronic versus adolescent-limited groups. An alternative approach for joint hypothesis testing that is statistically more powerful for a fixed significance level across tests utilizes a χ^2-based test of multiple contrasts. The degrees of freedom (d.f.) of this test equal the number of equality constraints being tested, which in the low IQ example is 2, or equivalently the number of different coefficients being tested minus 1.

The construction of this test is illustrated with the low IQ example. For notational convenience the rare group is indexed by 1, the adolescent-limited group by 2, the low chronic by 3, and the high chronic by 4, and z is used to denote low IQ. The hypothesis that $\theta_2^z = \theta_3^z = \theta_4^z$ can be tested by any of three equivalent statements of the null and alternative hypotheses:

Null 1: $\theta_2^z - \theta_3^z = 0$ and $\theta_2^z - \theta_4^z = 0$
Alternative 1: $\theta_2^z - \theta_3^z$ and/or $\theta_2^z - \theta_4^z \neq 0$

Null 2: $\theta_2^z - \theta_3^z = 0$ and $\theta_3^z - \theta_4^z = 0$
Alternative 2: $\theta_2^z - \theta_3^z$ and/or $\theta_3^z - \theta_4^z \neq 0$

Null 3: $\theta_2^z - \theta_4^z = 0$ and $\theta_3^z - \theta_4^z = 0$
Alternative 3: $\theta_2^z - \theta_4^z$ and/or $\theta_3^z - \theta_4^z \neq 0$

Let θ denote

$$\begin{bmatrix} \theta_2^z \\ \theta_3^z \\ \theta_4^z \end{bmatrix}$$

and $\hat{\theta}$ denote the counterpart vector of estimates. For the low IQ example

$$\hat{\theta} = \begin{bmatrix} .735 \\ 1.154 \\ 1.333 \end{bmatrix}.$$

Each version of the hypothesis test can be restated in matrix form:

Null: $H\theta = q$
Alternative: $H\theta \neq q$

where

$$q = \begin{bmatrix} 0 \\ 0 \end{bmatrix}$$

and H is a matrix that returns the designated equality/inequality tests when multiplied by θ. For the first formulation of the null and alternative hypothesis

$$H = \begin{bmatrix} 1 & -1 & 0 \\ 1 & 0 & -1 \end{bmatrix}.^4$$

The χ^2 test statistic is computed by:

$$\chi^2 = (H\hat{\theta} - q)'[H(V(\hat{\theta}))H']^{-1}[H\hat{\theta} - q], \qquad (6.6)$$

where $V(\hat{\theta})$ is the variance/covariance matrix of the parameter estimates in $\hat{\theta}$.

For the low IQ example, $V(\hat{\theta})$ is the remaining relevant quantity for computing the χ^2 test statistic. It equals:

$$\begin{bmatrix} .1620 & .0374 & .0467 \\ .0374 & .0240 & .0643 \\ .0467 & .0643 & .2830 \end{bmatrix}.$$

Substituting these quantities into equation 6.6 yields a χ^2 statistic of .98 with 2 d.f., which is far short of significance. This result implies that the hypothesis that low IQ has no differential impact across the delinquency trajectory groups is supported. Thus while the results in Table 6.2 show that low IQ is a risk factor for delinquency, the χ^2-based statistic implies that low IQ does not distinguish the specific developmental course of the delinquency. On the other hand, the companion test for the risk-taking variable is significant at the .05 level. This implies that risk taking is a significant predictor not only of delinquency but also of its specific trajectory.

Moving beyond the specific substantive implications of this example, the analysis also illustrates the utility of group-based trajectory modeling to conduct a form of two-stage analysis that distinguishes prevalence and intensity

---

4. For the second and third formulations of the hypotheses, H is, respectively, equal to:

$$\begin{bmatrix} 1 & -1 & 0 \\ 0 & 1 & -1 \end{bmatrix} \quad \text{and} \quad \begin{bmatrix} 1 & 0 & -1 \\ 0 & 1 & -1 \end{bmatrix}.$$

conditional upon prevalence—a distinction that is at least implicit in many investigations of phenomena with a developmental dimension. Prevalence refers to the presence or absence of a time-evolving phenomenon in individual population members. The aim of the prevalence component of the analysis is identification of factors that distinguishes between individuals who have or have not engaged in some activity (for example, smoked or not), or who have ever been outside the normal range or not (for example, have had high blood pressure or not). In the analysis of the London data, the prevalence stage was concerned with identification of variables that predicted membership in one of the three delinquency trajectories compared with the rare trajectory. Intensity refers to the developmental course of the phenomenon among those population members for which it is present. The focus of the intensity analysis is identification of characteristics that distinguish among alternative developmental trajectories of individuals for whom the phenomenon is deemed present. In the London analysis, this stage corresponded to the search for characteristics that distinguished among the three trajectories of more than rare delinquency.[5] The group-based trajectory model is ideally suited to support this type of two-stage analysis.

6.5 Assessing Magnitudes and Computing Group Membership Probabilities

Having identified individual-level characteristics that have a statistically significant association with the probability of group membership, two other important questions follow: (1) how large an impact does each such characteristic have on the probability of membership in each group, and (2) collectively, can these characteristics predict an individual's trajectory group membership with high probability?

The most commonly used metric for calibrating the magnitude of a specific variable on the probability of membership in a specified group is called

---

5. The prevalence or absence of a time-evolving phenomena in a specific individual is not always clear-cut. Many adolescents experiment with smoking but never smoke over a sustained period of time, and most boys occasionally fight. However, to consider the former "smokers" and the latter "violent delinquents" makes no sense and will obscure rather than illuminate the questions of why some adolescents become smokers and why some boys become violent delinquents.

the "odds ratio." Let x^m denote the mth individual-level characteristic included in the vector of individual characteristics that make up x_i. (The i subscript is suppressed in x^m to avoid a proliferation of unnecessary notation for this discussion.) The odds ratio measures the magnitude of the change in group membership probability for a specified group that is associated with a one-unit change in x^m. For variables measured on a 0/1 binary scale, for example, having a low IQ ($x^m = 1$) or not ($x^m = 0$), a one-unit change has a very concrete interpretation—the presence or absence of the characteristic. For each trajectory group j, the odds ratio for factor m (OR_j^m) is computed by:

$$OR_j^m = \frac{\pi_j(x^m = 1)/\pi_1(x^m = 1)}{\pi_j(x^m = 0)/\pi_1(x^m = 0)}. \tag{6.7}$$

For a specific group j, OR_j^m is the ratio of two odds. Its numerator is the odds of group j relative to the comparison group (that is, group 1 in the equation above) when $x^m = 1$. This quantity is measured by $\frac{\pi_j(x^m=1)}{\pi_1(x^m=1)}$. The denominator of OR_j^m is this same odds calculation except for $x^m = 0$. If $OR_j^m > 1$, this implies that $x^m = 1$ increases the odds of group j relative to group 1, and if $OR_j^m < 1$, it implies that the odds of j relative to group 1 are reduced.

The OR_j^m has two attractive features. It is easily computed: $OR_j^m = e^{\beta_j^m}$. To illustrate for the low IQ characteristic, OR_j^m for the high-chronic group is $e^{1.33} = 3.78$. This implies that low IQ substantially increases the odds of membership in the high-chronic group relative to the rare group. This calculation also illustrates another desirable feature of OR_j^m. It does not depend on the values of other predictors of trajectory group membership. Thus it is a measure of the magnitude of each of the predictor variables that is independent of the levels of the other variables. For the multinomial logit model, no other metric of magnitude has this very desirable property.

Balanced against the attractive features of OR_j^m is one major deficiency. It measures only relative change. Thus it is not a suitable metric for addressing the second question raised at the outset of this section—can the probability of membership in a specific group be known with high certainty on the basis of a specific set of individual-level characteristics? Section 2.4.1 described the calculations that are required to compute the probabilities of group membership in the basic model without predictors

Table 6.3   Predicted group membership probabilities (90% confidence intervals): London
data

| Scenarios | Group membership probability | | | |
	Rare	Adolescent limited	Low chronic	High chronic
1. No risks	.89	.045	.055	.006
	(.83, .96)	(.021, .093)	(.030, .098)	(.002, .016)
2. Low IQ only	.75	.079	.15	.020
	(.62, .83)	(.037, .165)	(.080, .25)	(.007, .052)
3. Criminal parents only	.70	.096	.17	.039
	(.56, .78)	(.041, .20)	(.073, .28)	(.015, .091)
4. High risk taking only	.71	.15	.090	.045
	(.58, .80)	(.076, .27)	(.045, .17)	(.021, .093)
5. Poor child rearing only	.80	.090	.087	.018
	(.69, .87)	(.043, .17)	(.044, .16)	(.006, .054)
6. All four risks	.079	.21	.22	.48
	(.033, .16)	(.081, .41)	(.089, .43)	(.25, .69)
Population base rate	.70	.12	.12	.06

of group membership probability. This section extends the earlier discussion
by describing the calculation of group membership probability as a function
of x_i.

To illustrate the end product of the probability calculations, Table 6.3 reports estimates of group membership probabilities for the London data for
six scenarios involving the level of the four predictor variables—low IQ, having a parent with a criminal record, high risk taking, and poor child rear-
ing. Scenario 1 assumes that all are 0. This is equivalent to calculating group
membership probability for individuals with none of the above risk factors
for delinquency. Scenarios 2–5 report these same probabilities for individuals
with only one of the four risk factors included in the model. In scenario 6 the
group membership probabilities are computed for individuals with all four of
the delinquency risks.

The calculations illustrate the concept of cumulative risk (Rutter et al.,
1975). Rutter argued that in most circumstances no single risk factor is decisive in determining an individual's vulnerability to psychopathology, but
that the accumulation of such risks is decisive. The calculations show that

each risk factor increases the probability of membership in one or more of the delinquent trajectory groups, but no single factor dramatically shifts the probabilities away from those in the no-risk scenario. For example, consider scenario 3. The model predicts that the probability of membership in the rare group is .70 for individuals who have at least one parent with a criminal record but who have none of the other risk factors. The counterpart prediction for the high-chronic group for these individuals is .039. In contrast, the predicted probabilities of membership in the rare- and high-chronic groups for individuals with no risks, including criminal parents, are, respectively, .89 and .006. Thus the criminal-parents risk factor materially reduces the rare group probability and increases the high-chronic group probability. Still the basic ordering of the probabilities remains—the rare group is much more likely than the high-chronic group. However, the presence of all four risks does result in a dramatic shift. The probability of membership in the high-chronic group increases from nearly 0 in the no-risk scenario to .48 in the all-four-risks scenario.

Note, however, that even in the all-risks scenario, the probability of membership in the high-chronic group is still less than .5. This finding can be explained by the population base rates. Because the high-chronic group only comprises 6% of the entire population, even the presence of multiple risk factors does not provide overwhelming evidence that an individual belongs in this trajectory. The difficulty of predicting membership in the high-chronic group with high probability makes clear that the prediction of extreme outcomes, at the individual level, is very difficult. Still the dramatic shift in probability away from the rare trajectory should not go unnoticed. With no risks the predicted probability of membership in this group is .89, but with all the risks the predicted probability for the rare group is only .079. Thus the model predicts that when all four risks are present, individuals have a very high probability of following one of the three trajectories of heightened criminality.

The analysis reported in Table 6.3 makes clear that the predicted probabilities can communicate a wealth of important insights about the phenomenon under investigation, and also can provide a potentially valuable tool for risk assessment. The actual basis of these calculations is illustrated for scenarios 1 and 6. The coefficient estimates reported in Table 6.2 provide the basis for computing an index that can be thought of as a propensity score for membership in each of the trajectory groups. Maintaining the indexing system defined earlier (where $1 =$ rare, $2 =$ adolescent limited, and so on), let $S_{ij} = x_i \hat{\theta}_j$ denote individual i's estimated propensity score for trajectory group j. Because the rare group serves as the comparison group, $S_{i1} = 0$ in all scenarios. For scenario 1, x_i is 0 for all risk factors. Thus S_{ij} equals the intercept estimate for each trajectory: -2.986 for the adolescent limited, -2.787 for the low chronics, and -4.970 for the high chronics. The resulting group membership probabilities are computed by:

$$\pi_1 = \frac{e^0}{e^0 + e^{-2.986} + e^{-2.787} + e^{-4.970}} = .89$$

$$\pi_2 = \frac{e^{-2.986}}{e^0 + e^{-2.986} + e^{-2.787} + e^{-4.970}} = .045$$

$$\pi_3 = \frac{e^{-2.787}}{e^0 + e^{-2.986} + e^{-2.787} + e^{-4.970}} = .055$$

$$\pi_4 = \frac{e^{-4.970}}{e^0 + e^{-2.986} + e^{-2.787} + e^{-4.970}} = .006.$$

Note that these "intercept-based" calculations mirror those performed in section 2.4.1. However, their interpretation is entirely different. The calculations from section 2.4.1 estimate the base rate of the four trajectory groups in the population. The above calculations estimate the probability of group membership when no risk factors are present. Thus with no risks, the estimated probability of membership in the rare group of .89 is higher than the estimated population base rate for this group of .70. Similarly, in the no-risk scenario, probability of membership in the high-chronic group, near 0, is far smaller than the estimated population base rate of high chronics in the population of .06.

The calculations for the all-risks scenario are conceptually identical. Because each of the variables in this illustration is coded in a binary format, for the all-risk scenario all $x^m = 1$. Consequently S_{ij} for a specific group is simply the sum of the coefficient estimates for that group. For the adolescent-limited group, $S_{i2} = -2.986 + .735 + 1.011 + 1.438 + .793 = .991$; for the low-chronic group, $S_{i3} = -2.787 + 1.154 + 1.380 + .715 + .563 = 1.025$; and for the high-chronic group, $S_{i4} = -4.970 + 1.333 + 2.078 + 2.207 + 1.160 = 1.808$. If the predictor variables were defined on a continuous scale, another approach would be required to define scenario values of x_i (for example, one standard deviation below the mean and one standard deviation above the mean).

6.6 Calculating Confidence Intervals for the Probabilities and Their Associated Trajectories

The probability calculations described in the prior section are based on the estimates of θ_j, $\hat{\theta}_j$, not the true values. Thus the predicted probabilities suffer from the same sampling errors as the estimates of θ_j. Confidence intervals are designed to communicate the impact of sampling error on the precision of statistical estimates. This section describes a procedure for computing confidence intervals for the predicted probabilities.[6] It also demonstrates that this same procedure can be used to compute a confidence interval for the estimates of a group's predicted trajectory by age.

Table 6.3 also reports 90% confidence intervals for each probability calculation. The confidence intervals for these probabilities are not directly computable by the usual calculations based on the standard errors of a parameter estimate, for two reasons.[7] First, and most fundamentally, the probabilities are not a linear function of the parameter estimates. The standard approach can only be applied to linear combinations of parameter estimates. Second, the probability estimates are a function of multiple parameter estimates. Thus the computation of the confidence interval must take into account the covariances of the multiple estimates.

There are several alternatives for calculating confidence intervals that accommodate these important technical problems. The approach demonstrated here is called the parametric bootstrap technique. This procedure, which was first proposed by Efron (1979), simulates the sampling distribution of the probability estimates as follows. Let $\hat{\theta}$ denote a vector composed of the multinomial logit parameter estimates θ_j for each group j, and let $V(\hat{\theta})$ denote the estimated matrix of $\hat{\theta}$'s variances and covariances. Because $\hat{\theta}$ is the product of maximum likelihood estimation, it is a consistent estimate of θ and

---

6. Another source of error is model misspecification. It is important to understand that confidence intervals do not capture the impact of this source of error, which in most analyses of nonexperimental data is likely at least as large as sampling error.

7. For example, the usual calculation for a 90% confidence interval is the parameter estimate plus/minus 1.65 times its standard error.

itself is asymptotically distributed according to a multivariate normal distribution. Because of these two properties, $\hat{\theta}$ and $V(\hat{\theta})$ can be used to create a computer-simulated random sample of estimates of θ. Each entry in the simulated sample is a random draw from a multivariate normal distribution with mean, $\hat{\theta}_j$, and variance/covariance, $V(\hat{\theta})$. The simulated estimates of θ are then used to generate estimates of the probability of interest based on the types of calculations demonstrated in section 6.5. The probability estimates are rank ordered to create a simulated sampling distribution of the scenario probability. This rank ordering forms the basis for defining the end points of confidence intervals of any desired certainty. For example, a 90% confidence interval is the lower and upper 5th percentiles of this distribution whereas a 98% confidence interval is defined by the lower and upper 1st percentiles of the distribution.

Consider the computation of the group membership probability confidence intervals for the all-risk scenario, scenario 6. For this scenario the group membership probabilities depend upon all the parameter estimates reported in Table 6.2. The parameter estimates as well as their variances and covariances were entered into a simulation program that generated 10,000 random draws from a multivariate normal distribution with a mean and variance/covariance defined by these parameters. The 10,000 draws were then used to generate 10,000 replications of the computations for computing group membership probabilities under scenario 6 that were described in section 6.5. The 10,000 probability estimates were rank ordered for each trajectory group. The 90% confidence intervals reported in Table 6.3 are the 5th and 95th percentiles of these rank orderings.

Observe that, unlike the typical confidence interval, the bootstrapped intervals are asymmetric. This asymmetry is most pronounced for the point estimates of group membership probability that are either small or large. For example, in scenario 6 the point estimate of the probability of membership in the rare group is .079. The lower bound on the 90% confidence interval is .033 (.046 probability points smaller), whereas the upper bound is .16 (.081 probability points higher). The reason for this asymmetry is that the point estimate of the probability of membership in the rare group for this scenario, .079, is close to the lower theoretical bound of a probability, 0. Therefore there is more potential for an upside error than for a downside error. Because the bootstrap method does not assume linearity but rather explicitly models nonlinearities, the mechanics of the method takes into account any asymmetries in the possibility of upside and downside error.

Table 6.4   Ninety percent confidence intervals for the predicted offending rate (λ) at selected ages for the high-chronic trajectory group

Age	Predicted λ	90% confidence interval
10	.72	(.52, .95)
15	1.69	(1.46, 1.93)
20	1.87	(1.62, 2.26)
25	.96	(.76, 1.21)
30	.24	(.15, .41)

This same simulation approach can also be utilized to compute confidence intervals for the trajectories themselves. Table 6.4 reports confidence intervals for the predicted rate of conviction for the high-chronic group at ages 10, 15, 20, 25, and 30. Consider the calculations that underlay the age 15 confidence interval. The London model was estimated using the Poisson form of the trajectory model, and the high-chronic trajectory is specified to follow a quadratic function of age whereby $\ln(\lambda_t^j) = \beta_0^j + \beta_1^j Age_{it} + \beta_2^j Age_{it}^2$. The interval for age 15 was created by drawing 10,000 estimates of the parameters β_0^j, β_1^j, and β_2^j that define the quadratic trajectory on $\ln(\lambda)$. The estimates were generated using the same procedure described above. These 10,000 estimates were used to replicate the calculation $\lambda = e^{\beta_0 + 1.5\beta_1 + 2.25\beta_2}$ 10,000 times. Again, the 90% confidence interval is the 5th and 95th percentile of a rank ordering of these estimates.

6.7 Model Selection

The introduction of predictors of the probability of group membership into the model potentially complicates the model selection search process described in Chapter 4. In particular, it adds a third dimension—predictors of trajectory group membership—to the model search space beyond the two discussed in Chapter 4, number of groups and the order of the polynomial equation describing each group's trajectory.

As a practical matter, however, a joint search for the optimal number and order of groups along with predictors of group membership probability is unnecessary. The introduction of predictors of group membership

Table 6.5 Predicted offending rate (λ) at selected ages for the four-group London model with and without predictors of trajectory group membership

	Rare		Adolescent limited	
Age	With predictors	Without predictors	With predictors	Without predictors
12	.01	.01	.24	.20
18	.01	.01	.46	.44
24	.01	.01	.00	.00
30	.01	.01	.00	.00

	Low chronic		High chronic	
Age	With predictors	Without predictors	With predictors	Without predictors
12	.16	.16	1.05	1.10
18	.45	.47	1.93	1.96
24	.50	.52	1.19	1.17
30	.20	.21	.25	.23

probability typically has almost no impact on the form of the trajectories themselves. Table 6.5 illustrates the insensitivity of trajectory estimates to the introduction of predictors of probability of trajectory group membership. For the four-group London model it reports estimates of λ at selected ages for models with and without the four risk factors for trajectory group membership. There is virtually no difference in the predicted rate of offending, λ, at each age. Conceptually, the reason for the stability of the trajectories is that the trajectories are defined by a time-varying variable, whereas the predictors of trajectory group membership are time invariant. Thus they do not include information that will affect the actual shape of a trajectory. From a statistical perspective, their informational role is limited to differentiating which of the time paths (trajectories) an individual is most likely to follow. They do not define the specific form of that trajectory over time.

If predictors of group membership are added to the model, an efficient three-stage procedure is recommended. First, using the guidelines developed in Chapter 4, identify the preferred number of groups as well as the order of the trajectories for a model without predictors of trajectory group membership. The focus of the second stage is the identification of significant predictors of group membership probability. In this stage multinomial logit models are estimated, relating group assignment to hypothesized predictors of group membership. The group membership identifications required for conducting these analyses are based on maximum posterior probability assignments from the first-stage model without predictors. A large number of statistical software packages are available for estimating such multinomial logit models. In the third stage, the final model is estimated. It jointly estimates the parameters defining the trajectories and the probabilities of group membership. The number and order of the trajectories are the products of the stage-one search, whereas the predictors of the probabilities of group membership are the products of the second-stage search.

The search for the best predictors of trajectory group membership could also be conducted using the joint-estimation procedure utilized in stage three. The software required to estimate the model is easy to use and the efficiency of estimation is also relatively good. Although estimation time will depend on data-set size, number of groups and covariates, and the speed of the computer, the computation time is generally only several minutes. For analyses in which hypotheses are well formed, such computation time is inconsequential, as very few runs will have to be made for the joint estimate. However, in analyses in which hypotheses are less well formed, or which are generally exploratory, much more effort will be put into model fitting. In these circumstances computation times of even a few minutes per run may be very cumbersome. Since modern computer estimation of a conventional multinomial logit model, such as those used in the stage-two analysis, is nearly instantaneous, the added computation time for the joint estimation represents a heavy penalty as opposed to deferring to the final stage.

Some readers might wonder about the necessity of even doing the final, third-stage estimation. Experience has shown that the statistical tests based on the assumption that membership is known with certainty are not seriously compromised by modest levels of assignment error (Roeder, Lynch, and Nagin, 1999). Thus too much can be made of the assignment error problem. However, despite the practical insignificance of the assignment error problem in many circumstances, the third-stage model estimation is recommended for three reasons. First, it is easily performed. Second, it ensures that the standard errors underlying statistical tests are properly computed in circumstances in which the impact of classification error is not trivial. An analysis reported in section 8.9 demonstrates such a circumstance. Third, if the analysis involves statistical tests of the type outlined in section 6.4 or requires the generation of confidence intervals based on the simulation procedure outlined in section 6.6, then correct estimates of parameter variances and covariances are required.

6.8 Cautionary Comments

There are two major points of caution on the interpretation and use of a trajectory model that includes predictors of probability of group membership. First, in discussing the results of the above demonstration analyses, the parameter estimates have been described as measuring "impacts" or "effects." It is important to remember that the conventional cautions about drawing causal inferences from nonexperimental data apply equally to the problem setting of group-based modeling. Use of multivariate statistical methods only reduces the chances that measured associations are spurious. The terms "impact" and "change" are used only to connote that group membership covaries with these factors.

The second caution concerns the calculation of the posterior probabilities of group membership in a model that includes predictors of group membership probability. The posterior probability calculations are affected by all variables that predict trajectory group membership. Among these are the values of all variables included in the specification of the multinomial logit function that determines the probability of group membership. Consequently, posterior probabilities of group membership will not be the same for individuals with identical values of the response variable, Y_i, but with differing values of the trajectory group predictor variables, x_i. For example, in the four-group London model reported in Table 6.2, individuals with no convictions and none of the risks for delinquency have a posterior probability of membership in the rare group that is nearly certain: .99. By contrast, there is one individual in the sample who also has no convictions but has all four of these risks. His posterior probability of membership in the rare group is still high, .71, but far short of certainty.

The example of the individual with four risk factors but no convictions illustrates two important lessons. First, predictions of a specific individual's developmental course on the basis of early risk and protective factors are far from certain. Just as this very high risk individual wound up having no convictions, other individuals with no risk factors had many convictions. Second, if group assignments based on the maximum posterior probability rule are being used to create profiles of group members, the assignments should be based on a model that includes no predictors of the probability of group membership. This approach to creating profiles ensures that classifications are based solely on the conformance of the individual's behavior with the alternative trajectory forms. If classification is based on a model with predictors of trajectory group membership, the profiles will be contaminated with an element of circularity—the profiles will be partially a statistical product of the very same predictors that the profiles themselves are intended to identify.

7

❖

Adding Covariates to the Trajectories Themselves

7.1 Overview

Trajectories describe the long-term course of a behavior or outcome. In Chapter 6 the basic model specification was generalized to allow the probability of trajectory group membership to vary as a function of individual-level characteristics. The purpose was to provide the statistical capability to identify characteristics that predict a behavior's developmental course. Logically such predictors should be established by the time of the initial period of the trajectories. In this chapter the focus shifts to a model generalization designed to analyze whether events that occur *during* the course of a trajectory alter the trajectory itself. The aim is to provide trajectory group-specific estimates of whether major life transitions such as the birth of a child, interventions such as counseling, or changes in the external environment such as moving from a high-poverty to a low-poverty neighborhood alter the developmental course of the outcome under study. The model generalization can also be used to test for cohort effects in multiple cohort designs and to analyze whether variables that vary over a continuum, such as treatment exposure time, are also associated with changes in the trajectories.

In combination with the Chapter 6 model generalization, the model extension developed in this chapter provides a statistical tool for distinguishing whether and by how much the developmental course of a behavior or outcome over a specific period of time is influenced by two conceptually distinct sets of forces—(1) preexisting tendencies or vulnerabilities and (2) events that occur during the period of the trajectory's unfolding (for example, medical treatments). This combined modeling capability is illustrated with an analysis of trajectories of adolescent delinquency. The analysis examines whether grade retention and family breakup during childhood predicts membership in a trajectory of high delinquency during adolescence, and also whether the occurrence of the same two events during adolescence alters the trajectories of delinquency themselves.

While the model extension is motivated by substantive issues that are central to the human development literature, it can also be usefully applied to analyzing impacts in many other problem domains. For example, the extension could be used to examine the effects of an advertising campaign or price change on trajectories of product or service use.

Section 7.2 lays out two alternative approaches for modeling the impact of an event that occurs during the course of the outcome under study and explains the basis for the choice between the two alternatives. Section 7.3 describes the technical details of this approach, which involves expanding the specification of a trajectory to include variables beyond age or time. Section 7.4 reports the illustrative application described above. Section 7.5 describes a procedure for conducting tests of whether the estimated effects of an event such as family dissolution vary by trajectory group. Section 7.6 demonstrates how the model extension can also be used to test for cohort effects in longitudinal data sets composed of multiple cohorts of individuals. Section 7.7 closes with a discussion of the challenge of distinguishing cause from effect in the context of a group-based trajectory model.

7.2 Modeling the Influence of Events That Occur during the Measurement Period of the Trajectory

Consider the problem of estimating the impact of parents' divorcing when a child is 5 to 15 years old on the child's physical aggression over that age range. How should one go about modeling the potential impact of this event on a child's trajectory of physical aggression? In the context of a group-based model, there are two fundamentally different approaches. One is to specify a model that permits a test of whether the event alters the child's trajectory. Analytically, this approach treats the individual's trajectory group membership as fixed. The information on the physical aggression of trajectory group members who do and do not have parents that divorce forms the basis for inferring the impact of divorce on the developmental course of physical aggression in that group. Another approach for modeling the impact of divorce is to specify a model that permits a test of whether parental divorce triggers a change in trajectory group membership. Analytically, this approach treats the trajectories as fixed entities but allows for the possibility that life events may cause individuals to change trajectory group. There is no right answer to the question of which of these modeling strategies is better. Both are conceptually valid approaches to modeling change. For several reasons, the former approach has been adopted.

The literature on human development over the life course has been an important source of inspiration for the methodology described in this book. Sampson and Laub (1992:66) observe that "trajectories refer to the long-term patterns and consequences of behavior." They go on to observe that "transitions are marked by specific life events . . . that are embedded in trajectories and evolve over shorter time spans." This description of trajectories and transitions is neatly captured by the first modeling approach but not by the second.

The first approach also conforms with a key tenet of the literature on development over the life course. This tenet holds that developmental history conditions the response to events which Elder (1985:31–32) calls "turning points, . . . a change in state that is more or less abrupt." From a statistical perspective, the precept that "development matters" implies that the magnitude or even the sign of a turning point's impact may depend upon a person's developmental course. For example, Nagin et al. (2003) found that grade retention had little impact on the physical aggression of individuals following either the chronic or the low-physical-aggression trajectories shown in Figure 1.2, but substantially exacerbated the physical aggression of individuals following the moderate or high declining trajectories.

Estimation of the impact of an event on an outcome of interest requires the statistical construction of the counterfactual—what the outcome would have been absent the occurrence of the event. In a randomized experiment the outcomes of control group members form the basis for estimating the counterfactual. In nonexperimental data the statistical construction of the counterfactual poses very difficult challenges. Group-based trajectory models based on nonexperimental data are not immune to these challenges. However, the modeling strategy of embedding turning points into the specification of the trajectory itself has several notable advantages over the alternative "changing-trajectory-group" formulation. Because impact estimates are trajectory-group specific, the estimates are based only on within-trajectory group differences in whether and when individuals experience the event of interest (for example, parents' divorcing) in the statistical construction of the counterfactual. By statistically focusing on within-group variation, the statistical estimate of the turning point's impact is limited to individuals with similar developmental histories. This modeling strategy identifies interactions between developmental history and a turning point's impact. The strategy also helps to avoid the selection argument that persons who experience the event are systematically different from those who do not. At least in terms of their developmental history, trajectory group members are similar.

The argument of homogeneity of trajectory group members is predicated on one key but implicit assumption—that the event does not fundamentally alter the behavior of most individuals. Stated differently, the model assumes that within a trajectory group change is incremental, not dramatic; the event may cause a deviation from the long-term average behavior of most group members, but the deviation is not so large that the average trajectory for the group bears no resemblance to the new trajectory of individuals affected by the event. The illustrative analysis reported in section 7.4 suggests that the incremental conception reasonably reflects the impact of grade retention and divorce on trajectories of adolescent delinquency. Other events, however, such as medical treatments, may have an impact that is transformative, not incremental. For such effects the assumption of incremental change may be inappropriate.

7.3 Adding Variables beyond Age or Time to Specification of the Trajectories Themselves

Figure 7.1 provides a graphical depiction of the model generalization. Using the notation from Chapter 6, x_m denotes predictors of the probability of trajectory group membership. Events measured contemporaneously with the trajectory itself that might alter its course are denoted by z_{lt}. Generalizing the specification of the trajectory to include z_{lt} is the topic of this section.

In the discussion that follows, z_{lt} is described exclusively as a 0/1 indicator variable that measures, for example, whether or not the individual is treated. It is important to emphasize, however, that the extension is not limited to the addition of binary variables to specification of the trajectory. The variable z_{lt} can be measured on any scale. For instance, it could be a count variable (for example, number of treatments) or a continuous-scale variable (for example, duration of treatment).

Observe that z_{lt} is subscripted by l and t. The l subscript is meant to make clear that the model generalization allows an examination of more than one type of contemporaneous influence on the trajectory. The t subscript denotes

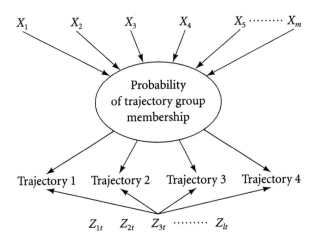

Figure 7.1   The overall model.

time, because the value of z_{lt} may change over time (for example, an individual can go into and out of treatment). However, z_{lt} is not required to be time vary-ing. For example, z_{lt} might distinguish cohort membership in a multicohort longitudinal study. Its inclusion in the specification of the trajectory provides the basis for testing for cohort effects. An example of such an application is demonstrated in section 7.6.

In the basic group model, a trajectory is described by a polynomial function of age or time. For the censored normal and logit model forms, the trajectory is specified in terms of a latent variable, y_t^*:

$$y_t^* = \beta_0^j + \beta_1^j Age_t + \beta_2^j Age_t^2 + \beta_3^j Age_t^3 + \varepsilon_t.^1 \tag{7.1}$$

The addition of the covariates z_{lt} to the specification of y_t^* is accomplished by including them as covariates in equation 7.1:

$$
\begin{aligned}
y_t^* = {} & \beta_0^j + \beta_1^j Age_t + \beta_2^j Age_t^2 + \beta_3^j Age_t^3 \\
& + \alpha_1^j z_{1t} + \alpha_2^j z_{2t} + \cdots + \alpha_L^j z_{Lt} + \varepsilon_t.
\end{aligned}
\tag{7.2}
$$

---

1. To avoid a proliferation of unnecessary notation, the subscript i denoting individuals has been suppressed.

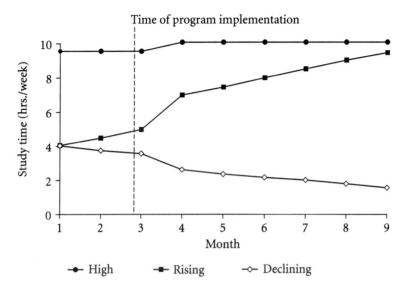

Figure 7.2 Hypothetical impact of a study habits program on trajectories of study time.

The model's estimated coefficients can be interpreted just like those of a conventional regression—the estimates measure the change in the response variable associated with changes in the explanatory variables.

Observe that the additional trajectory parameters, $\alpha_1^j, \alpha_2^j, \ldots, \alpha_L^j$, are superscripted by j. This implies that each of these parameters is specific to each trajectory group just like the parameters $\beta_0^j, \beta_1^j, \beta_2^j$, and β_3^j, which define the developmental course of the outcome over age. Thus if a specific covariate is measuring the status of an individual's involvement with an intervention (for example, in treatment or not) or activity (for example, has a job or not), the model provides an estimate of the effect of the intervention or activity that is trajectory-group specific.

The group-specific coefficient estimates are designed to capture dependencies between the effect of variables of interest and the developmental course of the outcome. The value of testing for dependencies of this form may be illustrated with a hypothetical example. Suppose a program for improving the study habits of high school students was initiated in the third month of a nine-month academic year. Figure 7.2 depicts the possible impact of the program on three hypothetical trajectories of average weekly study time. One trajectory is defined by a pattern of high but stable study time (labeled "high" in the figure). For this group it might be found that the program had no material impact, because its students already had good study habits. For students on the "rising" trajectory, the program is depicted as boosting their upward increase in study time. The third trajectory is labeled "declining." For these students, who were already disengaging from school prior to the third month, the program might exacerbate their disengagement. By permitting α_i^j to vary freely across trajectory groups, the model provides the capability for identifying such developmentally related dependencies in potential impact.

The introduction of covariates beyond age into the specification of the trajectory also has implications for the interpretation of parameters defining the polynomial in age. In a model without covariates, the trajectory does not condition on any event that might cause variation around the trajectory. Thus the trajectories in a noncovariate model can be thought of as measuring the prototypical development path of trajectory group members, averaged over all the contingencies that might cause individual variation about this developmental course. With the introduction of covariates, the estimated parameters in age have a different interpretation. They specify the expected developmental course for the case where all of the covariates equal zero. For the study-time illustration, this case corresponds to months 1–3, when the program was not being administered, or to students who did not participate in the program. Thus the β parameters defining the trajectory in age are *not* comparable in the models with and without covariates. Indeed if the covariates of interest do influence the trajectory, this guarantees that the age parameter estimates with and without other covariates are not comparable.

7.4 An Example of Adding Time-Varying Covariates to the Trajectory Specification

Nagin et al. (2003) first demonstrated the generalized model in the context of an analysis of the impact of grade retention (that is, requiring the child to repeat a grade level) on physical aggression in childhood. The application described below, which is based on the Montreal data, examines the potential impact of grade retention and family breakup on trajectories of violent delinquency in adolescence.

The application utilizes an index of violent delinquency that is the sum of the self-reported frequency of an individual's involvement in seven types of

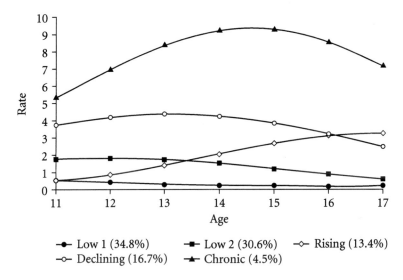

Figure 7.3 Trajectories of violent delinquency (basic model).

violent delinquency: threatening to attack someone, fist fighting, attacking someone who is innocent, gang fighting, throwing objects at people, carrying weapons, and using weapons in a fight. The trajectories were estimated as a Poisson model.

Figure 7.3 shows the resulting trajectories from ages 11 to 17 for a five-group model with no covariates other than age in the specification of the trajectories and no predictors of trajectory group membership. Two trajectories that account for an estimated 65.4% of the population remain low and also decline throughout adolescence. They are labeled "low 1" and "low 2." The "rising" group, estimated to account for 13.4% of the population, begins adolescence with similarly low violent delinquency but subsequently rises steeply. Two groups begin with a high rate of violence but subsequently follow very divergent paths, one group declines (and hence is labeled "declining") whereas the other group (labeled "chronic") remains high through adolescence.

We next consider whether the delinquency trajectories from ages 11 to 17 seem to be altered by the experience of first-time grade retention and/or separation from the subject's biological parents. There is much evidence that both these stressors are associated with heightened delinquency (Foster et al., 2003; Maguin and Loeber, 1996; Nagin et al., 2003; Pagani et al., 2001). To test for such associations the specification of the group-specific trajectories are expanded as follows:

$$\ln(\lambda_t^j) = \beta_0^j + \beta_1^j Age_t + \beta_2^j Age_t^2 + \alpha_1^j Fail_t + \alpha_2^j Separation_t,$$

where $Fail_t$ and $Separation_t$ are indicator variables, measuring each individual's retention and parental breakup status at age t. Specifically, $Fail_t$ equals 1 in all periods subsequent to an individual's first being retained at grade level and 0 in periods prior to retention. This definition of $Fail_t$ tests for whether there is an enduring impact on delinquency of the initial experience of grade retention.[2] $Separation_t$ is defined to equal 1 in all periods in which the boy is not living with both of his biological parents and equal to 0 in periods in which he is living with them. Thus if the biological parents go through periods of living and not living together, then $Separation_t$ may change multiple times over the observation period. In contrast, $Fail_t$ is defined so that it can only change value once (that is, when and if the boy is retained at a grade level for the first time after the age of 11). $Fail_t$ and $Separation_t$ correspond to z_{lt} in equation 7.2 and Figure 7.1 because they are potential turning points in an individual's trajectory.

The generalized model also includes four predictors of the probability of trajectory group membership. These predictors correspond to x_m in Figure 7.1. Two are counterparts of $Fail_t$ and $Separation_t$ but were measured prior to age 11. One, called $Fail_{10}$, equals 1 if the boy was retained by age 10, and 0 otherwise. Similarly, $Separation_{10}$ equals 1 if the boy's biological parents ever separated by age 10. The other predictor variables are low IQ and high physical aggression at age 6. Low IQ is an indicator variable distinguishing the boys in the lower quartile of the sample's IQ distribution. High physical aggression at age 6 distinguishes the boys in the upper quartile of the age 6 teacher ratings of physical aggression that were also used in estimating the trajectories in Figure 1.2.

The model's parameter estimates are reported in Table 7.1. Grade retention was associated with statistically significant increases in violent delinquency for each trajectory group. By contrast, family breakup was only associated with a

---

2. Alternative specifications that interacted $Fail_t$ with time from the retention event would allow an examination of whether the effect changed with time (for example, attenuated). Still further elaboration of the specification could test whether subsequent events of grade retention amplified the effect of the initial event. Such elaborations, though substantively important, are beyond the scope of an illustrative analysis.

Table 7.1 The impact of grade retention and family breakup on trajectories of violent delinquency

Variable	Coefficient estimate	z-score
Low 1 trajectory		
Intercept	13.26	3.27
Age	−18.95	−3.05
Age^2	5.76	2.47
Grade retention (>10)	.365	2.28
Family breakup (>10)	.391	2.30
Low 2 trajectory		
Intercept	−3.45	−2.10
Age	5.99	2.46
Age^2	−2.52	−2.84
Grade retention (>10)	.362	5.79
Family breakup (>10)	−.045	−.60
Rising trajectory		
Intercept	−6.56	−3.38
Age	8.70	3.20
Age^2	−2.42	−2.56
Grade retention (>10)	.202	2.99
Family breakup (>10)	.125	1.60
Declining trajectory		
Intercept	−8.52	5.40
Age	15.90	6.66
Age^2	−6.39	−7.15
Grade retention (>10)	.274	4.78
Family breakup (>10)	.078	1.28
Chronic trajectory		
Intercept	−6.29	−5.04
Age	11.64	6.42
Age^2	−4.12	−6.35
Grade retention (>10)	.287	5.40
Family breakup (>10)	−.014	−.25

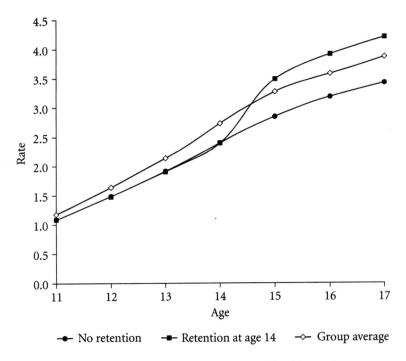

Figure 7.4   The impact of grade retention on the rising trajectory.

significant increase in violent delinquency for one group (low 1). Thus the findings imply that grade retention in adolescence was associated with subsequent increases in the violent delinquency of each trajectory group, whereas family breakup was not.

Figure 7.4 depicts graphically the impact of grade retention on the rising trajectory. Within the rising trajectory, subtrajectories for three scenarios based on retention are shown. One scenario (labeled "no retention") uses the parameter estimates for the rising trajectory to predict the expected offending rate from ages 11 to 17 under the assumption that the boy is not retained during this time period. The second trajectory (labeled "retention at age 14") depicts an alternative scenario in which the boy is first retained at age 14 and thus from age 15 onward is behind grade level. Observe that these two trajectories are identical through age 14 but at age 15 the expected rate of violent delinquency for the retention scenario increases by about 1.0 act compared with the continued nonretention scenario. The third trajectory, labeled the "group average," uses the weighted average of the *Fail$_t$* variable to trace out the expected trajectory of individuals following the rising trajectory.[3]

Prior to age 14, the group average trajectory lies above the two other trajectories, because a portion of the individuals in the group have already been retained, whereas no retention has occurred yet in either of the other two scenarios. After age 14, the group average is sandwiched between the non-retention and retention-at-age-14 trajectories, because it reflects a composite trajectory of individuals who have and have not experienced grade retention. Figure 7.4 illustrates the capability of the group-based methodology to communicate the findings from a complicated statistical model in a more easily comprehended graphical format.

The figure also speaks to the discussion in section 7.2 on the two alternative modeling strategies for estimating the impact of an event such as grade retention on the trajectory of the outcome variable. One was allowing the event to alter each group's trajectory and the other was allowing it to trigger changes in trajectory group membership. The former strategy, used here, was argued to be more appropriate for modeling incremental rather than seminal changes in trajectories. For grade retention, the findings reported in Figure 7.4 support the incremental conception of change in which the prior pattern of development not only conditions the response to the event but also circumscribes its magnitude. Because of the salience of the issue of whether impacts are incremental or dramatic, it is recommended that the counterpart of Figure 7.4 be created for all applications of the model generalization described in this chapter. Not only is the figure an effective device for communicating the implications of abstract statistical findings, it also serves to clarify whether an appropriate statistical model of change is being used.

Table 7.2 reports estimates of the four predictors of trajectory group membership. Early grade retention was not a significant predictor of membership in any of the groups, and early family breakup only predicted membership in the declining group relative to the low 1 group. Like grade retention, low IQ was not a significant predictor of membership in any trajectory group. However, high physical aggression at age 6 predicted a significant increase in

---

3. The weighted average is computed according to equation 4.3, with the weights measured by each individual's posterior probability of membership in the rising trajectory group.

Table 7.2 The impact of grade retention and family breakup on the probability of trajectory group membership (low 1 contrast group)

Variable	Coefficient estimate	z-score
Low 2 trajectory		
Intercept	.225	1.48
Grade retention (≤ 10)	−.073	−.26
Family breakup (<10)	.205	.68
Low IQ	.254	1.07
High physical aggression at 6	.105	.40
Rising trajectory		
Intercept	−.785	−4.02
Grade retention (≤ 10)	−.149	−.44
Family breakup (<10)	.515	1.58
Low IQ	.316	1.08
High physical aggression at 6	−.123	−.37
Declining trajectory		
Intercept	−1.94	−7.68
Grade retention (≤ 10)	−.326	−.78
Family breakup (<10)	.779	2.08
Low IQ	.123	.33
High physical aggression at 6	1.14	3.34
Chronic trajectory		
Intercept	−.813	−4.23
Grade retention (≤ 10)	−.235	−.70
Family breakup (<10)	−.282	−.74
Low IQ	.290	1.01
High physical aggression at 6	.643	2.24

the probability of membership in the two trajectories that began adolescence with high rates of violent delinquency.

The results suggest that grade retention in adolescence is associated with a pronounced increase in violent delinquency for all trajectory groups, but that early grade retention does not in itself predict heightened delinquency in adolescence. This finding illustrates the usefulness of the expanded model in clearly distinguishing the enduring impacts of preexisting individual-level characteristics, such as early life experiences, from the impact of events that occur contemporaneous with the phenomenon under study.

7.5 Testing for Differences across Trajectory Groups and over Time

An important strength of group-based trajectory modeling is that the model provides trajectory-group-specific estimates of key model parameters. This provides the opportunity for testing whether the impact estimates for turning-point events, such as grade retention, vary across trajectory groups.

In the violent delinquency example, the coefficient estimates for the retention variables reported in Table 7.1 indicate only limited evidence of group-specific dependencies. The estimates for the low 1 and low 2 groups were virtually identical, .365 and .362, respectively, which, in turn, were only modestly larger than the estimates for the rising group (.202), the declining group (.274), and the chronic group (.287).

A formal statistical test of whether these five estimates are significantly different in magnitude can be performed using the same testing procedure demonstrated in section 6.4. For this application, one of several equivalent forms of the Null and Alternative hypotheses is:

Null: $\alpha_1^1 - \alpha_1^2 = 0$ and $\alpha_1^1 - \alpha_1^3 = 0$ and $\alpha_1^1 - \alpha_1^4 = 0$ and
$\alpha_1^1 - \alpha_1^5 = 0$

Alternative: $\alpha_1^1 - \alpha_1^2 \neq 0$ and/or $\alpha_1^1 - \alpha_1^3 \neq 0$ and/or $\alpha_1^1 - \alpha_1^4 \neq 0$
and/or $\alpha_1^1 - \alpha_1^5 \neq 0$

The associated Wald-based χ^2 test statistic (d.f. $= 4$) equals 3.84. This falls far short of significance for even $\alpha = .10$.

Thus in this application there is no evidence that the magnitude of the effect of grade retention on violent delinquency varies across trajectory group. However, the magnitude might depend upon the age at which the retention occurs. Such age dependencies are a central theme in the literature on life course studies. Elder (1998:6) observes that "the personal impact of any change depends on where people are in their lives at the time of the change." For key life events such as marriage or parenthood, age dependencies are obvious—marriage and parenthood at ages 16 versus 30 have manifestly different implications for the life course (Hagan and Palloni, 1990).

To test for age dependencies within each trajectory group, the definition of $Fail_t$ was expanded to distinguish between retention during the ages from 11 through 14 ($Fail11\_14_t$), the typical ending age for middle school, and retention from age 15 through 17 ($Fail15\_17_t$). For this revised specification the following model was estimated:

$$\ln(\lambda_t^j) = \beta_0^j + \beta_1^j Age_t + \beta_2^j Age_t^2 + \alpha_1^j Fail11\_14_t + \alpha_2^j Fail15\_17_t, \quad (7.3)$$

where $Fail11\_14_t$ and $Fail15\_17_t$ are binary variables.[4] $Fail11\_14_t$ and $Fail15\_17_t$ were specified to allow for separate estimates of the impact of grade retention for the age intervals 11 to 14, and 15 to 17. Specifically, $Fail11\_14_t$ distinguished boys who first failed between ages 11 and 14. For these boys the variable equaled 0 for all ages prior to the retention and equaled 1 for all ages after the retention. For boys who never failed or failed after age 14, this variable equaled 0 for all ages from 11 to 17. $Fail15\_17_t$ distinguished boys who first failed at age 15 or later. For these boys the variable equaled 0 for all ages prior to the retention and equaled 1 for all ages after the retention. For boys who never failed or failed outside of ages 15 to 17, this variable equaled 0 for all ages from 11 to 17.

To illustrate the specification of these indicator variables, consider two hypothetical cases: (1) a boy who was first retained at age 12, and (2) a boy who was first retained at age 16. For the first example, $Fail11\_14_t$ would equal 0 at age 11 but from age 12 to age 17 would equal 1. $Fail15\_17_t$ would equal 0 throughout the measurement period from age 11 to age 17, because this variable was reserved for capturing the ongoing effects of failure at ages 15 to 17. For the second example, $Fail15\_17_t$ would equal 0 until age 16, when it would equal 1 for that age and also age 17, the last year over which the trajectory is defined. $Fail11\_14_t$ would equal 0 at all ages because the first retention occurred outside ages 11 to 14.

Table 7.3 reports the ten estimates of the impact of grade retention that were produced by this model. For the declining and chronic groups, the estimates of each of the age-grade impact estimates were statistically significant for a one-tailed test at $\alpha = .05$. Furthermore, for each group the estimates for

---

4. Because the impact of family breakup was statistically insignificant in four of the five groups, it was dropped from the specification.

Table 7.3 Testing for age dependencies in the impact of grade retention on trajectories of violent delinquency

Group	Variable	Coefficient estimate	z-score
Low 1	Retention ≤ 14	.375	2.16
	Retention > 14	1.532	3.46
Low 2	Retention ≤ 14	.347	5.06
	Retention > 14	.073	0.31
Rising	Retention ≤ 14	.227	2.81
	Retention > 14	.004	0.03
Declining	Retention ≤ 14	.273	4.24
	Retention > 14	.332	1.85
Chronic	Retention ≤ 14	.294	5.50
	Retention > 14	.229	2.31

the two age groups were of about equal magnitude. By contrast, for the low 1, low 2, and rising groups there do appear to be substantial age dependencies. For example, for the rising group the age 14 or younger impact estimate was highly significant and equaled .227, whereas the age 15 or older estimate was only .004 and not even remotely close to being statistically significant. The same pattern is also present for the low 2 group. By contrast, the pattern is reversed for the low 1 group: both grade-retention impact estimates are statistically significant, but the magnitude of the 15 or older estimate is far larger than the 14 or younger estimate. Section 6.4 laid out the z-score-based test for testing the inequality of the parameters α_1^j and α_2^j in equation 7.3. On the basis of this test we can in fact conclude that the estimates of α_1^j and α_2^j for the low 1, low 2, and rising groups are significantly different from each other. This result implies that the exacerbating impact of grade retention on violent delinquency is age dependent, but that this age dependency varies by trajectory group. For the low 2 and rising groups the impact of retention attenuates with age, for the low 1 group it worsens with age, and for the chronic and declining groups there is no apparent age dependency. The analysis illustrates how the group-based trajectory framework can be used to identify such age dependencies that themselves depend upon developmental history.

7.6 Testing for Cohort Effects

Longitudinal studies are often made up of multiple cohorts that reflect either differences in the age of subjects at the outset of the study or differences in the time that subjects began to be monitored (for example, different release cohorts from hospitalization). In such multiple cohort studies, it is common practice to test for cohort effects that reflect differences across cohorts in their developmental trajectories. It is important to account for cohort effects if the data on the cohorts are combined for the purpose of constructing an overall trajectory model.

This section demonstrates the use of the model generalization described by equation 7.2 to test for such cohort effects. The specification of equation 7.2 anticipates the augmentation of the basic trajectory model in age with another covariate that also varies with time (for example, grade retention status). However, the covariate may also be a time-invariant variable, such as cohort membership.

This demonstration utilizes data from the Rochester Youth Development Study (RYDS). The RYDS examined a sample of two grade cohorts—seventh- and eighth-grade students in the 1987–88 academic year from Rochester, New York. Students at high risk for serious delinquency and drug use were over-sampled, but the entire school population was represented in the study. For an overview of the RYDS, see Thornberry et al. (2003).

In previous analyses of the self-reported delinquency data from RYDS, Bushway, Thornberry, and Krohn (2003) found that a six-group, Poisson-based model provided the best representation of the trajectories of general delinquency. For this demonstration, the Bushway et al. model was expanded to include a grade-cohort indicator variable to test for cohort effects in each of these trajectories. The specific form of the model was:

$$\ln(\lambda_t^j) = \beta_0^j + \beta_1^j Age_{it} + \beta_2^j Age_{it}^2 + \alpha_1^j cohort_i, \qquad (7.4)$$

where $cohort_i$ equals 1 for individuals from the eighth-grade cohort and 0 for individuals in the seventh-grade cohort.[5]

---

5. Cohort effects can be manifested in many ways. The model specification in equation 7.4 tests for cohort effects that are reflected in an upward or downward shift in each trajectory group across cohorts. A more general specification of cohort effects would test not only for shifts but also for differences across cohorts in the time path of the trajectories themselves. Such a test would require that equation 7.4 be expanded to include interactions between cohort membership and age. A model that included interactions with both the age and

Table 7.4 Cohort effect estimates for the Rochester Youth Development Study

Trajectory	Estimate of cohort effect (α_1^j)	z-score
Gradual desistors [a]	.544	2.85
Slow-uptake chronics	−.010	−.12
Late starters	.468	2.79
Low-level offender	.799	3.42
Bell-shaped desistors [a]	−.054	−.37
High-level chronics	.194	1.56

a. *Desistance* is a term used by criminologists to describe cessation from committing crimes.

Table 7.4 reports estimates of α_1^j for the six trajectory groups. Observe that there is evidence of statistically significant cohort effects, but only for three of the six trajectories. As determined by analyses not reported here, the cohort effect in a single-group model is statistically significant, but the findings from this group-based analysis suggest that this effect is not universal within the sampled population. Rather it is limited to population segments making up three trajectory groups.

7.7 Distinguishing Cause from Effect: The Challenge of Endogeneity

Throughout this chapter the discussion has used terms like "impact" or "effect on" to describe the statistical association between a covariate, such as grade retention, and the form of a trajectory. As already emphasized in Chapter 6, the group-based trajectory framework is not immune to the hazards of drawing causal inferences from nonexperimental data. In the context of the model extension developed in this chapter, the most salient obstacle to causal inference is distinguishing cause from effect—does grade retention cause violent delinquency, is it a consequence of violent delinquency, or both? In econometric parlance, such reciprocal relationships yield problems of endogeneity. Failure to account for endogeneity can seriously compromise statistical findings by confounding cause-and-effect relationships.

the age^2 terms would test whether the cohorts follow entirely different trajectories. Until the implications for model identification of this generalized specification are investigated, this test is not recommended.

This section describes an approach to generalizing this chapter's model extension to account for endogeneity. The discussion is intended as an outline for future research, because the extensions are neither actually demonstrated nor fully developed.

To determine whether personal experiences or interventions alter trajectories, we must consider the process that generates these events. Because the goal is to establish whether such events change the outcome under study, the literature on causal inference commonly refers to them as *treatments*. In this context, the term *endogenous treatments* means that the treatment is assigned on the basis of behavioral outcomes that are of interest to the researcher. In contrast, *exogenous treatments*, also known as *strongly ignorable* treatment assignments (Rosenbaum and Rubin, 1983), are independent of these outcomes.

The distinction between exogenous and endogenous treatment assignment is subtle but also fundamental to making valid inferences about treatment effects. Consider the problem of using nonexperimental data to infer the impact of counseling on a psychiatric disorder. Individuals seek out counseling for many reasons. A stylized model of this decision is outlined for the purpose of highlighting the statistical difference between exogenous and endogenous treatments.

Suppose that a major factor in the decision to enter counseling is the support and encouragement of family members and close friends. Further suppose that such support independently has a salutary impact on the individual's mental health. Under these circumstances if a statistical model does not account for social support, the impact of treatment will be exaggerated, because it will also reflect the salutary impact of supportive family and friends.

A treatment is said to be exogenous if the statistical model of the individual's mental health includes a sufficient level of controls for supportive family and friends that the difference between those who receive and do not receive counseling is attributable to factors that have no direct impact on mental health (for example, the extent of insurance coverage for mental health services). Rosenbaum and Rubin use the term "strongly ignorable" assignment to describe exogenous assignment in order to emphasize the idea that the residual set of variables that explain why some are treated and others are not can be ignored in the statistical model without adverse consequences for bias.

If the assumption of strongly ignorable assignment is not tenable, the source of the endogeneity must be accounted for in the statistical model. Much statistical research has focused on developing methods to account for endogeneity. The solution involves: (1) specifying a tractable model that accounts for the influence of the outcome of interest (for example, depression) on the probability of treatment (for example, hospitalization), and (2) using *instrumental variables* that create treatment variation independent of the behavioral outcomes of interest. Finding strong and valid instruments is a case-specific problem whose solution, if it exists, depends on the available data. Thus the focus in this section is on (1).

Specification of a model that accounts for the treatment-assignment process requires that the basic model be expanded to reflect the impact of trajectory group membership on the probability of experiencing a specified treatment. Two models of the treatment assignment process are laid out in this section. In one model, treatment assignment is based on knowledge of trajectory group membership. The other model assumes that group membership is not known and must be inferred from past behavior.

These two models are specified in the context of the simplified environment of a binary treatment, D_t (1 = treatment, 0 = no treatment), that is applied in period τ and may determine outcomes in period τ and beyond. The models build from the framework discussed throughout the book—namely, the probability of membership in group j, $\pi_j(x)$, is a function of observed individual characteristics, x, and the probability distribution of the outcome of interest, denoted by $p^j(y_t \mid age_t, D_t)$, which is conditional on group j membership and is a function of observed age and treatment.[6]

The endogeneity of D_t requires that we also specify its conditional distribution. The first model to be considered assumes that treatment assignment probability depends upon trajectory group membership, but that treatment assignment is exogenous within a trajectory group. This model is intended to account for the possibility that treatment rates systematically vary across trajectory groups in a fashion that obscures the efficacy of the treatment. For example, if individuals in trajectories of high depression are more likely to receive treatments involving hospitalization, the efficacy of hospitalization will likely be obscured by a comparison of the outcomes of depression patients who were and were not hospitalized. In addition, this model allows treatment probability to also depend upon age; individual characteristics that predict trajectory group membership, x; and one or more instrumental variables, w. For this model the probability of treatment is denoted by $p(D_t \mid j, Age_i, x, w)$.

---

6. Suppression of the subscript i denoting individuals continues.

For a statistical model to account for endogeneity it must specify the joint probability distribution of y_t and D_t, $p(y_t, D_t)$, which for this model equals:

$$\sum_{j=1}^{K} \pi_j(x) \prod_{t=\tau}^{T} \left[p^j(y_t \mid Age_t, D_t) \cdot p(D_i \mid j, Age_i, x, w; \gamma) \right]. \quad (7.5)$$

The "assignment based on group membership" model assumes that trajectory group membership is known to the person responsible for assigning the treatment. If the treatment assignment decision is made by the individual himself (for example, whether to seek treatment for depression), this is a plausible model structure. If the assignment decision is made by an independent third party, however, the assumption that group membership is known is less plausible. In this circumstance a more realistic model is one in which group membership is inferred on the basis of prior behavior.

Thus the second model formulation drops the assumption that membership in group j is known and replaces it with the assumption that group membership is inferred from prior behavioral outcomes. Specifically, it is assumed that $p(D_t \mid Y(\tau - 1), Age_t, x, z)$, where $Y(\tau - 1)$ denotes the longitudinal sequence of behaviors recorded through period $\tau - 1$. The likelihood function for each individual for periods τ and beyond is as follows:

$$\sum_{j=1}^{J} \pi_j(x) \prod_{t=\tau}^{T} \left[p^j(y_t \mid Age_t, D_t; \beta_j) \cdot p(D_t \mid Y(\tau - 1), Age_t, x, z) \right]. \quad (7.6)$$

For prior periods, the likelihood is as before.

For the membership-inferred formulation of the assignment process, the endogeneity of treatments arises only from the inclusion of past outcomes, $Y(\tau - 1)$, as determinants of treatment probability. To make this problem more tractable, the role of outcomes, age, and x is modeled as operating solely through the posterior probabilities of group membership, $P(j \mid Y(\tau - 1), Age, x)$. Thus the conditional distribution of treatments reduces to

$$P(D_t \mid \Pr(j \mid Y(\tau - 1), Age, x), z),$$

where, as before:

$$P(j \mid Y(\tau - 1), Age, x) = \frac{P^j(Y(\tau - 1) \mid Age)\pi_j(x)}{\sum_{k=1}^{K} P(Y^k(\tau - 1) \mid Age)\pi_k(x)}.$$

As indicated at the outset of this section, both of these formulations have yet to be formally developed and applied. Their implementation is a key item on the agenda for further development of the group-based trajectory framework. They have this high-priority status because a more confident basis for causal inference in applications of the group-based trajectory method will return large dividends for scientific inquiry, public policy, and clinical practice.

Note, however, that both of these model formulations solve the endogeneity problem only in the limited sense that if the modeling assumptions that underlie them are correct, the resulting estimates of the treatment effect will not be contaminated by the impact of the outcome of interest on the likelihood of receiving treatment. If our assumptions are *not* correct, we have not escaped the endogeneity problem. In any specific application, these modeling assumptions, which form the conditions for identification of the treatment effect, will invariably be a source of disagreement. Some may question whether the treatment assignment process is being correctly modeled. Others may question whether the instrumental variables are truly independent of the outcome of interest. Note, however, that such challenges are not unique to causal inference with the group-based trajectory method. Rather they are reflective of the difficulty of drawing causal inferences from nonexperimental data. Further, the problem is not impervious to statistical analysis.

Over the past two decades pioneering work by statisticians and econometricians (cf. Angrist and Imbens, 1995; Manski, 1995; Rosenbaum and Rubin, 1983; Rosenbaum, 1995) has done much to clarify the formidable conditions required for valid causal inference from nonexperimental data. In so doing, this work has clarified the potential fragility of treatment-effect estimates based on modeling assumptions. This theoretical research has also served to heighten appreciation of the power of a true randomized experiment.

In light of this research on causal inference, concern about the difficulty of using group-based modeling to formally account for endogenous treatments is understandable. Notwithstanding, it is important to keep in mind the alternative to not pursuing this line of research for untangling cause from effect. This alternative will rarely be the "gold standard" for establishing causality—experiments with random assignment. Rather, it will be continued analysis of nonexperimental data with statistical methods that ignore the problem of endogeneity.

To be concrete, consider a meta-analysis of corporal punishment by Elizabeth Gershoff that appeared in *Psychological Bulletin*. Gershoff (2002:565) included "determining causal directions" as a key topic for future research. She observed: "Correlational designs cannot rule out the possibility that child behavior problems elicit corporal punishment more than corporal punishment causes such problems." She also points out that "although some experimental studies of corporal punishment have been conducted . . . , the ethics of [random assignment] would challenge most institutional review boards." Thus, in the case of corporal punishment, scientific headway on the problem of "determining causal directions" is not likely to come from randomized experiments. Rather it will come from application of the types of model extensions laid out in this section.

Corporal punishment is not an anomalous example of a "treatment" that is largely beyond the reach of experimental study. Other examples are parental separation, child neglect, grade retention, bullying, social ostracism, illicit drug use, and poverty. Progress in understanding the causal impact of such experiences requires the development of statistical methods that account for endogneity. The appropriate standard for judging whether these methods offer value-added is not randomized experiments but the status quo approaches used in most social science research for drawing causal inferences from non-experimental data.

8

Dual Trajectory Analysis

8.1 Overview

Prior chapters have focused on modeling the trajectory of a single outcome. This chapter demonstrates the use of the group-based trajectory framework to model the developmental course of two distinct but related outcomes. The resulting dual trajectory model provides a rich, yet easily comprehended, statistical summary of the developmental linkages between the two outcomes of interest. It can be used to analyze the connections between the developmental trajectories of two outcomes that are evolving contemporaneously (such as depression and alcohol use) or that evolve over different time periods that may or not overlap (such as prosocial behavior in childhood and school achievement in adolescence).

The dual model has three key outputs: (1) trajectory groups for both measurement series; (2) the probability of membership in each such trajectory group; and (3) probabilities linking membership in trajectory groups across behaviors. The linking probabilities are the key advance of the dual model. Compared with the use of a single summary statistic to measure the association of two outcomes, the linking probabilities provide a far more detailed and varied summary of the developmental connections between the two outcomes under study. The dual model can also be used to analyze how the joint probabilities vary with individual-level characteristics.

The dual model was first presented in Nagin and Tremblay (2001b). The motivation for the model was to provide a new statistical tool for analyzing two prominent themes in developmental psychopathology, developmental criminology, and psychiatry—comorbidity and heterotypic continuity. Comorbidity refers to the contemporaneous occurrence of two or more undesirable conditions, such as conduct disorder and hyperactivity during childhood

(Angold, Costello, and Erkanli, 1999; Nagin and Tremblay, 1999), or anxiety and depression in adulthood (Kessler et al., 1994). The interrelationship of two or more behaviors over nonoverlapping periods in time is also of significant interest in developmental science. In personality psychology such temporal interdependencies have been described by the term "heterotypic continuity" (Caspi, 1998; Kagan, 1969). Heterotypic continuity refers to a propensity for engaging in a generic form of behavior that reveals itself in different ways over life stages. For example, a propensity for shyness may manifest itself by a reluctance to approach strangers during early childhood, avoidance of group social events during adolescence, and the choice of a profession in adulthood that does not require interaction with the public. The form of the social avoidance is different, but the constant is a reluctance to interact with strangers.

Because of the changing form of a trait's manifestation, use of the same measurement scale at different stages of life is generally inappropriate for capturing such behavioral propensities. For example, in my own work with Richard Tremblay on the developmental course of physical aggression, we have examined the connection between physical aggression in childhood and violent delinquency in adolescence (Nagin and Tremblay, 1999, 2002; Brame, Nagin, and Tremblay, 2001). The former was measured by teacher reports of the child's tendency to bully and fight with his classmates and the latter was measured by the self-reports of the individuals themselves on the frequency of their engaging in various forms of violent delinquency such as gang fighting and using a weapon. Because the two scales measure different behaviors and are based on different reporting sources, they are not easily combined into a single scale. Yet both scales are intended to measure a propensity for physical aggression. The dual model is designed to relate the two measurement scales but without combining them into a single metric.

Although the initial motivation for the dual model was couched in the terminology of development science, potential applications of the model extend into diverse problem domains in which the central concern is overlap in the temporal evolution of two outcomes or behaviors. Two examples include the intertemporal connections of kidney failure and impaired vision in diabetics and text messaging and voice mail usage rate among cell phone users. Thus readers are again reminded to think beyond the specific content of the application examples and consider them as exemplars of a style of analysis that can be applied in substantively distant problem domains.

Section 8.2 discusses the problem of relating two series of measurement for the purpose of measuring comorbidity or heterotypic continuity. Section 8.3 reports an illustrative application of the dual model. The purpose is to provide context for the derivation of the likelihood function of the dual model in section 8.4. Section 8.5 reports a more extended application that illustrates a variety of valuable analyses that can be conducted with the model's parameter estimates. Section 8.6 demonstrates a number of useful calculations involving the probabilities that link trajectories across behaviors. Section 8.7 generalizes the dual model so that the linking probabilities can depend on individual-level characteristics, and section 8.8 demonstrates the generalization with an illustrative analysis. Section 8.9 closes with a discussion of the limitations of an alternative approach to estimating the linking probabilities.

8.2 The Problem of Summarizing the Relationship between Two Distinct but Related Series of Measurements

Comorbidity and heterotypic continuity are typically represented by a single summary statistic, usually a correlation or an odds ratio, that measures the degree of overlap of the two behaviors or symptoms of interest (for example, hyperactivity and conduct disorder at age 6) or, alternatively, relates the two distinct behaviors measured at different life stages (for example, physical aggression at age 5 and violent delinquency at age 15).[1]

Figure 8.1 depicts the essence of the data summary problem in such analyses. Panel A characterizes the conventional approach to summarizing the co-occurrence of two behaviors. For comorbidity analysis, up to T summary measures of association can be computed—one for each of the T measurement periods. For example, if series X and Z, respectively, measured depression and anxiety over T periods, up to T correlation coefficients could be

---

1. Examples of research using this conventional measurement strategy in comorbidity analysis include: Costello et al. (1988), Fergusson, Horwood, and Lynskey (1993), Haapasalo et al. (2000), Lewinsohn et al. (1993), and Valez, Johnson, and Cohen (1989). Similar examples of heterotypic continuity analysis include: Backteman and Magnusson (1981), Caspi (1998), Farrington (1990), Huesmann, Eron, Lefkowitz, and Walder (1984), Loeber and LeBlanc (1990), and Olweus (1979).

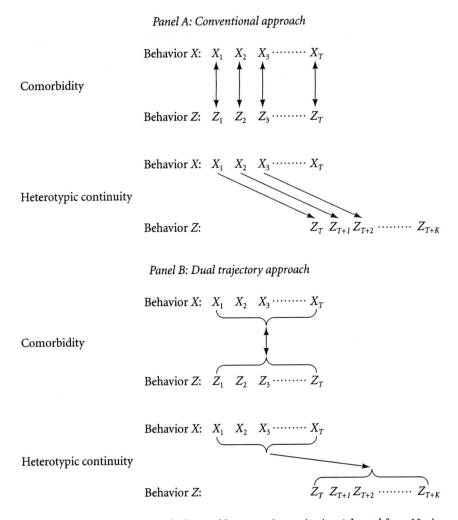

Figure 8.1   Measuring comorbidity and heterotypic continuity. Adapted from Nagin
and Tremblay (2001b).

computed to represent comorbidity for each period. For heterotypic continuity analysis, the number of possible combinations is even larger because each
of the T measurements of behavior X can be related to any of the K measurements of behavior Z from period T forward.

The conventional approach to measuring behavioral overlap in psychopathology suffers from several important limitations. Most important, it

makes inefficient use of longitudinal data, because the measures of association utilize at most only two assessment periods. In light of the enormous cost of conducting longitudinal studies, it is ironic that the analysis ultimately reduces to a correlation of two periods of data. It is also paradoxical, because a key rationale for tracking individuals for more than two assessment periods is to provide the capacity to trace more than a linear change in the developmental course. Yet this capacity is greatly dissipated by conventional summary statistics for measuring comorbidity and heterotypic continuity.

In some other application domains more effective use is made of the longitudinal character of the data. For example, studies of the long-term impacts of poverty distinguish between transient and sustained poverty (Duncan and Brooks-Gunn, 1997; McLanahan and Sandefur, 1994; Pagani et al., 1997). Similarly, analyses of the impact of household structure on child development have distinguished not only alternative household structures but also number of transitions between these structures (McCord, 1982; Juby and Farrington, 2001; Fergusson, Horwood, and Lynskey, 1993).

However, even these studies suffer from a second important limitation. The customary interpretation of a summary statistic relating two variables, whether it be a correlation coefficient or a multiple regression coefficient, is that its magnitude applies equally to all individuals within the population under study (Brame, Nagin, and Tremblay, 2001). For example, suppose the correlation between involvement in antisocial behavior at ages 8 and 14 was found to be 0.6. Most commonly, this correlation is interpreted as applying to all population members. However, there is a more complicated but more realistic alternative—it is an average correlation calculated over heterogeneous subpopulations. For some subpopulations, there may be very little association, while for other subpopulations, the association may be much larger (e.g., Magnusson and Bergman, 1990; Pulkkinen and Tremblay, 1992).

The dual model aims to address the various limitations of conventional approaches for analyzing two series of measurements. The essence of the approach is depicted in panel B of Figure 8.1. It relates all measurements of the two behaviors of interest in a single summary statistical model. As previously noted, the key components of the resulting dual model are trajectory groups for both of the measurement series, the probability of membership in each such trajectory group, and probabilities that link membership in trajectory groups across behaviors.

The dual trajectory model is an important advance over conventional approaches for measuring comorbidity or heterotypic continuity for several reasons. First, by summarizing the developmental course of behaviors of interest in the form of trajectory groups the model is exploiting the longitudinal character of the data. Thus the dual model is capturing the dynamic dimension of the overlap between the behaviors whereas the conventional approach does not. Second, by summarizing the linkages across the trajectory groups for each behavior in the form of an array of probabilities rather than in the form of a single summary statistic, the model provides a statistical basis for communicating not only average tendencies but also deviations from the average tendencies. The result is a far richer summary of the pattern of interconnection in the developmental course of the two behaviors.

8.3 An Example: The Linkage of Trajectories of Violent Delinquency and Number of Sexual Partners from Ages 13 to 17

The three key outputs of the dual model are illustrated with an analysis of the linkage between violent delinquency from ages 13 to 17 and number of sexual partners per year over this same age range. The model is estimated with data from the Montreal-based longitudinal study. Figure 8.2 displays the form of the trajectory groups identified for these two behaviors.

Panel A shows the trajectories for violent delinquency. The five trajectories are a product of the Poisson-based model and measure the expected rate of violent delinquency by age for each group. They are very similar to the trajectories reported in Figure 7.3, which are also based on the Montreal study. The trajectories in that figure begin at age 11; for this analysis the starting age is 13, the first age at which the study participants were asked about their sexual activities.

The two largest trajectory groups, labeled the low 1 and 2 groups, account for nearly 66% of the population. The remaining one-third, who engage in more than occasional violence, are split among three groups: a chronic group (6.8%), which follows the classic hump-shaped trajectory of delinquency; a declining group (10.8%), which starts at a high rate at age 13 but declines thereafter; and a rising group (16.5%), which is low at age 13 but rises thereafter to a level that is about half that of the chronic group.

Panel B shows four trajectories for the number of sexual partners in the past year, based on respondent self-reports. One group, estimated to make up

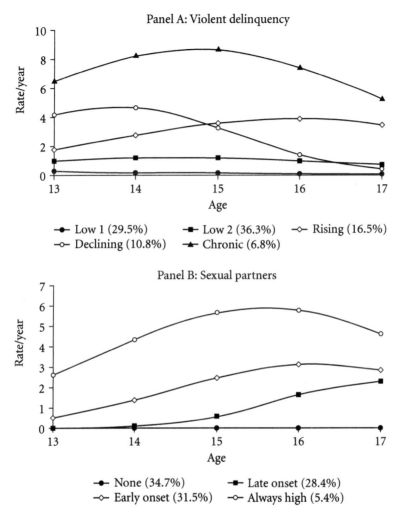

Figure 8.2 A dual trajectory model of violent delinquency and number of sexual partners from ages 13 to 17.

about 35% of the population, reports no sexual activity over ages 13 to 17. This group is labeled "none." Two other groups, each estimated to account for about 30% of the population, report rising numbers of sexual partners per year over this period. The groups are distinguished by the age of onset of sexual activity. Members of the late-onset group predominantly appear to initiate sex at about age 15 to 16, whereas the initiation age for the early-

onset group is about age 13 to 14. The final group displays a high level of
sexual activity throughout the age range. This always-high group is estimated
to include about 5% of the population.

Table 8.1 reports the key innovation of the joint trajectory model—three
alternative representations of the linkage between the violent delinquency
and sexual partners trajectories. One is the probability of membership in
each of the violent delinquency trajectories, conditional upon membership
in each of the sexual partners trajectory groups. These probabilities are reported in panel A. Because the probabilities are conditional upon membership
in a given sexual partners trajectory group, each column of probabilities in
panel A sums to 1. Panel B reports the reverse set of conditional probabilities: the probability of membership in each of the sexual partners trajectories
conditional upon membership in each of the violent delinquency trajectory
groups. In this panel, each row of probabilities sums to 1. The third form
of representation, reported in panel C, is the joint probability of membership in a specific violent delinquency trajectory and a specific trajectory of
number of sexual partners. This panel enumerates all the possible combinations of violent delinquency and sexual partners trajectory groups. Thus the
twenty joint probabilities sum to 1. Denoting the violent trajectory groups by
k and sexual partners trajectories by j, the first form of representation is $\pi_{k|j}$
(that is, the probability of k given j), the second is $\pi_{j|k}$ (that is, the prob-
ability of j given k), and the third is π_{jk} (that is, the joint probability of j
and k).

However represented, the results show a strong interrelationship between
the developmental trajectories for these two behaviors. Panel A shows that
the boys who are not sexually active from ages 13 to 17 are least likely to
be members of the three higher trajectories of violent delinquency. Indeed
their probability of membership in the chronic trajectory is nearly zero.
By contrast, the boys who follow the always-high sexual activity trajectory
have a negligible chance of belonging to either of the two low-violent delinquency trajectory groups, and nearly a two-thirds chance of following the
trajectory of chronic-violent delinquency. The late- and early-onset groups
are in between. For members of these sexual partners trajectories, the probability of their following any specific violent trajectory group is far less
certain than for the two other groups. This implies greater heterogeneity in
the developmental course of their violence during adolescence. Compared
with simply correlating the number of acts of violent delinquency with the
number of sexual partners each year from age 13 to age 17, the dual model

Table 8.1   The interrelationship from ages 13 to 17 of violent delinquency and number of
             sexual partners

A. Probability of delinquency group k conditional on sexual partners group j ($\pi_{k|j}$)

Violent delinquency group	Sexual partners group			
	None	Late onset	Early onset	Always high
Low 1	.54	.30	.08	.00
Low 2	.34	.47	.36	.00
Rising	.06	.13	.31	.22
Declining	.06	.09	.17	.16
Chronic	.00	.02	.09	.62

B. Probability of sexual partners group j conditional on delinquency group k ($\pi_{j|k}$)

Violent delinquency group	Sexual partners group			
	None	Late onset	Early onset	Always high
Low 1	.63	.29	.08	.00
Low 2	.33	.37	.31	.00
Rising	.12	.22	.59	.07
Declining	.20	.24	.49	.08
Chronic	.02	.07	.42	.49

C. Joint probability of sexual partners group j and delinquency group k (π_{jk})

Violent delinquency group	Sexual partners group			
	None	Late onset	Early onset	Always high
Low 1	.19	.08	.02	.00
Low 2	.12	.13	.11	.00
Rising	.02	.04	.10	.01
Declining	.02	.03	.05	.01
Chronic	.00	.00	.03	.03

provides a far richer, yet still comprehensible, summary of the relationships in
the data.

We turn now to the derivation of the statistical model that formed the basis
for this analysis.

8.4 Derivation of the Likelihood Function for the Dual Trajectory Model

The likelihood function for the dual model builds upon the basic assumptions of the single trajectory model. Let $Y_1 = \{y_{11}, y_{12}, y_{13}, \ldots, y_{1T_1}\}$ and $Y_2 = \{y_{21}, y_{22}, y_{23}, \ldots, y_{2T_2}\}$ denote the two longitudinal series to be modeled in a dual trajectory format. As illustrated by panel B of Figure 8.1, the model does not require that the measurements be contemporaneous or even that the length of the measurement periods be the same (that is, $T_1 \neq T_2$).

The assumption of conditional independence given group membership, which underlies the single trajectory model, is maintained. Thus $f^j(Y_1) = \prod^{T_1} f_t^j(y_{1t})$ and $h^j(Y_2) = \prod^{T_2} h_t^j(y_{2t})$, where $f(*)$ and $h(*)$ are suitably defined probability distributions given the form of the data (for example, Poisson for count data). Note that the distributions defining $f(*)$ and $h(*)$ need not be the same. Thus while in the previous example both $f(*)$ and $h(*)$ took the form of a Poisson distribution, this is not required. For example, in an illustration described in section 8.5, $h(*)$ follows the Poisson distribution and $f(*)$ follows the censored normal distribution.

Figure 8.3 presents two conceptual models for joining the trajectories of $f^j(Y_1)$ and $h^j(Y_2)$. In the constrained model, each trajectory for Y_1 (for example, childhood physical aggression) is uniquely associated with a trajectory for Y_2 (for example, adolescent violence). This model was first demonstrated in Brame, Nagin, and Tremblay (2001). Figure 8.4 shows two of the seven combined trajectories that were reported in that analysis. Both groups dis-

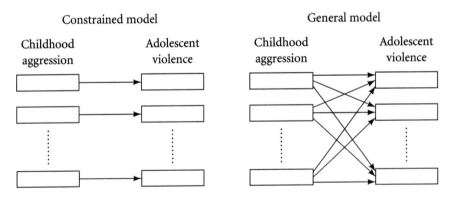

Figure 8.3   Two dual trajectory models.

play a consistently high level of physical aggression from ages 6 to 13. Despite the similarity of their childhood aggression trajectories, the two groups display markedly different trajectories of aggression in adolescence. At age 13 the self-reported violent delinquency of one group is higher than that of any other group at any age. Their violence rises steadily to a peak at age 15 and thereafter declines. This group was called the high childhood aggression/high adolescent violence group and was estimated to account for about 3% of the

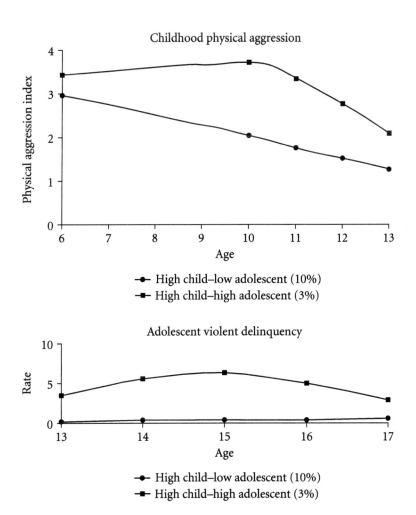

Figure 8.4   Illustration of the constrained version of the dual trajectory model.

population. In contrast, the second group is composed of individuals who report a negligible level of violence in their adolescence, despite their high aggression in childhood. This group, which was called the high childhood aggression/low adolescent violence group was estimated to make up 10% of the population.

The second, more general model shown in Figure 8.3 relaxes the constraint of a unique identification of trajectories across Y_1 and Y_2. Instead the linkages between the trajectories for Y_1 and Y_2 are described in probabilistic terms. The multiple arrows linking the trajectories reflect the probabilities that characterize the linkage. This means that researchers need not assume the form of linkages between two different outcomes ex ante. The violent delinquency and sexual partners trajectory analysis (see Table 8.1) is an example of the general model.

The probabilities that describe the linkage across the trajectory for the two outcomes, $P(j \mid k)$, $P(k \mid j)$, and $P(j\&k)$, provide explicit metrics for describing the degree of overlap in the developmental course of the two outcomes in both the constrained and the general model. With these probabilities in hand, a researcher can ask questions such as: Is the probability of membership in a specific trajectory group for Y_2 independent of trajectory group membership for Y_1? Is the joint probability of membership in the extreme trajectory groups of Y_1 and Y_2 comparatively large or small? The answer to the former question is important for assessing whether there is actually a linkage between the developmental courses of Y_1 and Y_2, and the answer to the latter is important for estimating the required size (and cost-benefit) of a program targeted at an extreme group.

Compared with the constrained model, the one downside of the general model is that it is more complex to calculate—a whole new set of probabilities are added to the model. Balanced against this increased complexity is the enriched description of the overlap between the trajectories for the two behaviors.

8.4.1 Likelihood Function for the Constrained Model

The constrained model assumes that there are J unique trajectories for representing the combined developmental course of Y_1 and Y_2. It is assumed that, conditional on membership in the jth group, Y_1 and Y_2 are independently distributed with $P^j(Y_1, Y_2) = f^j(Y_1)h^j(Y_2)$. Thus the unconditional distribution of Y_1 and Y_2 sums across the conditional distributions, $P^j(Y_1, Y_2)$, with each such conditional distribution weighted by π_j:

$$P(Y_1, Y_2) = \sum_j \pi_j f^j(Y_1) h^j(Y_2). \tag{8.1}$$

As in the trajectory model for a single outcome variable, the trajectories are described by polynomial functions of age or time. However, because a group is defined by trajectories for two outcomes, Y_1 and Y_2, two sets of trajectory group specific parameters are estimated, one for each outcome.

8.4.2 Likelihood for the General Model

The general model assumes that the J trajectories groups for Y_1 are probabilistically linked with K trajectory groups for Y_2. As with the constrained model, the general model assumes that, conditional on j and k, Y_1 and Y_2 are independently distributed, $P_{jk}(Y_1, Y_2) = f^j(Y_1) h^k(Y_2)$. Thus the unconditional likelihood function of Y_1 and Y_2 for each individual i sums across $P_{jk}(Y_1, Y_2)$ with each such conditional distribution weighted by π_{jk} (that is, the joint probability of membership in trajectory group j for Y_1 and trajectory group k for Y_2):

$$P(Y_1, Y_2) = \sum_j \sum_k \pi_{jk} f^j(Y_1) h^k(Y_2). \tag{8.2}$$

An alternative and equivalent form of the likelihood function builds from the result that $\pi_{jk} = \pi_{k|j} \pi_j$ and substitutes $\pi_{k|j} \pi_j$ for π_{jk}. Thus

$$\begin{aligned} P(Y_1, Y_2) &= \sum_j \sum_k \pi_{k|j} \pi_j f^j(Y_1) h^k(Y_2) \\ &= \sum_j \pi_j f^j(Y_1) \sum_k \pi_{k|j} h^k(Y_2). \end{aligned} \tag{8.3}$$

Observe that this second likelihood function has a sequential construction—each group j of Y_1 is linked to each group k of Y_2 via a conditional probability $\pi_{k|j}$. For problems in which Y_1 temporally precedes Y_2, this formulation is a natural representation of their temporal ordering. Regardless of temporal sequence, however, still another equivalent formulation conditionally links each group k to each group j via the conditional probability $\pi_{j|k}$. For this formulation the likelihood function for each individual i is:

$$P(Y_1, Y_2) = \sum_k \pi_k h^k(Y_1) \sum_j \pi_{j|k} f^j(Y_1). \qquad (8.4)$$

8.5 Another Example: The Linkage between Childhood Physical Aggression and Adolescent Violence

This example revisits the linkage between childhood physical aggression and violent delinquency in adolescence that was used above to illustrate the constrained model, but this time in the context of the general model. The example's purpose is twofold: (1) to demonstrate the application of dual trajectory modeling to the analysis of data over two adjacent time periods, and (2) to elaborate upon a variety of useful calculations and subsidiary analyses that can be conducted with the outputs of the dual model.

Figure 8.5 reports the childhood physical aggression trajectories from ages 6 to 13. The shapes and sizes of the childhood trajectories are very similar to

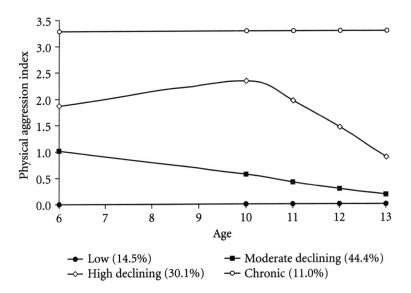

Figure 8.5 Physical aggression trajectories from ages 6 to 13.

those reported in Figure 1.2 for the age period 6 to 15. The one exception concerns the size of the chronic group, which is nearly three times larger than in the earlier analysis, 11% versus 4%. The increased size of the chronic group is attributable to the two-year truncation in the observation period in this analysis. Some individuals in the chronic group may not clearly enter the period of declining physical aggression that distinguishes the chronic group from the high-declining group until age 13 or later.

The trajectories for violent delinquency are not depicted, because they are virtually identical to those reported in Figure 8.2. It should be noted, however, that they are, in fact, very slightly changed because they were jointly estimated with a different Y_2—childhood physical aggression, not number of sexual partners in adolescence.

How do the adolescent violent delinquency trajectory groups link up with the childhood physical aggression trajectories? Table 8.2 reports the conditional probability of "transitioning" from each of the age 6–13 physical aggression trajectory groups to the various age 13–17 violent delinquency trajectory groups. Denoting the trajectories for childhood physical aggression by j and adolescent violent delinquency by k, these probabilities correspond to $\pi_{k|j}$ in the prior discussion of the derivation of the likelihood. For example, the estimated probability of an individual in the moderate declining childhood group (that is, $j = 2$) transitioning to either the low 1 or 2 adolescent trajectory group (that is, $k = 1$ or 2) is .731. By contrast, the probability of his transitioning to the chronic group is less than .019.

The transition probabilities conform to long-standing results on the continuity of problem behaviors. Across the childhood physical aggression groups, the low-childhood group is most likely to transit to the low 1 or 2 adolescent trajectories (.895), whereas the chronic-childhood group is least likely to

Table 8.2   Probability of adolescent trajectory group membership conditional on childhood trajectory group

Childhood group	Adolescent group			
	Low 1 and 2	Rising	Declining	Chronic
Low	.895	.091	.014	.000
Moderate declining	.731	.133	.117	.019
High declining	.528	.171	.189	.112
Chronic	.304	.270	.206	.220

transit to the low 1 or 2 adolescent groups (.304). In between are the moderate and high-declining childhood physical aggression groups with probabilities of .73 and .53, respectively. Conversely, the low-childhood group is least likely to join any of the three high-adolescent trajectory groups (.105 = .091 + .014 + .000) and the childhood chronics are most likely to transit to these trajectories (.696 = .270 + .206 + .220).

The transition probabilities are also consistent with prior research, which finds that physical aggression generally declines as age increases (Broidy et al., 2003; Tremblay et al., 1999). For all groups, including the childhood chronics, the most likely transition is to the low 1 or 2 adolescent trajectory groups. Further, with the exception of the chronic-childhood group, this probability exceeds .5. Conversely, the probability of boys in the two lowest childhood groups transiting to the chronic-adolescent group is negligible. Still, a sizable minority of individuals in the two lowest childhood trajectory groups transit into one of the three higher adolescent trajectory groups—10% and 27%, respectively, for the low and moderate-declining childhood groups.

This discussion was intended to illustrate the richness of information contained in the estimates of $\pi_{k|j}$. All of this would be lost if the analysis used only a single summary statistic such as a correlation to communicate the connections over time in two behavioral outcomes. An even fuller description of the interconnections of the developmental trajectories of Y_1 and Y_2 can be obtained from consideration of three other probabilities—π_{jk}, $\pi_{j|k}$, and π_k.

8.6 Calculating π_{jk}, $\pi_{j|k}$, and π_k

Because childhood physical aggression temporally precedes violence in adolescence, it is natural to represent the connection between the trajectories in child and adolescence by $\pi_{k|j}$, the probability of violent delinquency trajectory group k given childhood trajectory j. However, the two alternative representations of the interconnection, $\pi_{j|k}$ and π_{jk}, are also of interest. The former measures the probability of childhood trajectory j given membership in adolescent trajectory group k. This probability provides the basis for describing the composition of each adolescent violent trajectory group in terms of the representation of each childhood trajectory group. The latter probability measures the joint probability of belonging to a specific childhood trajectory j and adolescent trajectory k. This section describes the necessary calculations for estimating both these probabilities. In addition it details the calculations required to compute the probability of membership in each of the k groups of Y_2, π_k.

The trajectory estimation software used to estimate the model described in the prior section is based on the representation of the likelihood shown in equation 8.3. With this representation, two sets of probabilities are direct products of model estimation, π_j and $\pi_{k|j}$. With these estimates in hand, $\pi_{j|k}$, π_{jk}, and π_k can be calculated by the following relationships:

$$\pi_k = \sum_j \pi_{k|j}\pi_j \quad k = 1, \ldots, K, \tag{8.5}$$

$$\pi_{jk} = \pi_{k|j}\pi_j, \tag{8.6}$$

and

$$\pi_{j|k} = \pi_{k|j}\frac{\pi_j}{\pi_k}. \tag{8.7}$$

Equation 8.5 specifies the calculation for computing the probability of membership in each of the k trajectory groups for Y_2. From equation 8.6 it can be seen that each component of the sum in equation 8.5 is the joint probability of membership in trajectory group j and k, $\pi_{jk}(=\pi_{k|j}\pi_j)$. To compute π_k for a fixed k, the joint probabilities are summed over the j trajectory groups for Y_1. Because a member in trajectory group k must have also been a member of one of the J groups for Y_1, the sum of the joint probabilities, π_{jk}, over the J groups that make up Y_1 equals π_k.

The calculation of π_k is illustrated for the declining violent delinquency adolescent group and for the chronic violent adolescent group. For this demonstration the former trajectory is denoted by $k = 4$ and the latter group by $k = 5$. The childhood trajectories are denoted by $j = 1$ for the low trajectory, $j = 2$ for the moderate-declining trajectory, $j = 3$ for the high-declining trajectory, and $j = 4$ for the chronic trajectory. To perform these calculations, we need π_j for each childhood group. As reported in Figure 8.5, $\pi_1 = .145$, $\pi_2 = .444$, $\pi_3 = .301$, and $\pi_4 = .110$. Table 8.2 reports the required conditional probabilities. For the declining violent delinquency group, these are $\pi_{4|1} = .014$, $\pi_{4|2} = .117$, $\pi_{4|3} = .189$, and $\pi_{4|4} = .206$. For the chronic delinquency group the counterpart probabilities are $\pi_{5|1} = .000$, $\pi_{5|2} = .019$,

Table 8.3 Percentage of adolescent trajectory group membership contributed by each childhood trajectory group

Childhood physical aggression groups (ages 6–13)	Adolescent violent trajectory groups (ages 13–17)	
	Chronic only	Chronic and declining and rising
Low	0	4.3
Moderate declining	12.8	33.8
High declining	50.9	40.2
Chronic	36.4	21.7

$\pi_{5|3} = .112$, and $\pi_{4|4} = .220$. On the basis of equation 8.5, the probability of membership in the declining violent delinquency group, π_4, is calculated by $.014 * .145 + .117 * .444 + .189 * .301 + .206 * .110 = .133$. The first term in the sum, $.014 * .145 (= .00203)$, is the joint probability of membership in the declining-violent group in adolescence and in the low group in childhood. The second term, $.117 * .444 (= .052)$, is the joint probability of membership in the declining-violent group in adolescence and in the moderate-declining group in childhood. The third and fourth terms are the counterpart joint probabilities, but for the high-declining and chronic-childhood groups, respectively. The sum of these joint probabilities across the four childhood groups equals the total probability of membership in the declining-adolescent group.

The logic of the calculation for the chronic violent delinquency group, π_5, is conceptually equivalent, but all of the joint probabilities in the sum pertain to that group. The specific calculation of π_5 is $.000 * .145 + .019 * .444 + .112 * .301 + .220 * .110 = .066$.

We turn now to the calculation of $\pi_{j|k}$. Table 8.3 reports estimates of $\pi_{j|k}$ for the chronic violent trajectory group and for the combination of the chronic, declining, and rising groups. These estimates of $\pi_{j|k}$ measure the contribution of each of the childhood trajectory groups to these alternative combinations of adolescent trajectories. For example, the low and moderate-declining childhood groups, which make up 58.9% of the total childhood population, contribute only 12.8% of the population of the adolescent chronics. In contrast, their contribution to the combined population of the adolescent chronics, decliners, and risers is a more substantial 38.1%.

Both these calculations were performed using equation 8.7. First, consider the calculation of proportion of the adolescent chronics who were in the two lowest childhood aggression trajectory groups, .128. This proportion is the sum of two probabilities: (1) the probability of having been a member of the low childhood group given membership in the chronic adolescent group, $\pi_{j=1|k=5}$, and (2) the probability of having been a member of the moderate-declining childhood group given membership in the chronic adolescent group, $\pi_{j=2|k=5}$. According to equation 8.7,

$$\pi_{j=1|k=5} = \pi_{k=5|j=1} \frac{\pi_{j=1}}{\pi_{k=5}} = .00 * \frac{.145}{.066} = .000$$

and

$$\pi_{j=2|k=5} = \pi_{k=5|j=2} \frac{\pi_{j=2}}{\pi_{k=5}} = .019 * \frac{.444}{.066} = .128.$$

The calculation of the contributions of the childhood groups to a combination of adolescent groups requires an adaptation of equation 8.7. Consider the calculation of the contribution of the moderate-declining group ($j = 2$) to the combination of the rising ($k = 3$), high-declining ($k = 4$), or the chronic ($k = 5$) adolescent groups. This contribution is measured by the probability $\pi_{j=2|k=3, 4, \text{ or } 5}$. According to equation 8.7,

$$\pi_{j=2|k=3, 4, \text{ or } 5} = \pi_{k=3, 4, \text{ or } 5|j=2} \frac{\pi_{j=2}}{\pi_{k=3, 4, \text{ or } 5}} = .269 * \frac{.444}{.354} = .337.$$

The quantities used in this calculation were obtained as follows. The probability $\pi_{j=2} = .444$ is a direct product of model estimation, as previously discussed. The probability of membership in each of the adolescent groups, k, is calculated by equation 8.5. As already demonstrated, $\pi_{k=4} = .135$ and $\pi_{k=5} = .066$. Application of equation 8.5 to the rising group results in an estimate of $\pi_{k=3} = .153$. Thus $\pi_{k=3, 4, \text{ or } 5} = .354 (= .153 + .135 + .066)$. The final ingredient required for the calculation is $\pi_{k=3, 4, \text{ or } 5|j=2}$. This conditional probability is the sum of the conditional probabilities of transition from the moderate-declining childhood group to the rising, declining, and chronic adolescent groups. From Table 8.2 these probabilities are, respectively, .133, .117, and .019. Therefore $\pi_{k=3, 4, \text{ or } 5|j=2} = .269$.

Although calculating these probabilities requires some additional effort, the information that they provide is important for conveying statistical findings in a manner that is easily understood. The probabilities can also be useful to practitioners in assigning treatments to targeted subpopulations. For example, a school administrator could use the probabilities to help determine which children should be enrolled in adolescent violence-prevention programs on the basis of early childhood behavior.

8.7 Generalizing the Model to Include Covariates in the Probabilities Linking Trajectories between Y_1 and Y_2

Chapter 6 demonstrated a model generalization that allowed the probability of trajectory group membership, π_j, to vary as a function of individual-level variables. This section extends this same generalization to the transition probabilities $\pi_{k|j}$. The variables associated with $\pi_{k|j}$ can measure long-standing characteristics of individuals or their circumstances. They can also measure events at or near the time of the transition. If both types of predictors of $\pi_{k|j}$ are included, the model extension provides a statistical capability for distinguishing the impacts of long-standing individual differences and more proximate events in determining transitions across trajectories.

In the context of the illustrative example from the prior section, this capability would help to answer such fundamental questions as: What factors, if any, explain the differences in adolescent violence of individuals who followed the same trajectory of childhood physical aggression? Is the divergence attributable to long-standing individual differences that first manifest themselves at the important developmental transition from childhood to adolescence? Alternatively, is the divergence attributable to experiences during the transition to adolescence that trigger a separation of theretofore similar trajectories of development? A comparable set of questions could be framed about any behavior or outcome that evolves over time. Thus this model generalization has many important applications.

Recall that the generalization developed in Chapter 6 used the multinomial logit function to specify the linkage between a vector of individual characteristics, x_i, and probability of trajectory group membership, $\pi_j(x_i)$. The generalization described here again relies on application of this probability function.

As a prelude to the description of this generalization, the estimation of π_j and $\pi_{k|j}$ without covariates is first discussed. The form of the likelihood function specified by equation 8.3 involves the estimation of both sets of probabilities. For the same reasons discussed in section 2.4.1, π_j and $\pi_{k|j}$ were estimated using multinomial logit functions without covariates:[2]

$$\pi_j = e^{\theta^0_j} \bigg/ \sum_j e^{\theta^0_j} \tag{8.8}$$

and

$$\pi_{k|j} = e^{\gamma^0_{k|j}} \bigg/ \sum_k e^{\gamma^0_{k|j}} \quad j = 1, \ldots, J. \tag{8.9}$$

While equations 8.8 and 8.9 follow the same functional form, they differ in one important respect—estimation of the former requires the estimation of many fewer parameters than the latter. Equation 8.8 specifies J probabilities, one for each of the J trajectory groups of Y_1. Estimation of equation 8.8 requires the estimation of $J - 1$ parameters, each corresponding to one of $J - 1$ trajectory groups. Recall from the discussion in section 2.4.1 that an additional parameter is not required for the Jth group, because its probability can be computed by 1 minus the sum of the probabilities for the $J - 1$ other groups. By contrast, equation 8.9 specifies $J * K$ probabilities. For each of Y_1's J trajectory groups, there are a total of K transition probabilities, one for each of Y_2's K groups. Thus for *each* group j, a total of $K - 1$ parameters must be estimated, each corresponding to one of the $K - 1$ trajectory groups of Y_2. Again the transition probability to the Kth group can be calculated as 1 minus the sum of the probabilities for the other $K - 1$ groups. Thus, in total, estimation of the transition probabilities described by equation 8.9 requires the estimation of $J * (K - 1)$ parameters—one set of $K - 1$ parameters for each of the J groups of Y_1.

The difference in number of model parameters required to specify π_j and $\pi_{k|j}$ without covariates has important implications for the specification of a model that allows π_j and $\pi_{k|j}$ to vary as a function of covariates. Let x_i

---

2. Briefly, the reasons are to guarantee that the estimated probabilities are in the theoretically required 0-to-1 interval and to build a model specification that lends itself to the inclusion of predictors of trajectory group membership.

and w_i denote sets of potential predictors of π_j and $\pi_{k|j}$, respectively. The two sets may be made up of variables that are identical, partially overlapping, or nonoverlapping. As in Chapter 6, this generalization of the dual model assumes that π_j follows the multinomial logit function:

$$\pi_j(x_i) = \frac{e^{x_i\theta_j}}{\sum\limits_j e^{x_i\theta_j}}. \tag{8.10}$$

To help to make clearly a point about the specification of $\pi_{k|j}(w_i)$, equation 8.10 can be rewritten in a form that more obviously ties it to equation 8.8:

$$\pi_j(x_i) = e^{\theta_j^0 + \theta_j' x_i} \Big/ \sum\limits_j e^{\theta_j^0 + \theta_j' x_i}. \tag{8.10'}$$

This alternative format makes it clear that for each group j, θ_j includes two components—an intercept, θ_j^0, and a set of parameters, θ_j', that measure the impact of each variable included in x_i on the probability of group j, relative to the reference group. Thus, if x_i included five predictors of trajectory group membership and $J = 4$, a total of eighteen parameters would be estimated. The total includes three estimates of θ_j^0 plus fifteen estimates of θ_j' composed of a set of five parameters for each of the three nonreference groups.[3]

This example illustrates an important feature of logit models: because θ_j' is group specific, one set of parameters must be estimated for each trajectory group. As a result there is a risk that the number of parameters in the model may outstrip the information in the data that is required for their estimation. Stated in formal statistical terms, parameter proliferation ultimately results in problems of statistical power even for large data sets.

The risk of parameter proliferation is particularly acute if the equivalent generalization is applied to equation 8.9, whereby:

$$\pi_{k|j}(w_i) = e^{\gamma_{k|j}^0 + \gamma_{k|j}' w_i} \Big/ \sum\limits_k e^{\gamma_{k|j}^0 + \gamma_{k|j}' w_i} \quad j = 1, \ldots, J. \tag{8.11}$$

---

3. Recall from the Chapter 6 discussion that without loss of generality the parameters for the reference group can be set equal to 0.

This risk is most easily illustrated with an example. Consider again the childhood physical aggression and adolescent violence illustration from section 8.5. This model includes four trajectories of childhood physical aggression ($J = 4$) and five trajectories of adolescent violent delinquency ($K = 5$). Suppose w_i included five characteristics that might affect the probability of transitioning from a given trajectory j of Y_1 to each trajectory group k of Y_2. For each of Y_1's J trajectory groups this specification requires the estimation of a total of twenty-four logit parameters—four estimates of $\gamma^0_{k|j}$ plus a set of five parameters that make up $\gamma'_{k|j}$ for each of the four noncontrast delinquency groups.[4] Thus, across the four childhood physical aggression groups, equation 8.11 requires the estimation of a total of ninety-six parameters. Even in a large longitudinal data set, such as the Montreal study, this is more parameters than can be feasibly estimated.

One way to streamline the model is to assume that effects of the variables included in w_i do not depend upon the trajectory group membership for Y_1. Under this assumption the various values of $\gamma'_{k|j}$ are equal across the J trajectory groups in Y_1, and therefore they can be denoted by γ'_k. Conceptually, this modification amounts to assuming that the influence of a particular variable on the probability of transition to a specific trajectory group k of Y_2 as measured by γ'_k does not interact with trajectory membership for Y_1. For the above example, this reduces the number of required parameters from ninety-six to thirty-six. With the introduction of the no-interaction constraint, equation 8.11 can be restated as:

$$\pi_{k|j}(w_i) = e^{\gamma^0_{k|j} + \gamma'_k w_i} \bigg/ \sum_k e^{\gamma^0_{k|jk} + \gamma'_k w_i} \quad j = 1, \ldots, J. \quad (8.12)$$

Note that the no-interaction model continues to allow the intercepts, $\gamma'_{k|j}$, to vary freely across Y_1's J trajectories. Consequently, the transition probabilities, $\pi_{k|j}$, will be different for two individuals with identical characteristics w_i but who had followed different trajectories for behavior Y_1. Thus the no-interaction model still allows the trajectory that is followed for Y_1 to influence the probability of trajectory group membership for Y_2 even controlling for the variables in w_i.

---

4. Because w_i measures five characteristics, $\gamma'_{k|j}$ for each noncontrast group includes five parameter estimates. Thus the specification requires six parameters for each of the noncontrast groups—$\gamma^\theta_{k|j}$ plus $\gamma'_{k|j}$.

Indeed in the special circumstance in which the factors included in w_i have no impact on the transition probabilities (that is, $\gamma'_k = 0$), equation 8.12 reduces to its original form without covariates, equation 8.9. This circumstance has special substantive implications. It implies that the transition across trajectories for the behaviors Y_1 and Y_2 is wholly determined by the developmental trajectory that is followed for the earlier behavior Y_1.

8.8 An Example of a Model That Includes Covariates in the Specification of π_j and $\pi_{k|j}$

The model extension developed in the prior section is illustrated with the childhood physical aggression and adolescent violence example. For this illustration an index was created that is the sum of five binary indicators of risk factors for physical aggression: subject's mother has less than a tenth-grade education, subject's mother began childbearing as a teenager, subject's parents separated by age 6, subject is in the lowest quartile of the IQ distribution, and subject was held back in school prior to age 10. This index is the sole element of x_i, but in general x_i could include multiple predictors.

This same risk index is also included in w_i to test whether these risk factors predict a transition to the higher-level violent delinquency trajectories after controlling for membership in the childhood physical aggression trajectory group. Also included in w_i is a binary indicator variable equal to 1 for boys who first experienced grade retention at age 11 or 12.[5]

These two components of w_i were selected to demonstrate the use of the model to examine two conceptually distinct explanations of why persons in the same childhood trajectory may follow different trajectories in adolescence. One explanation is that preexisting individual characteristics may be decisive in determining outcomes in adolescence. The risk factor index is made up of such potential characteristics, and its inclusion in the model allows a test of the idea that risk factors established early in life have an enduring impact on development. Our first hypothesis is that individuals who are high on this index are more likely to transition to a high violence trajectory in adolescence, even after controlling for childhood trajectory group membership. A

---

5. Nagin et al. (2003) and Pagani et al. (2001) found that grade retention is associated with a subsequent escalation in violence.

second hypothesis is that an event occurring at or near the period of transition from the childhood trajectory to the adolescent trajectory is decisive in determining the adolescent trajectory that is subsequently followed. This alternative explanation shifts the focus of attention away from long-standing individual differences to important events in the individual's life that occur while the trajectory itself is evolving. The first-time grade retention at age 11 or 12 is a possible example of such an event. Its inclusion in the model allows a test of the hypothesis that grade retention just prior to the transition to adolescence increases the probability of movement to a trajectory of high violence in adolescence, controlling for childhood trajectory of physical aggression.

Panel A of Table 8.4 reports parameter estimates of θ_j^0 and θ_j'. These parameters define the probability of membership in the four childhood physical aggression trajectory groups. They are the conceptual equivalent of the results reported in Table 6.2 on the linkage of various risk factors to trajectory group membership in the London data. The results indicate that for each trajectory group the risk index (labeled "Risk" in Table 8.4) is positively and significantly associated with an increase in the probability of membership in the moderate-declining, high-declining, and chronic trajectory groups relative to the low group. For example, using the calculation procedures demonstrated in Chapter 6, an increase in the index from 0, its minimum, to 5, its maximum, increases the probability of membership in the chronic childhood group from .02 to .41. Also observe that the magnitude of the risk-index coefficient estimate is successively larger from the moderate-declining group to the high-declining group to the chronic group. This implies that the risk index has a progressively larger impact on the probability of membership in the successively higher childhood physical aggression trajectories.

Panel B reports estimates of $\gamma_{k|j}^0$ and γ_k'. Consider first the estimates of γ_k', which measure the impact of the risk index and grade retention on the probability of transition to the various violent delinquency trajectories. Observe that none of the risk-index coefficient estimates are even remotely close to statistical significance. This implies that these early risks do not predict membership in the violent delinquency trajectory group, *controlling* for childhood physical aggression trajectory. Note, however, that first-time grade retention at age 11 or 12 is significantly associated with an increased risk of transition to the rising and chronic trajectories of violent delinquency in adolescence. In the context of the prior discussion of explanations for individual variation in transition probabilities, the findings imply that preexisting vulnerabilities

Table 8.4 Predictions of the probabilities of childhood physical aggression trajectories and of the probabilities of transition to trajectories of adolescent violent delinquency

Panel A: Childhood physical aggression trajectory (low trajectory is comparison group)

Variable	Coefficient	z-score
Moderate declining		
Intercept	.810	4.29
Risk	.416	2.52
High declining		
Intercept	−.326	−1.36
Risk	.923	5.64
Chronic		
Intercept	−2.73	−3.11
Risk	1.38	5.74

Panel B: Transition to adolescent violence trajectory (low 1 is comparison group)

Variable	Coefficient	z-score
Low 2 ($k = 2$)		
Risk	.030	.29
Fail 11–12	.540	1.40
$\gamma_{2|1}$ (low phys. agg.)	−.229	−.79
$\gamma_{2|2}$ (mod. decline)	−.099	−.46
$\gamma_{2|3}$ (high decline)	1.42	3.13
$\gamma_{2|4}$ (chronic)	−3.144	−1.34
Rising ($k = 3$)		
Risk	−.025	−.18
Fail 11–12	.902	2.15
$\gamma_{3|1}$	−1.662	−3.61
$\gamma_{3|2}$	−1.127	−3.68
$\gamma_{3|3}$	.561	.98
$\gamma_{3|4}$	.711	.74
Declining ($k = 4$)		
Risk	−.020	−.15
Fail 11–12	.322	.67
$\gamma_{4|1}$	−3.885	−1.43
$\gamma_{4|2}$	−1.084	−3.51
$\gamma_{4|3}$	.768	1.45
$\gamma_{4|4}$	.844	.94

Table 8.4   (continued)

Panel B: Transition to adolescent violence trajectory (continued)

Variable	Coefficient	z-score
Chronic ($k = 5$)		
Risk	.084	.48
Fail 11–12	1.050	2.13
$\gamma_{5\|1}$	−14.82	−.07
$\gamma_{5\|2}$	−3.135	−5.61
$\gamma_{5\|3}$	−.047	−.07
$\gamma_{5\|4}$	.256	.26

do not directly influence the transition from the childhood trajectory to the adolescent trajectory. By contrast, the contemporaneous event of grade retention during or just before transition to adolescence appears to be a decisive influence.

The three key findings of this illustrative analysis are: (1) preexisting vulnerabilities do not seem to influence the transition; from childhood physical trajectory to the adolescent violence trajectory; (2) the contemporaneous event of grade retention does seem to influence this transition; and (3) controlling for the impact of grade retention and preexisting vulnerabilities, low childhood physical aggression predicts low adolescent violence, and conversely high childhood physical aggression predicts a transition to high adolescence violence. More broadly, the analysis is intended to illustrate an approach to analyzing intertemporal connections in trajectories of distinct but related behaviors that can be applied in wide-ranging problem domains.

8.9 A Comparison of Estimates from the Dual Model and Cross-Classification Analysis

An alternative approach to estimating $\pi_{k|j}$, $\pi_{j|k}$, and π_{jk} involves the cross-tabulation of group memberships from single trajectory models. This alternative can be accomplished as follows: (1) estimate the separate trajectory models for Y_1 and Y_2; (2) on the basis of the posterior probabilities of group membership, sort the sample members into the trajectory groups for Y_1 and

Y_2 to which they most likely belong; and (3) cross-tabulate the group membership counts to estimate $\pi_{k|j}$, $\pi_{j|k}$, and π_{jk}.

This approach has two hazards that are avoided by the dual trajectory model. Such a "classify–analyze" strategy will not produce consistent estimates of the above probabilities. The size of the bias will depend upon the classification error as reflected in the posterior probabilities of group membership. If the error is small, the size of the bias will be small. If the classification error is large, however, the bias may become sizable. Second, the cross-tabulation strategy does not provide a valid basis for computing the standard errors of the estimates of $\pi_{k|j}$, $\pi_{j|k}$, and π_{jk}. Specifically, because the standard errors do not account for uncertainty in group membership, they will be too small. Consequently, confidence intervals for the probability estimates will be too narrow. As a result, the intervals will impart a false sense of confidence in the precision of the probability estimates. In contrast, the dual model provides consistent estimates of all required standard errors and of the probabilities themselves.

Table 8.5 compares estimates of $\pi_{k|j}$ from the dual model and from the cross-tabulation strategy for the childhood physical aggression and adolescent violence model without covariates. Estimates of $\pi_{k|j}$ based on these two approaches are reported for the moderate-declining and chronic childhood trajectories. These two groups are, respectively, the largest and smallest childhood trajectories. In total, 432 individuals were assigned to the former group, whereas only 85 individuals were assigned to the latter. Also, the average posterior probability of assignment for the moderate group is higher than for the chronic group, .85 versus .75. Thus the assignments to the moderate childhood group are less prone to classification error than the assignments to the chronic group.

For the moderate-declining group, the correspondence between the estimates of $\pi_{k|j}$ from the dual model and the cross-tabulation approach is reasonably good, but far from exact. The dual model estimates the probability of transition from the moderate childhood trajectory to the low 1 adolescent trajectory at .389. The estimate from the cross-tabulation approach is .315, nearly 20% smaller. Conversely, the estimate of $\pi_{k|j}$ from cross-tabulation for the transition to the low 2 trajectory (.410) is about 20% larger than the estimate from the dual model (.342). On the other hand, the two methods produce very similar estimates of $\pi_{k|j}$ for the higher delinquency trajectories. Note, however, that the 90% confidence intervals from the dual model are larger than those for the cross-tabulation model. As noted, this reflects the fact that the standard errors from the cross-tabulation approach are too small.

Table 8.5 A comparison of $\pi_{k|j}$ estimates and 90% confidence intervals from the dual model and from cross-tabulations

Childhood trajectory	Estimator	Low 1	Low 2	Rising	Declining	Chronic
				Adolescent trajectory		
Moderate declining	Dual model	.389	.342	.133	.117	.019
		(.321, .454)	(.279, .404)	(.099, .185)	(.076, .171)	(.007, .046)
	Cross-tabulation (*N* = 432)	.315	.410	.130	.109	.037
		(.278, .354)	(.370, .450)	(.104, .159)	(.085, .137)	(.023, .056)
Chronic	Dual model	.066	.238	.270	.206	.220
		(.018, .195)	(.117, .389)	(.154, .393)	(.102, .345)	(.127, .323)
	Cross-tabulation (*N* = 85)	.094	.412	.177	.153	.165
		(.048, .163)	(.322, .507)	(.112, .259)	(.093, .232)	(.102, .245)

For the chronic group, the correspondence between the alternative estimates of $\pi_{k|j}$ is poor. For example, the cross-tabulation approach vastly overestimates the probability of transition to one of the two low delinquency trajectories——.506 from cross-tabulation versus .304 from the dual model. Further, the confidence intervals from the cross-tabulation approach are substantially narrower than the intervals from the dual model. The poor performance of the cross-tabulation approach for the chronic childhood group reflects the combination of the group's small sample size and modest assignment accuracy. Thus, given the ease of estimating the correct model using the dual estimation method, it seems to be clearly preferable to cross-classification analysis.

9

❖

Concluding Observations

9.1 Overview

This book has described the construction and application of a group-based statistical model for analyzing developmental trajectories. All models involve approximations. As developed in Chapter 3, the key modeling assumption in the group-based trajectory framework is the use of groups to approximate a more complex underlying reality. This concluding chapter returns to the theme of groups as approximations. Section 9.2 cautions against the reification of statistical groups by emphasizing the limits of statistical approximation when applied to specific individuals. Section 9.3 closes by reiterating the ongoing theme of this book: groups are a useful vehicle for constructing a compact and informative summary of population heterogeneity in complex longitudinal data sets.

9.2 Reification of Groups

Categorical groupings are used as basic organizing devices in countless numbers of everyday human activities, even though the groups have no more reality than they do in statistical modeling. Everyday communications are filled with queries requiring a categorical response—for example, "did you have a good day?" or "is Smith a pleasant person?" Both the questioner and the respondent know that the query is about a fictional category. Days are rarely all good or bad, and people are not entirely pleasant or unpleasant. Nevertheless, such queries remain a staple of everyday communications because both parties understand that a categorical response provides a succinct summary that can be elaborated upon if necessary.

The use of groups as a summary heuristic for more complex realities is not limited to mundane human interactions. Groups with no literal reality are used as organizing devices in innumerable activities that are crucial to the effective functioning of modern societies. For example, group-based conceptualizations are pervasive in medicine and the law. Depression is a diagnostic category even though its symptoms range over a continuous spectrum. Similarly, the criminal law requires that a defendant be competent to stand trial, yet competence is not a well-defined state.

Groups are also used as an approximating device in science. In biology, for example, the species classifications are a form of approximation. In correspondence with Charles Darwin ten years prior to the publication of *Origin of Species*, Hugh Strickland, a leading zoologist and geologist who was trying to change traditions in zoological nomenclature, observed: "Of course you will understand that by *type-species* I only mean a conventional distinction, referring only to *words*, not to *things*; and like human titles, only used as a matter of convenience. Nature knows no more *type-species* or 'typical groups' than she does of Dukes and Marquesses. Swainson indeed, & other Quinarians talk very mysteriously about 'types' as if the latter got their coronets from Nature & not from Man. But all that appears to me to be 'fudge' " (Burkhurdt and Smith, 1988:216).

The pervasive use of group-based thinking in explaining the world around us and in structuring our economic and social institutions is testimony to the foundational role of groups in human cognition. Psychologists use the term "schemas" as a label for describing the cognitive role of groups. Anderson (1980:128) defines schemas as "large complex units of knowledge that organize much of what we know about general categories of objects, classes of events, and *types of people*" (emphasis added). Anderson (1980:129) goes on to observe: "Schematic thought is a powerful way to process complex sets of information. However, schematic thought is subject to biases and distortion." In the context of the present discussion one such cognitive distortion is the reification of groups as nonexistent realities.

The risk of reification is particularly great when the groups are identified using a statistical method like the one described in this book. The group's reality is reinforced by the patina of scientific objectivity that accompanies statistical analysis and by the very language that is used to describe the statistical findings, for example, "group 1, which represents x% of the population, is best labeled . . . "

The tendency to reify groups has important risks. One is in the conduct of public policy. If a group is small and its behavior is socially undesirable, such as committing crimes, the reification of the group as a distinct entity—rather than as an extreme on a continuum—may provoke draconian responses to the behavior, by creating the impression of a bright line of separation between "them" and "us." Human history is replete with tragic instances in which a fictional, group-based separation is the first step in the dehumanization of "them." Two other risks are not inherently insidious but still important. One is that reification creates the impression of the immutability of the groups. This risk is the subject of section 9.2.1. Reification may also prompt a fruitless search for individual-level assessment procedures to identify definitively members of the extreme group ex ante, for the purpose of preemptively averting the harm that these individuals would otherwise inflict. This risk is the subject of section 9.2.2.

9.2.1 Groups Are Not Immutable

Chapter 4 described the interplay of formal statistical criteria and subjective judgment that is required for making a well-founded decision on the number of groups to include in a model. Because the groups are intended as an approximation of a more complex underlying reality, the objective is not to identify the "true" number of groups. Instead, the aim is to identify as simple a model as possible that displays the distinctive features of the population distribution of trajectories.

The number of groups and the shape of each group's trajectory are not fixed realities. Both of these features of the full model may be altered by the size of the data set that is used for estimating the model. In a longitudinal data set, size is defined on two dimensions, the number of cases/individuals in the data set and the number of periods for which cases/individuals are monitored. The impact of these two dimensions of size on the number and shapes of the trajectories in the preferred model is an understudied topic, but enough has been done to suggest two tentative conclusions. Sampson, Laub, and Eggleston (2004) and D'Unger et al. (1998) analyzed whether the number of trajectories in the preferred model was affected by the number of individuals included in the estimation sample. Both analyses found that beyond a minimum threshold involving 300 to 500 cases, the number of trajectory groups in the preferred model did not change. Eggleston, Laub, and Sampson (2004) conducted an extensive sensitivity analysis on the impact of varying the number of periods over which the trajectories were estimated. The results of this analysis are instructive and deserve special attention.

The Eggleston, Laub, and Sampson (ELS) analysis was based on a classic longitudinal data set assembled by Sheldon and Eleanor Glueck (1968) and subsequently augmented by Sampson and Laub (1993) and Laub and Sampson (2003). The ELS analysis was based on the arrest histories from age 7 to 70 of 500 men who in their youth, circa 1930, had been remanded to a Boston area reform school. ELS analyzed the impact of estimating trajectory models over progressively longer follow-up periods. The shortest follow-up period was from ages 7 to 25 and the longest was from ages 7 to 70.

In a nutshell, ELS found the following: the preferred model for a follow-up period as short as age 7 to 32 and for as long as age 7 to 70 involved six groups. The shapes of the six trajectories in the preferred model were similar across analyses. Still, a more than doubling of the follow-up time period did have an impact. ELS found that the peak age of criminality and the individual-level group membership of several trajectory groups were materially affected by the length of the follow-up period.

These sensitivities provide important insight into the importance of the length of the follow-up period in analyses of longitudinal data, whether with the group-based trajectory modeling or with standard growth curve modeling (Nagin, 2004). The trajectory groups that were most affected by extending the length of the follow-up period were precisely those groups for which a longer follow-up period is desirable, namely, groups composed of individuals who are still offending at the close of the follow-up period. Thus ELS found that while some individuals who were offending at a high-rate up to age 32 continued to follow a trajectory of high-rate offending in subsequent decades, others "shifted" to trajectories characterized by rapid decline in the post–age 32 analyses. On the other hand, there was far greater stability in the groups in which the offending rate was near zero by the close of the observation period. For example, individuals who were following trajectories characterized by negligible offending rates by age 32 continued to follow these same trajectories in analyses involving longer follow-up periods.

The ELS findings suggest two conclusions that transcend the study of the developmental course of criminal behavior. First, the uncertainty of trajectory group membership of individuals who remained active offenders at the close of the observation period is a reminder that even though the past is prologue to the future, the past does not determine the future. Second, researchers who conduct longitudinal studies regularly argue for the importance of continuing assessments of study participants. The raison d'être for continued data collection is that the phenomenon under study has yet to unfold entirely. The uncertainties in trajectory group membership documented by ELS give testimony to the importance of continued tracking and measurement until the phenomenon under study has fully unfolded. Indeed, the ELS analyses illustrate two fundamental lessons of statistics—more and better data allows for more refined statistical inferences and a statistical model is a characterization of collected data, not of uncollected data.

This basic lesson of statistical science is illustrated with the physical aggression trajectory model based on the Montreal longitudinal study. Panel A of Figure 9.1 reports the four-group model that has been repeatedly referred to throughout this book. As described in Chapter 4, this was the preferred model based on the Bayesian Information Criterion. The model in panel A utilizes all of the teacher-based physical aggression assessments from age 6 to age 15. If the analysis is restricted only to the assessments up to age 13, the preferred model based on the Bayesian Information Criterion involves only the three groups depicted in panel B.

It is instructive to compare the inferences that can be drawn from these two models. Both models suggest that physical aggression is either stable or declining from kindergarten into adolescence. To be sure, the high-declining trajectory in both models shows a very small increase from age 6 to age 10, but the dominant pattern is decline. The sizes of the three groups that are common to both models—the low group, the moderate-declining group, and the high-declining group—are also not materially different. The only important difference between the two models is that without the ages 14 and 15 data, the small chronic group has yet to emerge with sufficient clarity for statistical identification.

Table 9.1 provides another perspective on the impact of extending the observation window to age 15. For each model, individuals were assigned to a trajectory group based on the maximum posterior probability assignment rule. Table 9.1 reports cross-tabulations of trajectory group membership with various predictors and correlates of physical aggression. Observe that for the three groups that are common to both models, the mean values of the variables are nearly identical. This reflects the high degree of overlap in the identities

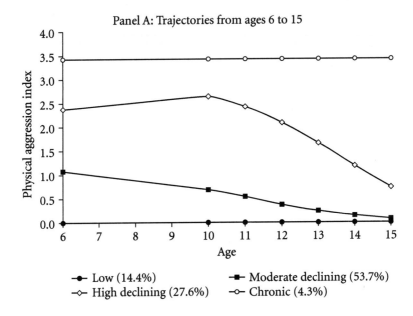

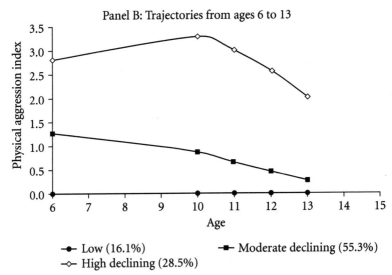

Figure 9.1   Trajectories of physical aggression from ages 6 to 15 and from ages 6 to 13.

Table 9.1 Comparison of group membership characteristics for a 3-group, age 6–13 model versus a 4-group, age 6–15 model (physical aggression, Montreal data)

	Group						
	Rare		Low decline		High decline		Chronic
Variable	3 Grp 6–13	4 Grp 6–15	3 Grp 6–13	4 Grp 6–15	3 Grp 6–13	4 Grp 6–15	4 Grp 6–15
Low IQ (%)	19.9	20.0	26.5	25.0	40.8	41.1	41.9
Teen mother (%)	13.9	12.4	22.2	21.7	32.1	30.0	51.6
Sexual partners at age 13 (ave.)	.13	.11	.25	.23	.55	.49	1.17
Violent delinquency (ave.)	.7	.7	1.1	1.0	2.1	1.9	3.6

of individuals assigned to the three groups across the two models. Also observe that the chronic group in the four-group model is much more prone to early sexual behavior and has far higher self-reported violent delinquency than any of the other groups. Finally, it is noteworthy that the teenage-mother risk factor but not the low-IQ risk factor distinguishes the chronic group from the high-declining group. This finding anticipates a key result in Nagin and Tremblay (2001a) that only mother characteristics, namely teen onset of child-bearing and low education, distinguish the high-declining trajectory group from the chronic group.

This comparison of the preferred three-group physical aggression model, based on the ages 6 to 13 data, with the preferred four-group model, based on the ages 6 to 15 data, illustrates two important points. First, the groups that make up a group-based trajectory model are not immutable entities. They are instead statistical devices for summarizing key features of the data used in the analysis, in the former case the physical aggression data from ages 6 to 13 and in the latter the data from ages 6 to 15. Second, and more fundamentally, the analysis illustrates that more data allow for more refined statistical inferences. The emergence of the chronic group in the ages 6 to 15 data does not contradict the three-group model based on the ages 6 to 13 data. To the contrary, it is an elaboration of the ages 6 to 13 model that becomes possible with the addition of two more years of assessment data. Similarly, the conclusion that only maternal characteristics distinguish the chronic and high-declining groups is a further demonstration of the capacity for more refined statistical inferences with more data.

9.2.2 Predicting an Individual's Trajectory Group Membership

It is important to distinguish two fundamentally different uses of a prediction analysis. One is to predict an individual's behavioral trajectory for the purpose of classifying him or her as a type. This use is the topic of the present discussion. The second use is to identify risk characteristics within the population at large which, if altered, might lead to better outcomes on average. This latter use does not require the targeting and categorization of specific individuals. It is important to distinguish these alternatives because the rationale for intervention to reduce population risk only requires a finding that the risk factor significantly increases the probability of the behavior. By contrast, a more exacting standard is required for prediction and categorization of individuals into an undesirable group.

The difficulty of predicting an individual's trajectory group is illustrated with an empirical example. One might wonder why such a demonstration is even necessary, in light of my stated view that the trajectory groups are statistical constructs, not realities. Although the groups are not realities per se, the clustering of individuals with similar trajectories is a reality. Thus it is reasonable to ask whether membership in the various clusters can be predicted ex ante with high probability.

Consider the problem of predicting membership in the four trajectory groups identified in the London data. Section 6.3 describes an analysis in which the probability of trajectory group membership was related to four classic risk factors for delinquency—low IQ, one or both parents having a criminal record, high risk-taking behavior, and poor parenting. Each factor was scored on a binary scale equal to 1 if the risk was present and 0 if not present. For the purposes of this demonstration, the four risk factors were summed to produce a single risk index ranging from 0 to 4. A score of 0 corresponded to an individual's having none of the risks and a score of 4 corresponded to an individual's having all of the risks. In between were individuals with one, two, or three of the risks. The four-group London model was reestimated using this single-risk index as a predictor of trajectory group membership in lieu of the four distinct risk factors.

The index has a pronounced statistical relationship with the probability of trajectory group membership, in terms of both the statistical significance and the magnitude of the risk-index coefficient estimates. Table 9.2 reports the probabilities of membership in each of the four trajectory groups that are im-

Table 9.2 Probability of trajectory group membership as a function of number of risks (London data)

Number of risks	Trajectory group			
	Rare	Adolescent limited	Low chronic	High chronic
0	.90	.04	.05	.01
1	.75	.10	.12	.03
2	.49	.19	.21	.11
3	.22	.24	.25	.28
4	.07	.22	.22	.49

plied by the coefficient estimates for individuals with zero through four risk factors. The results demonstrate that the risk index has a very pronounced impact on the probability of group membership. At one extreme, the predicted probability of membership in the rare and high-chronic trajectories for individuals with no risks is .90 and .01, respectively. For individuals with four risks the probability of the rare trajectory drops to .07 and the probability of the high-chronic trajectory increases to .49.

Although the risk index has a large impact on the probability of trajectory group membership, it is not so significant as to distinguish group membership with near certainty in the criminal trajectory groups. To be sure, membership in the rare group is very certain, .90, for individuals with no risks, but the base-rate probability for this group is already very high, .70. The real challenge from both a technical and a policy perspective is prediction of membership in a small group. In particular, identification of individuals destined to follow the high-chronic trajectory, who make up an estimated 6% of the population, could pay high social dividends. However, even with four risks, the probability of membership in this group does not exceed .5. With three risks it drops to less than .3.

Figure 9.2 provides a graphical perspective on the prediction problem and on the pitfall of reification of group identity. Panel A shows the four trajectories identified in Table 9.2. These trajectories have been described in earlier chapters, so it is sufficient to note that they are distinctive in their levels, rate of rise and fall, and peaks of maximum offending rate. Now consider the problem of predicting ex ante the trajectories of individuals with varying number

Panel A: Trajectories of convictions

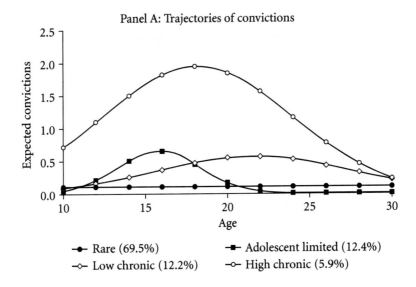

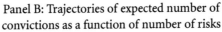

Panel B: Trajectories of expected number of
convictions as a function of number of risks

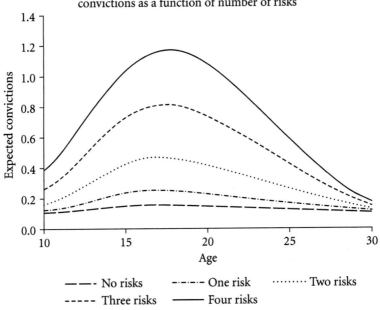

Figure 9.2   Predicting trajectories of conviction for the London data.

of risk factors. Even if the groups are thought of as real entities, Table 9.2 demonstrates that it is not possible ex ante to assign individuals definitively to a specific trajectory on the basis of a number of risk factors. It is only possible ex ante to construct an *expected* trajectory. For each number of risk factors, the expected trajectory is the product of weighting the trajectories shown in panel A with the probabilities reported in Table 9.2. For example, consider the expected rate of offending at age 18 for individuals with three risk factors. According to the model's parameter estimates, the predicted age 18 rate of offending (that is, λ_{18}) is .01 for the rare group, .46 for the adolescent-limited group, .47 for the low-chronic group, and 1.94 for the high-chronic group. As shown in Table 9.2, for individuals with three risks, the probabilities of membership in the rare, adolescent-limited, low-chronic, and high-chronic groups are, respectively, .22, .24, .25, and .28. The expected rate of offending at age 18 for individuals with three risks, $E(\lambda_{18} \mid 3 \text{ risks})$, weights the predicted rate at age 18 for each group by the probability of that group. Thus $E(\lambda_{18} \mid 3 \text{ risks})$ equals .77($= .22 * .01 + .24 * .46 + .25 * .47 + .28 * 1.94$). This calculation is repeated at each age to construct an expected trajectory for the group with three risk factors.

Panel B of Figure 9.2 reports the predicted trajectories of individuals with zero to four risk factors. As the number of risks increases, the trajectories predict ever higher levels of the expected offending rate, λ, at each age. However, the distinctive paths of offending that are so apparent in panel A are no longer present in panel B. Instead, the expected offending rate varies as a function of the number of risks over a smooth continuum.

The contrast between the trajectories in panels A and B has two important implications. First, even if the world were made up of literally distinct groups, ex ante the predicted trajectories of individuals would likely be distributed over a continuum, even if classification probabilities seemed to have a high capacity to discriminate group membership. This conclusion is still another reminder of the pitfall of reifying groups. The second implication reverses this logic. Even if an outcome varies ex ante with a predictor variable according to a smooth continuum, it may still be the case that there are highly distinctive trajectories of that outcome that are systematically related to the predictor variable. Thus taxonomic theories that predict distinctive trajectories with distinctive causes may still be valid, even if the putative causes ex ante do not clearly predict distinct trajectories.

9.2.3 Ex Ante Prediction of Distinct Trajectories

The importance of this second point deserves special emphasis, because it has fundamental implications for statistical inference. Consider the Moffitt (1993) taxonomic theory of antisocial behavior. Moffitt predicts two distinct trajectories—a life-course-persistent trajectory and an adolescent-limited trajectory. Panel A of Figure 9.3 provides a depiction of Moffitt's account of these two trajectories. The life-course-persistent trajectory is flat and high, whereas the adolescent-limited trajectory rises and then falls with age. Moffitt predicts that the life-course-persistent group will make up only about 5% of the population. However, her theory also predicts that the probability of following this trajectory is highest for individuals with various neurological deficits who experienced adversity in early childhood.

Sampson and Laub (2003) challenge Moffitt's theory on many grounds. The purpose here is not to wade into the debate about the validity of her taxonomic theory, but rather to clarify a possible misinterpretation of Sampson and Laub's line of argument. They create an index of risks that is conceptually similar to that developed for the London data. In an analysis of the Glueck data, Sampson and Laub demonstrate that people who are high on this risk index also have higher rates of arrest over the life span. This finding accords with the just-described findings for the London men. Sampson and Laub also found that the trajectory of offending of the high-risk men paralleled that of the lower-risk men. Across all crime types it first rose to a peak at about age 23 and then began a steady decline. The parallel trajectories of the high- and low-risk men should not be interpreted, in and of itself, as implying that there is no life-course-persistent trajectory.

Returning to the thumbnail sketch of the Moffiit theory, suppose that in fact the world was composed only of the two trajectories she described and that the probability of following the life-course-persistent trajectory was increased tenfold to .5 for individuals suffering from the risks that she outlines. Panel B of Figure 9.3 shows the expected trajectory of this high-risk group. Its shape is remarkably similar to that of the adolescent-limited group: it rises and then falls and also reaches a peak at the same age. The only material difference is that at each age the predicted rate of antisocial behavior is higher than for the pure adolescent-limited trajectory. Thus even though an individual in the high-risk group is an order of magnitude more likely to follow a trajectory of chronic antisocial behavior, as a group, these high-risk individuals still

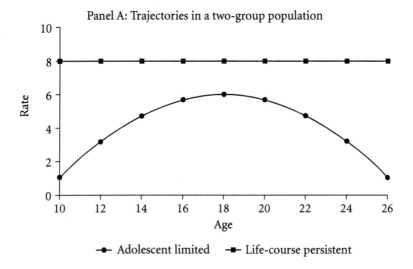

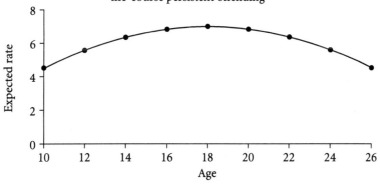

Figure 9.3 The ex ante prediction of distinct trajectories.

follow the classic hump-shaped age-crime curve. There is no inherent contra-
diction in this conclusion. It simply reflects the fact that even if some set of
characteristics increases the probability that individuals will follow a particular developmental trajectory, not all individuals with those characteristics will
follow that trajectory. Just as in the analysis of the London data reported in Fig-

ure 9.2, the expected trajectory of all individuals with those characteristics will be a weighted average of the entire set of trajectories that they ultimately follow. As a result, the expected trajectory in panel B of Figure 9.3 is an amalgam of the chronic trajectory and the adolescent-limited trajectories. The observation that the expected trajectory resembles the adolescent-limited trajectory neither proves nor disproves the existence of the chronic trajectory, nor is it at odds with the prediction that individuals with specific vulnerabilities are at greater risk of following that trajectory.

Of course, the hypothetical trajectories in Figure 9.3 do not demonstrate Moffitt's taxonomic theory. That is not their purpose. Their purpose is to reiterate the point that the population may be made up of distinctive clusters of trajectories with distinctive causes or predictors, even if the putative causes/predictors ex ante do not clearly predict distinct trajectories.

9.3 Summarizing Population Heterogeneity in Complex Longitudinal Data Sets

A hallmark of modern longitudinal studies is the variety and richness of measurements that are made of a study's subjects and their circumstances. Less often acknowledged is that this abundance of information is accompanied by a difficult companion—complexity. Commonly, researchers are confronted with the dilemma of how best to explore and communicate the rich set of measurements at their disposal without becoming so bogged down in complexity that the lessons to be learned from the data are lost on them and their audience.

An important motivation for my commitment to developing and promoting the group-based trajectory method is the belief that alternative methods for analyzing development in longitudinal data sets too often leave the researcher with a Hobson's choice of balancing comprehensibility against an adequate exploration of complexity. Group-based trajectory modeling does not solve the problem of balancing comprehensibility and complexity. It does, however, improve a researcher's ability to identify, summarize, and communicate complex patterns in longitudinal data.

By grounding the statistical analysis in a group-based framework, it benefits from the many advantages of schematic thought that have been documented by cognitive psychologists. Just as schematic thought is a "powerful way to process complex sets of information" (Anderson, 1980:128), trajectory groups are a powerful device for summarizing complex longitudinal data sets. Individual-level heterogeneity in developmental trajectories is described by a small number of groups that are defined by their size and shape. The group's size is expressed in terms of its percentage representation in the population and its shape by an equation that is easily represented in a graphical form. The gain in comprehension that attends a graphical, group-based data summary is hard to overstate. Pure parametric data summaries are so abstract that their meaning in substantive terms is commonly lost not only on the audience for the findings but on the researchers themselves. Trajectory groups also provide an objective basis for summarizing other related measurements in a compact and cognitively manageable form. An example of this type of summary is the group profiles based on the posterior probabilities of group membership. Finally, trajectory groups provide a basis for identifying and succinctly communicating complex linkages that are commonly lost in alternative forms of analysis. The transition probabilities from the dual trajectory model, described in Chapter 8, exemplify this capability. The transition probabilities provide the basis for a far more varied and subtle description of the interconnections among the trajectories for the two outcomes of interest than is possible with a single summary statistic such as a correlation or a regression coefficient.

Summarizing data requires reduction. Reduction requires approximation. In the case of group-based models, the approximation involves the grouping of individuals who are not entirely homogeneous. The return for this form of approximation is a greatly expanded capability for creating dense, yet comprehensible, descriptions of groups of people through time.

References

Akaike, H. 1974. "A New Look at Statistical Model Identification." *IEEE Transactions on Automatic Control*, 19: 716–723.

Anderson, J. R. 1980. *Cognitive Psychology and Its Implications*. San Francisco: Freeman and Co.

Angold A., E. J. Costello, and A. Erkanli. 1999. "Comorbidity." *Journal of Child Psychology and Psychiatry*, 40: 57–87.

Angrist, J. D., and G. W. Imbens. 1995. "Two-Stage Least Squares Estimation of Average Causal Effects in Models with Variable Treatment Intensity." *Journal of the American Statistical Association*, 90: 431–442.

Backteman, G., and D. Magnusson. 1981. "Longitudinal Stability of Personality Characteristics." *Journal of Personality*, 49: 148–160.

Bauer, D. J., and P. Curran. 2003a. "Distributional Assumptions of the Growth Mixture Models: Implications for Over-extraction of Latent Trajectory Classes." *Psychological Methods*, 8: 338–363.

———. 2003b. "Overextraction of Latent Trajectory Classes: Much Ado about Nothing? Reply to Rindskopf 2003, Muthén 2003, and Cudeck and Henley 2003." *Psychological Methods*, 8: 384–392.

———. 2004. "The Integration of Continuous and Discrete Latent Variable Models: Potential Problems and Promising Opportunities." *Psychological Methods*, 9: 3–29.

Baumol, W. 1992. "On My Attitudes: Sociopolitical and Methodological." In M. Szenberg, ed., *Eminent Economists: Their Life Philosophies*. Cambridge: Cambridge University Press.

Bergman, L. R. 1998. "A Pattern-Oriented Approach to Studying Individual Development: Snapshots and Processes." In R. B. Cairns, L. R. Bergman, and J. Kagan, eds., *Methods and Models for Studying the Individual.* Thousand Oaks, Calif.: Sage Publications.

Brame, R., D. S. Nagin, and R. E. Tremblay. 2001. "Developmental Trajectories of Physical Aggression from School Entry to Late Adolescence." *Journal of Child Psychology and Psychiatry,* 42: 503–512.

Brame, R., D. Nagin, and L. Wasserman. 2004. "Exploring Some Analytical Characteristics of Finite Mixture Models." Working paper. Carnegie Mellon University.

Broidy, L. M., D. Nagin, R. E. Tremblay, B. Brame, K. Dodge, D. Fergusson, J. Horwood, R. Loeber, R. Laird, D. Lynam, T. Moffitt, J. E. Bates, G. S. Pettit, and F. Vitaro. 2003. "Developmental Trajectories of Childhood Disruptive Behaviors and Adolescent Delinquency: A Six Site, Cross-National Study." *Developmental Psychology,* 39: 222–245.

Bryk, A. S., and S. W. Raudenbush. 1987. "Application of Hierarchical Linear Models to Assessing Change." *Psychology Bulletin,* 101: 147–158.

———. 1992. *Hierarchical Linear Models for Social and Behavioral Research: Application and Data Analysis Methods.* Newbury Park, Calif.: Sage Publications.

Burkhardt, F., and S. Smith, eds. 1988. *The Correspondence of Charles Darwin.* Vol. 4, *1847–1850.* Cambridge: Cambridge University Press.

Bushway, S., A. Piquero, L. Broidy, E. Cauffman, P. Mazerolle. 2001. "An Empirical Framework for Studying Desistance as a Process." *Criminology,* 39: 491–516.

Bushway, S., T. Thornberry, and M. Krohn. 2003. "Desistance as a Developmental Process: A Comparison of Static and Dynamic Approaches." *Journal of Quantitative Criminology,* 19: 129–153.

Cantor, N., and N. Genero. 1986. "Psychiatric Diagnosis and Natural Categorization: A Close Analogy." In T. Millon and G. Klerman, eds., *Contemporary Directions in Psychopathology.* New York: Guilford.

Carpenter, J., and J. Bithell. 2000. "Bootstrap Confidence Intervals: When, Which, What? A Practical Guide for Medical Statisticians." *Statistics in Medicine,* 19: 1141–1164.

Caspi, A. 1998. "Personality Development across the Life Course." In N. Eisenberg and W. Daom, eds., *Handbook of Child Psychology,* 5th ed., New York: Wiley.

Christ, M., R. Krishnan, D. Nagin, and O. Guenther. 2002. "Measuring Web Portal Utilization." Proceedings, 35th Hawaii International Conference on System Science (HICSS-35), Hilton Wailkoloa Village, HI.

Cloninger, R. C. 1986. "A Unified Biosocial Theory of Personality and Its Role in the Development of Anxiety States." *Psychiatric Developments*, 3: 167–225.

———. 1987. "A Systematic Method for Clinical Description and Classification of Personality Variants." *Archives of General Psychiatry*, 44: 573–588.

Costello, E. J., A. J. Costello, C. Edelbrock, B. J. Burns, M. K. Dulcan, D. Brent, and S. Janiszewski. 1988. "Psychiatric Disorders in Pediatric Primary Care: Prevalence and Risk Factors." *Archives of General Psychiatry*, 45: 1107–1116.

Cramér, H. 1946. *Mathematical Methods of Statistics*. Princeton, N.J.: Princeton University Press.

Duncan, G., and J. Brooks-Gunn. 1997. *Consequences of Growing Up Poor*. New York: Russell Sage Foundation.

D'Unger, A., K. Land, P. McCall, and D. Nagin. 1998. "How Many Latent Classes of Delinquent/Criminal Careers? Results from Mixed Poisson Regression Analyses of the London, Philadelphia, and Racine Cohorts Studies." *American Journal of Sociology*, 103: 1593–1630.

Efron, B. 1979. "Bootstrap Methods: Another Look at the Jackknife." *Annals of Statistics*, 7: 1–26.

Eggleston, E. P., J. H. Laub, and R. J. Sampson. 2004. "Methodological Sensitivities to Latent Class Analysis of Long-Term Criminal Trajectories." *Journal of Quantitative Criminology*, 20: 1–26.

Elder, Jr., G. H. 1985. "Perspectives on the Life Course." In G. H. Elder, Jr., ed., *Life Course Dynamics*. Ithaca, N.Y.: Cornell University Press.

———. 1998. "The Life Course as Developmental Theory." *Child Development*, 69: 1–12.

Everitt, B. S., and D. J. Hand. 1981. *Finite Mixture Distributions*. London: Chapman and Hall.

Farrington, D. P. 1986. "Age and Crime." In M. Tonry and N. Morris, eds., *Crime and Justice: An Annual Review of Research*. Vol. 7. Chicago: University of Chicago Press.

———. 1990. "Childhood Aggression and Adult Violence: Early Precursors and Later-Life Outcomes." In D. J. Pepler and K. H. Rubin, eds., *The Development of Childhood Aggression*. Hillsdale, N.J.: Lawrence-Erlbaum.

Farrington, D. P., and D. J. West. 1990. "The Cambridge Study in Delinquent Development: A Prospective Longitudinal Study of 411 Males." In H. Kerner and G. Kaiser, eds., *Criminality: Personality, Behavior, and Life History*. New York: Springer-Verlag.

Fergusson, D. M., L. J. Horwood, and M. T. Lynskey. 1993. "Prevalence and Co-morbidity of DSM-III-R Diagnoses in a Birth Cohort of 15-year-olds." *Journal of the American Academy of Child and Adolescent Psychiatry*, 32: 1127–1134.

Foster, H., D. Nagin, J. Hagan, E. Costello, and A. Angold. 2003. "Stress Histories of Poverty, Family Structure, and Child Conduct Disorder." Working paper. College Station: Texas A&M.

Gelman, A., and D. Rubin. 1999. "Evaluating and Using Statistical Methods in the Social Sciences: A Discussion of 'A Critique of the Bayesian Information Criterion for Model Selection.'" *Sociological Methods and Research*, 27: 403–410.

Gershoff, E. 2002. "Corporal Punishment by Parents and Associated Child Behaviors and Experiences: A Meta-Analytic and Theoretical Review." *Psychological Bulletin*, 128: 539–579.

Geweke, J. 1989. "Bayesian Inference in Econometric Models Using Monte Carlo Integration." *Econometrica*, 57: 1317–1339.

Ghosh, J. K., and P. K. Sen. 1985. "On the Asymptotic Performance of the Log Likelihood Ratio Statistic for the Mixture Model and Related Results." In L. M. LeCam and R. A. Olshen, eds., *Proceedings of the Berkeley Conference in Honor of Jerzy Neyman and Jack Kiefer*. Monterey, Calif.: Wadsworth.

Glueck, S., and E. Glueck. 1968. *Delinquents and Nondelinquents in Perspective*. New York: Commonwealth Fund.

Goldstein, H. 1995. *Multilevel Statistical Models*. 2nd ed. London: Edward Arnold.

Greene, W. H. 1990. *Econometric Analysis*. New York: Macmillan.

———. 1995. *Econometrics*. New York: Macmillan.

Haapasalo, J., and R. Tremblay. 1994. "Physically Aggressive Boys from Ages 6 to 12: Family Background, Parenting Behavior, and Prediction of Delinquency." *Journal of Consulting and Clinical Psychology*, 62: 1044–1052.

Haapasalo, J., R. E. Tremblay, B. Boulerice, and F. Vitaro. 2000. "Relative Advantages of Person- and Variable-Based Approaches for Predicting Problem Behaviors from Kindergarten Assessments." *Journal of Quantitative Criminology*, 16: 145–168.

Hagan, J., and A. Palloni. 1990. "The Social Reproduction of a Criminal Class in Working-Class London, circa 1950–1980." *American Journal of Sociology*, 96: 265–299.

Heckman, J., and B. Singer. 1984. "A Method for Minimizing the Impact of Distributional Assumptions in Econometric Models for Duration Data." *Econometrica*, 52: 271–320.

Hirschi, T., and M. R. Gottfredson. 1983. "Age and the Explanation of Crime." *American Journal of Sociology*, 89: 552–584.

Holyoak, K., and B. Spellman. 1993. "Thinking." *Annual Review of Psychology*, 4: 265–315.

Huesmann, L. R., L. D. Eron, M. M. Lefkowitz, and L. O. Walder. 1984. "Stability of Aggression over Time and Generations." *Developmental Psychology*, 20: 1120–1134.

Jones, B. L. 2001. "Analyzing Longitudinal Data with Mixture Models: A Trajectory Approach." Ph.D. dissertation, Carnegie Mellon University.

Jones, B. L., D. Nagin, and K. Roeder. 2001. "A SAS Procedure Based on Mixture Models for Estimating Developmental Trajectories." *Sociological Research and Methods*, 29: 374–393.

Juby, H., and D. P. Farrington. 2001. "Disentangling the Link between Disrupted Families and Delinquency." *British Journal of Criminology*, 41: 22–40.

Kagan, J. 1969. "The Three Faces of Continuity in Human Development." In D. A. Goslin, ed., *Handbook of Socialization Theory and Research*. Chicago: Rand McNally.

Kandel, D. B. 1975. "Stages in Adolescent Involvement in Drug Use." *Science*, 190: 912–914.

Kasen, S., P. Cohen, A. E. Skodol, J. G. Johnson, E. Smailes, and J. S. Brook. 2001. "Childhood Depression and Adult Personality Disorder—Alternative Pathways of Continuity." *Archives of General Psychiatry*, 58: 231–236.

Kass, R. E., and A. E. Raftery. 1995. "Bayes Factor." *Journal of the American Statistical Association*, 90: 773–795.

Kass, R. E., and L. Wasserman. 1995. "A Reference Bayesian Test for Nested Hypotheses and Its Relationship to the Schwarz Criterion." *Journal of the American Statistical Association*, 90: 928–934.

Kessler, R. C., K. A. McGonagle, S. Zhao, C. B. Nelson, M. Hughes, S. Eshleman, H. U. Wittchen, and K. S. Kendler. 1994. "Lifetime and 12-Month Prevalence of DSM-III-R Psychiatric Disorders in the United States: Results from the National Comorbidity Study." *Archives of General Psychiatry*, 51: 8–19.

Kochanska, G. 1997. "Multiple Pathways to Conscience for Children with Different Temperaments: From Toddlerhood to Age 5." *Developmental Psychology*, 33: 228–240.

Lacourse, E., D. Nagin, F. Vitaro, M. Claes, and R. E. Tremblay. 2003. "Developmental Trajectories of Boys' Delinquent Group Membership and Facilitation of Violent Behaviors during Adolescence." *Development and Psychopathology*, 15, 183–197.

Lambert, D. 1993. "Zero-Inflated Poisson Regression with an Application to Defects in Manufacturing." *Technometrics*, 34: 1–13.

Land, K., P. McCall, and D. Nagin. 1996. "A Comparison of Poisson, Negative Binomial, and Semiparametric Mixed Poisson Regression Models with Empirical Applications to Criminal Careers Data." *Sociological Methods and Research*, 24: 387–440.

Land, K., and D. Nagin. 1996. "Micro-Models of Criminal Careers: A Synthesis of the Criminal Careers and Life Course Approaches via Semiparametric Mixed Poisson Models with Empirical Applications." *Journal of Quantitative Criminology*, 12: 163–191.

Laub, J. H., D. Nagin, and R. Sampson. 1998. "Good Marriages and Trajectories of Change in Criminal Offending." *American Sociological Review*, 63: 225–238.

Laub, J. H., and R. Sampson. 2003. *Shared Beginnings, Divergent Lives: Delinquent Boys to Age 70*. Cambridge, Mass.: Harvard University Press.

Lewinsohn, P. M., H. Hops, R. E. Roberts, J. R. Seeley, and J. A. Andrews. 1993. "Adolescent Psychopathology: Prevalence and Incidence of Depression and Other DSM-III-R Disorders in High School Students." *Journal of Abnormal Psychology,* 102: 133–144.

Little, R. J. A., and D. B. Rubin. 1987. *Statistical Analysis of Missing Data.* New York: Wiley.

Lo, Y., N. Mendell, and D. Rubin. 2001. "Testing the Number of Components in a Normal Mixture." *Biometrica,* 88: 767–778.

Loeber, R. 1991. "Questions and Advances in the Study of Developmental Pathways." In D. Cicchetti and S. Toth, eds., *Models and Integrations.* Rochester Symposium on Developmental Psychopathology, Rochester, N.Y.: University of Rochester Press.

Loeber, R., and M. LeBlanc. 1990. "Toward a Developmental Criminology." In M. Tonry and N. Morris, eds., *Crime and Justice: An Annual Review of Research.* Vol. 20. Chicago: University of Chicago Press.

Loeber, R., and M. Stouthamer-Loeber. 1998. "Development of Juvenile Aggression and Violence: Some Common Misconceptions and Controversies." *American Psychologist*, 53: 242–259.

MacCallum, R. C., C. Kim, W. B. Malarkey, and J. K. Kiecolt-Glaser. 1997. "Studying Multivariate Change Using Multilevel Models and Latent Curve Models." *Multivariate Behavioral Research,* 32: 215–253.

Maddala, G. S. 1983. *Limited Dependent and Qualitative Variables in Econometrics.* New York: Cambridge University Press.

Magnusson, D. 1998. "The Logic and Implications of a Person-Oriented Approach." In R. B. Cairns, L. R. Bergman, and J. Kagan, eds., *Methods and Models for Studying the Individual.* Thousand Oaks, Calif.: Sage Publications.

Magnusson, D., and L. R. Bergman. 1990. "A Pattern Approach to the Study of Pathways from Childhood to Adulthood." In L. N. Robins and M. Rutter, eds., *Straight and Devious Pathways from Childhood to Adulthood.* New York: Cambridge University Press.

Maguin, E., and R. Loeber. 1996. "Academic Performance and Delinquency." In M. Tonry, ed., *Crime and Justice: An Annual Review*. Chicago: University of Chicago Press.

Manski, C. F. 1995. *Identification Problems in the Social Sciences.* Cambridge, Mass.: Harvard University Press.

Markman, E. M. 1989. *Categorization and Naming in Children: Problems of Induction.* Cambridge: MIT Press.

McArdle, J. J., and D. Epstein. 1987. "Latent Growth Curves within Developmental Structural Equation Models." *Child Development,* 58: 110– 113.

McCord, J. 1982. "A Longitudinal View of the Relationship between Paternal Absence and Crime." In J. Gunn and D. P. Farrington, eds., *Abnormal Offenders, Delinquency, and the Criminal Justice System.* New York: John Wiley.

McLachlan, G., and D. Peel. 2000. *Finite Mixture Models.* New York: Wiley.

McLanahan, S., and G. D. Sandefur. 1994. *Growing Up with a Single Parent.* Cambridge, Mass.: Harvard University Press.

Meredith, W., and J. Tisak. 1990. "Latent Curve Analysis." *Psychometrika,* 55: 107–122.

Moffitt, T. E. 1993. "Adolescence-Limited and Life-Course-Persistent Antisocial Behavior: A Developmental Taxonomy." *Psychological Review,* 100: 674–701.

Moffitt, T. E., A. Caspi, N. Dickson, P. Silva, and W. Stanton. 1996. "Childhood-Onset versus Adolescent-Onset Antisocial Conduct Problems in Males: Natural History from Ages 3 to 18."*Development and Psychopathology,* 8: 399–424.

Mustillo, S., C. Worthman, A. Erkanli, G. Keeler, A. Angold, and E. J. Costello. 2003. "Obesity and Psychiatric Disorder: Developmental Trajectories." *Pediatric* 111: 851–859.

Muthén, B. 1989. "Latent Variable Modeling in Heterogeneous Populations." *Psychometrika,* 54: 557–585.

———. 2001. "Second-Generation Structural Equation Modeling with a Combination of Categorical and Continuous Latent Variables: New Opportunities for Latent Class/Latent Curve Modeling." In A. Sayers and L. Collins, eds., *New Methods for the Analysis of Change.* Washington, D.C.: American Psychological Association.

Muthén, B., and K. Shedden. 1999. "Finite Mixture Modeling with Mixture Outcomes Using the EM Algorithm." *Biometrics,* 55: 463–469.

Muthén, L. K., and B. O. Muthén. 1998–2004. *Mplus User's Guide*. 3rd ed. Los Angeles: Muthén and Muthén.

Nagin, D. 1999. "Analyzing Developmental Trajectories: Semi-Parametric, Group-Based Approach." *Psychological Methods*, 4: 39–177.

———. 2004. "Response to 'Methodological Sensitivities to Latent Class Analysis of Long-Term Criminal Trajectories.'" *Journal of Quantitative Criminology*, 20: 27–36.

Nagin, D., D. Farrington, and T. Moffitt. 1995. "Life-Course Trajectories of Different Types of Offenders." *Criminology*, 33: 111–139.

Nagin, D. S., and K. C. Land. 1993. "Age, Criminal Careers, and Population Heterogeneity: Specification and Estimation of a Nonparametric, Mixed Poisson Model." *Criminology*, 31: 327–362.

Nagin, D., L. Pagani, R. Tremblay, and F. Vitaro. 2003. "Life Course Turning Points: A Case Study of the Effect of School Failure on Interpersonal Violence." *Development and Psychopathology*, 15: 343–361.

Nagin, D. S., and R. E. Tremblay. 1999. "Trajectories of Boys' Physical Aggression, Opposition, and Hyperactivity on the Path to Physically Violent and Nonviolent Juvenile Delinquency." *Child Development*, 70: 1181–1196.

———. 2001a. "Parental and Early Childhood Predictors of Persistent Physical Aggression in Boys from Kindergarten to High School." *Archives of General Psychiatry*, 58: 389–394.

———. 2001b. "Analyzing Developmental Trajectories of Distinct but Related Behaviors: A Group-Based Method." *Psychological Methods*, 6: 18–34.

———. 2002. "Most Fall but Not All: Changes in Physical Aggression from Childhood through Adolescence." Working paper. Carnegie Mellon University.

Olweus, D. 1979. "Stability of Aggressive Reaction Patterns in Males: A Review." *Psychological Bulletin*, 86: 852–875.

Pagani, L., B. Boulerice, and R. E. Tremblay. 1997. "The Influence of Poverty on Children's Classroom Placement and Behavior Problems." In G. J. Duncan and J. Brooks-Gunn, eds., *Consequences of Growing Up Poor*. New York: Russell Sage Foundation.

Pagani, L., R. E. Tremblay, F. Vitaro, B. Boulerice, and P. McDuff. 2001. "Effects of Grade Retention on Academic Performance and Behavioural Development." *Development and Psychopathology*, 13: 297–315.

Patterson, G. R., B. D. DeBaryshe, and E. Ramsey. 1989. "A Developmental Perspective on Antisocial Behavior." *American Psychologist*, 44: 329–335.

Patterson, G. R., M. S. Forgatch, K. L. Yoerger, and M. Stoolmiller. 1998. "Variables That Initiate and Maintain an Early-Onset Trajectory for Juvenile Offending." *Development and Psychopathology*, 10: 531–547.

Pulkkinen, L., and R. E. Tremblay. 1992. "Patterns of Boys' Social Adjustment in Two Cultures and at Different Ages: A Longitudinal Perspective." *International Journal of Behavioral Development*, 15: 527–553.

Raftery, A. E. 1995. "Bayesian Model Selection in Social Research." *Sociological Methodology*, 25: 111–164.

———. 1999. "Bayes Factors and BIC: Comment on 'A Critique of the Bayesian Information Criterion for Model Selection.'" *Sociological Methods and Research*, 3: 411–427.

Raudenbush, S. W. 2001. "Comparing-Personal Trajectories and Drawing Causal Inferences from Longitudinal Data." *Annual Review of Psychology*, 52: 501–525.

Roeder, K., K. Lynch, and D. Nagin. 1999. "Modeling Uncertainty in Latent Class Membership: A Case Study in Criminology." *Journal of the American Statistical Association*, 94: 766–776.

Rosenbaum, P. R. 1995. *Observational Studies*. New York: Springer-Verlag.

Rosenbaum, P., and D. Rubin. 1983. "The Central Role of the Propensity Score in Observational Studies for Causal Effects." *Biometrika*, 70: 41–55.

Rutter, M., B. Yule, D. Quintin, O. Rowlands, W. Yule, and W. Berger. 1975. "Attainment and Adjustment in Two Geographical Areas: The Prevalence of Psychiatric Disorder." *British Journal of Psychiatry*, 126: 493–509.

Sampson, R. J., and J. H. Laub. 1992. "Crime and Deviance in the Life Course." *Annual Review of Sociology*, 18: 63–84.

———. 1993. *Crime in the Making: Pathways and Turning Points through Life.* Cambridge, Mass.: Harvard University Press.

———. 2003. "Life Course Desisters? Trajectories of Crime among Delinquent Boys Followed to Age 70." *Criminology*, 41: 555–592.

Sampson, R. J., J. H. Laub, and E. P. Eggleston. 2004. "On the Robustness and Validity of Groups (Response to Daniel Nagin)." *Journal of Quantitative Criminology*, 20: 37–42.

Schafer, J. L., and J. W. Graham. 2002. "Missing Data: Our View of the State of the Art." *Psychological Methods,* 7: 147–177.

Schwarz, G. 1978. "Estimating Dimensions of a Model." *Annals of Statistics,* 6: 461–464.

Thiel, H. 1971. *Principles of Econometrics.* New York: Wiley.

Thornberry, T. P., A. J. Lizotte, M. D. Krohn, C. A. Smith, and P. K. Porter. 2003. "Causes and Consequences of Delinquency: Findings from the Rochester Youth Development Study." In T. Thornberry, and M. D. Krohn, eds., *Taking Stock of Delinquency: An Overview of Findings from Contemporary Longitudinal Studies.* New York: Kluwer Academic.

Titterington, D. M., A. F. M. Smith, and U. E. Makov. 1985. *Statistical Analysis of Finite Mixture Distributions.* New York: Wiley.

Tobin, J. 1958. "Estimation of Relationships for Limited Dependent Variables." *Econometrica,* 26: 24–36.

Tremblay, R. E., L. Desmarais-Gervais, C. Gagnon, and P. Charlebois. 1987. "The Preschool Behavior Questionnaire: Stability of Its Factor Structure between Culture, Sexes, Ages, and Socioeconomic Classes." *International Journal of Behavioral Development,* 10: 467–484.

Tremblay, R. E., C. Japek, D. Pérusse, P. McDuff, M. Boivin, M. Zoccolillo, and J. Montplaisir. 1999. "The Search for the Age of 'Onset' of Physical Aggression: Rousseau and Bandura Revisited." *Criminal Behaviour and Mental Health,* 9: 8–23.

Tyrka, A. R., J. A. Graber, and J. Brooks-Gunn. 2000. "The Development of Disordered Eating." In J. A. Sameroff, M. Lewis, and S. M. Miller, eds., *Handbook of Developmental Psychopathology,* 2nd ed. New York: Kluwer Academic/Plenum Publisher.

Valez, C., J. Johnson, and P. Cohen. 1989. "A Longitudinal Analysis of Selected Risk Factors of Childhood Psychopathology." *Journal of American Academy of Child and Adolescent Psychiatry,* 28: 861–864.

Wald, A. 1943. "Tests of Statistical Hypotheses Concerning Several Parameters When the Number of Observation Is Large." *Transactions of the American Mathematical Society,* 54: 426–482.

Warr, M. 2002. *Companions in Crime: The Social Aspects of Criminal Conduct.* New York: Cambridge University Press.

Wasserman, L. 2000. "Bayesian Model Selection and Model Averaging." *Journal of Mathematical Psychology*, 44: 92–107.

Weakland, D. L. 1999. "A Critique of the Bayesian Information Criterion for Model Selection." *Sociological Methods and Research*, 27: 359–397.

Weisburd, D., S. Bushway, C. Lum, and S. Yang. 2004. "Trajectories of Crime at Places: A Longitudinal Study of Street Segments in the City of Seattle." *Criminology*, 42: 283–322.

Willett, J. B., and A. G. Sayer. 1994. "Using Covariance Structure Analysis to Detect Correlates and Predictors of Individual Change over Time." *Psychological Bulletin*, 116: 363–381.

Wooldridge, J. M. 2002. *Econometric Analysis of Cross-Section and Panel Data.* Cambridge: MIT Press.

Index